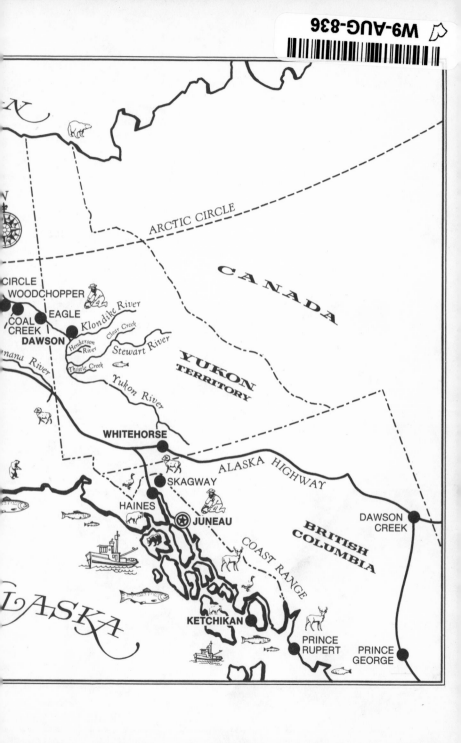

ARCTIC CIRCLE

CANADA

CIRCLE
WOODCHOPPER
EAGLE
COAL
CREEK
Klondike River
DAWSON
Clear Creek
Henderson River
Stewart River
Thistle Creek
nana River
Yukon River

YUKON
TERRITORY

WHITEHORSE

ALASKA HIGHWAY

SKAGWAY
HAINES
JUNEAU

COAST RANGE

DAWSON
CREEK

BRITISH
COLUMBIA

ALASKA

KETCHIKAN

PRINCE
RUPERT

PRINCE
GEORGE

North Country Challenge

North Country Challenge

by ERNEST N. PATTY

President Emeritus of the University of Alaska

DAVID McKAY COMPANY, Inc.   NEW YORK

NORTH COUNTRY CHALLENGE

COPYRIGHT © 1969 BY ERNEST N. PATTY

Library of Congress Catalog Card Number: 69-20203

MANUFACTURED IN THE UNITED STATES OF AMERICA

VAN REES PRESS • NEW YORK

To KAY

ACKNOWLEDGMENTS

THIS book was Kay's idea. Over the years she made notes and saved clippings of events around us. We spent many happy hours together planning it.

I am deeply indebted to Jean Muir for careful editorial revisions and suggestions which have greatly strengthened the narrative.

My son, Stanton H. Patty, read portions of the manuscript and offered many valuable suggestions.

I acknowledge my debt to our many friends in Alaska who shared these exciting days with us. I have made every effort to record the details accurately, but some of the descriptions are from memory and if any inadvertent errors have crept in, I hope they will forgive me. After all, if a man talks about himself, he is bound to tell a few unintentional lies.

CONTENTS

Photographs between pages 148 and 149

North Country Challenge

Chapter I

FIRST STEP INTO ADVENTURE

THE S.S. *Northwestern* of the Alaska Steamship Co. was nosing her way up the Inside Passage, three days out of Seattle. Sometimes as I leaned on the rail I felt almost intoxicated by the magnificence, by the sheer vastness and grandeur of the mountains soaring to landward, and sometimes I just wondered if I were behaving in a madcap fashion by bringing my wife and year-old son into so rugged and primitive a land.

It was September 1922, and we were on our way to Fairbanks in the heart of Alaska. A college was being organized there, the northernmost college on the North American continent, and I had been asked to join the first faculty and help develop the School of Mines.

Back in Washington State, where for a year I had been manager of a zinc mine near Northport, the prospect of pioneering a new college in the Far North had sounded interesting and adventurous. Besides, who knows? We might even make our fortunes up there. Alaska has always held a special allure for mining men. But as I watched that great wild land slipping past, I began to have qualms. I was taking my family to the farthest-north outpost of civili-

1

zation on the continent. North of Fairbanks there were just a few scattered villages, none of them with more than fifty whites. Fairbanks itself was only a small town of some fifteen hundred souls. There, I had been told, summer temperatures sometimes reached into the 90s, but during the long dark winters the thermometer frequently dropped to 50 below zero and occasionally to 60 below, a range of 150 degrees. I hoped our young son would not grow pasty-faced during those sun-starved winters.

An odd atmosphere of gloom seemed to surround us on the ship. Ever since we pulled away from the pier in Seattle, we had noticed a peculiar attitude on the part of the Alaskans aboard. No one showed the slightest enthusiasm for the new college. Whenever I mentioned to one of them that I was joining the faculty in Fairbanks, he would glance quickly from me to my dark-haired young wife, Kay. Then he would shake his head and say, "Well, I wish you luck."

When we met him in Spokane, the president of the new college, Dr. Charles E. Bunnell, had fired our imaginations with tales of life in the Far North and of the opportunities that were waiting there. As an undercurrent to all his talk there had been fine hopes and fine plans. Clearly, Dr. Bunnell expected the Alaska Agricultural College & School of Mines to be a great institution someday—the University of Alaska, unique in situation and possibilities.

By the time our ship had sailed past British Columbia and was skirting the coast of Alaska, I suspected that we had been oversold, that I had indeed gone off half-cocked. I was nearly sure of it after a conversation with a businessman from Juneau.

Kay had joined me at the rail. The breeze that riffled her hair brought the exhilarating scent of sea and forest and snowy peaks, but the Inside Passage stayed calm and unruffled, protected from the open ocean by a chain of mountainous islands that formed a barrier to the west. We were following a deep, twisting, glacier-carved trench. It was once a valley where the ice had gouged so deeply below sea level that the ocean had rushed in to drown it as the ice withdrew. The chisel marks of the ice were still fresh.

On the land side, the giant Coast Range rose in steep escarpments, cloaked with a dense rain forest of spruce and hemlock. We had followed this for hundreds of miles. The forest extended from the sea upward for two or three thousand feet. Above the timberline, bold cliffs reached thousands of feet higher to end in the jagged crestline of the range, a chain of peaks robed in a permanent ice cap with white pendants spilling down the mountainside and the valleys. At the moment we were passing the entrance of a large fjord with its finger extending far back into the range. Icebergs were floating by to tell us that the glacier which cut the fjord still lurked at the head of this mysterious channel. The whole scene had a beauty that sang to the soul, and I began to quote Byron: "How often we forget all time, when alone, admiring nature's universal throne, her woods, her wilds, her waters, the intense reply of hers to our intelligence."

Kay glinted her brown eyes toward me. "Are you getting in voice for your professorial job?" she asked, looking mirthful. "But you're going to teach mining, not English Lit. Remember?"

I was about to tell her that every good mining man I knew had some poetry in his soul, when someone cut in. "I hear you're going to Fairbanks to that college they're talking about." A stocky and rather belligerent-looking businessman from Juneau had moved up beside us. Before I had time to answer he went on, "I hope you bought a round-trip ticket, because you're sure as hell going to need it."

This man seemed determined to get some opinions off his chest. "Trying to start a college at Fairbanks is a great blunder," he announced, as if he were daring me to contradict him. "I doubt if it ever opens its doors. If it does, it won't last a year. Our young people want to go to the States for their college education and, what's more, they're entitled to see how the rest of the world lives."

By this time a grizzled old miner had joined our group. He was grinning widely as if he thought the whole conversation was a huge joke.

"Besides," the businessman went on, "it would be a damned sight less expensive for the territory if we financed their college expenses outside, instead of trying to provide funds for a college up there. And they'd get a better education, too."

That last remark stung. "You are overlooking one important factor," I retorted. "Many of your young people would not return. Alaska needs its young people. You are exporting your most valuable resource."

During the trip one overwhelming impression had been forming in my mind. This country was a rugged wilderness. It would defy generations of men to tame it. Man might hack out a little enclave for a mine, a salmon cannery, or a town, but if he moved away for a time, the lush undergrowth and the forest would move right back in and reclaim it.

Clearly the country's latent resources were tremendous. For the first time, we had come to recognize the sea as a great reservoir of life and wealth. At Ketchikan, our first port of call, where homes notched the steep mountainside, where canneries and cold-storage plants lined the harbor and little fishing boats danced across the waters on their way to and from the fishing grounds, we had gone ashore and in a nearby river had watched the salmon struggling upstream to spawn. All the way up the coast, from the offshore banks, we had seen boats bringing in their loads of halibut, and from almost every inlet and all along the coast, a gleaming tide of salmon was being carried to the canneries. At Petersburg we had watched men unloading tons of delicate Alaska shrimp.

The forests, too, which now came down to the water's edge untouched by a woodsman's axe, were a potential source of wealth. Someday pulp and sawmills would dot the coast we were passing. That timber could be a rich asset for centuries. But right now, in 1922, where were students coming from to fill a college?

"If it's such a hopeless venture, why was the college created in the first place?" I asked the man from Juneau.

He shrugged his shoulders irritably. "Politics," he said.

"Hell's bells, son," the old miner put in, "Fairbanks is a worked-out gold camp. In a few years it won't be anything but a fish camp on the river. Putting money into a college there is like pouring sand down a rat hole. It couldn't possibly work out."

I glanced at Kay and she made a rueful face. As for me, if at that moment I could have picked up our baby, taken my wife by the hand, and walked home, I probably would have done it. But at least we were young and resilient. As we told ourselves later, if we were off on a wild-goose chase, we might as well have as much fun out of it as possible.

Neither of us had ever taken an ocean voyage before. Every aspect of shipboard life was fascinating to us. Sometimes, when fog settled in the narrow Inside Passage, our ship would go pushing into it, whistle blasting. The sound, bouncing back from the mountains on each side, helped the captain keep his position in the tortuous channel, with its

5

hazards of islands and rocky pinnacles. Then oldtime Alaskans aboard would be full of harrowing stories about shipwrecks along the coast, stories that kept cropping up in our minds after we left the protection of the Inside Passage and, for the first time, were struck by the full force of an angry ocean. Two days later the *Northwestern* steamed into the calm of Prince William Sound, and when we came on deck, there—a quarter of a mile away—was the face of Columbia glacier, a great river of ice marching down the mountain. It must have been a mile wide with a face three hundred feet high. The captain stopped the ship to let loose a long blast from the ship's whistle. At the sound, great slabs of ice peeled off and went cascading down into the sea with a roar and a force that rocked our ship.

As soon as we touched port on Latouche Island, to load copper concentrates, I rushed ashore, hoping to hear a few encouraging words about the college in Fairbanks from Van Presely, manager of the Latouche mine. Instead, he was no more hopeful than any of the others had been, but as he said goodbye, he generously offered me a job at the mine, if the college failed. So at least we would not have to slink back to Seattle defeated.

Night was falling as we pulled away from the Latouche dock. Ernest, Jr., was asleep in the stateroom, so after dinner Kay and I climbed around the deck cargo and stood holding hands, on the bow of the ship. The noise of the exhaust was muted there. The ship seemed to glide without effort across the water. On each side, the channel was hemmed in by shadowy forests that tumbled down to the water's edge and faintly, above the timber, we could see rugged mountain ridges silhouetted against the darkening sky. I wondered if many men had crossed those ridges and if there might be rich veins of copper outcropping there.

Beside me I felt Kay tremble and was about to say,

6

"You're getting cold. Let's go in," when I saw her face. It was not cold which had caused that shudder. My stouthearted Kay was frightened. In that minute, I felt as if I could read her thoughts. For a week all we had seen was a tremendous wilderness with a few scattered towns and fishing villages. And there was the baby—very little and vulnerable. All my qualms returned to me. Fairbanks, I knew, had a good school, a small hospital, and two doctors. But if my wife or child ever needed major surgery they would have to endure the long trip to the States and that meant from ten to fourteen days travel, depending on train and steamer schedules. Even Anchorage, the nearest town to the south of Fairbanks, was two days away by train.

With a pang of conscience, I thought, "I've been reckless. I've made a stupid mistake."

Kay was staring ahead, where the channel seemed to grow narrower. Suddenly she turned her head around toward me. "I feel as if I were being carried down a dark passage with no return," she said and looked startled.

All the same, by the next morning we were both on top of the world again. Maybe it was the air, crisp and clear and heady with the chill of distant snows. Maybe it was just being young or the sense of finishing the first long lap of our journey. Yes, that was it, an apostrophe to youth.

The *Northwestern* eased her way between two rock pinnacles and we were in Resurrection Bay, in sight of Seward, the terminus of the Alaska Railroad. When the ship docked, Kay and I went trooping merrily off, bag, baggage, and baby. The sky and those glorious mountains were enough to lift anyone's heart. Fairbanks was somewhere behind those mountains, four hundred sixty land miles away.

It took us two days to get there. The train struggled up the Coast Range and then went switchbacking down again to tidewater at Turnagain Arm and Cook Inlet. Once we

7

saw a band of mountain goats grazing on a steep hillside, and once, after a series of frenzied blasts from the locomotive whistle, the train came to a jarring halt while the crew chased a moose off the tracks.

Sometime during the night our train labored up the second barrier, the Alaska Range. It was growing dark again on the second day by the time we had rolled across the broad Tanana Valley until we reached the little town of Nenana. Here we were put on a barge and ferried across the Tanana River where a little narrow-gauge train was waiting for us.

The weather was freezing. At the end of each coach there was a massive coal stove which the brakeman stoked until the heat was suffocating. But our feet stayed cold. The brakeman lighted oil lamps swinging overhead; the locomotive gave a silly little whistle, and we were away across the murky landscape toward Fairbanks, three hours ahead.

When I thought of Fairbanks I could understand why mining men are apt to be a superstitious lot. It is an example of that strange working out of chance, that synchronicity, that seems to be woven through so much mining lore.

Fairbanks was christened with a woman's tears, a woman, sitting on a riverbank, all her worldly goods heaped around her and nothing in sight but a tangled wilderness. That was in 1901. Her husband, "Captain" E. T. Barnette, had chartered a small sternwheeler, the *Lavelle Young,* to transport his supplies from St. Michel on the Bering Sea, up the Yukon River to its confluence with the Tanana. He was planning to establish a trading post on its upper reaches.

The water was low. Captain W. C. Adams, master of the *Lavelle Young,* was doubtful of reaching the upstream point that Barnette had in mind. So they made a bargain. When

8

they reached the point where low water prevented further progress, the outfit would be unloaded.

After nearly two thousand miles, the *Lavelle Young* was grounded on a sandbar in Chena Slough, a branch of the Tanana River. Over Barnette's furious objections, the captain dropped the boat downstream and unloaded the outfit on the riverbank. Years later, when Captain Adams told me the story, he said that as the steamer pulled away, Mrs. Barnette was sitting on a packing case, crying. Barnette had already grabbed his axe to cut cabin logs for a shelter.

That absolute wilderness was peopled only by an occasional traveling band of Indians. As far as they knew there was not another white person within one hundred fifty miles. One hell of a spot for a trading post, as Captain Adams, disappearing around the bend, admitted to himself.

A few hours later, miraculously, the Barnette's first customer arrived, a wiry little Italian prospector named Felix Pedro. He came bursting out of the brush with an empty stomach. How was he to know then that his name was destined to live in the history of Alaska mining? For months Pedro had been searching unsuccessfully for the location where, the summer before, working out of Circle City on the Yukon, he had found a creek that showed many colors of placer gold. Finally he had reached a ridge where the mountains gave way to the broad floor of the Tanana Valley, from which the Alaska Range leaped abruptly, some ninety miles away.

His supplies were growing low and he had been living mostly on his rifle. It was time to start the long trek back to Circle City. No one knows why he picked the creek that is now named after him. It may have been pure luck, his turn-about point. As he panned the gravels along the stream where at intervals the overburden had been eroded and gravel bars exposed, a string of fine colors appeared in

9

his gold pan. To an experienced prospector like Pedro, those fine colors of gold strongly suggested that the bottom gravels, resting on bedrock, would contain a rich paystreak of coarser gold. The heavy gold would work its way deep into the gravel, leaving only small colors near the surface.

He wanted desperately to stay all winter, to build a cabin, sink holes and check his discovery. But his food supply by that time was perilously low. In his eagerness he had overstayed himself, and his very existence was in danger. Even if he left at once he might not survive the long trip across the mountains. While he mulled over his dilemma, something happened that made him sure Fate itself was taking an interest in his affairs. In the distance he saw the smoke of a steamboat on the slough.

All the time that Captain Adams was backing the sternwheeler off the sandbar, dropping down river, arguing with Barnette, and unloading supplies, Pedro was pelting down the ridge and across the lowlands toward them. There were no trails and dense underbrush slowed his progress. By the time he struggled, panting, to the riverbank, the steamboat had vanished. But at that moment, his moment of black despair, another incredible thing happened. Quite near at hand he heard the ring of Barnette's axe, and there was a whole trading post of goods ready to supply him.

Pedro packed his new supplies back to his creek and yet he sank no prospect hole that winter. Instead he wandered about the area, panning gravel bars on streams in nearby valleys, as yet unmapped and unnamed. Summer had come before he returned to the creek where he had found gold and started to sink a shaft. He worked for weeks, thawing a shaft with wood fires and hot rocks down through frozen muck and gravel, his excitement growing wtih each day's work. He had never before laid eyes on gravel so rich. By that time he was working feverishly. Finally he reached bedrock. Concentrated there was a seven-foot layer of gold-bearing gravel, washed down from quartz veins concealed in the mountains at the head of his creek. It was gold beyond his most fevered dreams.

News of Pedro's rich strike in the Tanana country seeped out during the winter by "Moccasin telegraph." The news traveled up the Yukon to the Forty Mile and on to Dawson in the Klondike. Prospectors loaded up their dog sleds and headed for the new diggings. By the following summer, hundreds of men were digging and sluicing dumps of gold-bearing gravel that they had mined during the winter. With the opening of river transportation, steamboats brought in more men and tons of supplies, mining machinery, horses, wagons, and cattle on the hoof. Docks were built and the settlement around Barnette's prosperous trading post grew into a small log cabin town. At a miner's meeting, the new town was named Fairbanks, after the country's vice-president. Pedro had discovered the largest placer gold district in Alaska. From $40,000 in gold recovered in 1903, production leaped to $600,000 in 1904, to $6 million in 1905 after the big mining plants were in place, and reached $9 million in 1906.

Fairbanks was just twenty years old when our belongings were dumped on the railroad station platform. It was a cold, blustery night, and Kay and I were both full of misgivings as I hoisted Ernest Jr. piggyback on my shoulders and so trudged across the Chena River bridge to spend our first night at the Nordale Hotel.

The glitter had long since gone out of the gold rush, but the next morning, when we set out for breakfast, I could see that Fairbanks still had all the earmarks of a mining camp —unpaved streets, wooden sidewalks, false fronts on buildings in the business district, log cabin homes, no water lines or sewers. At the Model Cafe, big bare-fisted men were

11

sitting at the counter, eating steak for breakfast, shoulders bulging under heavy woolen sweaters.

The smallest coin in use, we discovered, was a 25-cent piece. I had accumulated a good deal of small change during the trip and tried to get rid of it when I paid for our breakfasts. Mrs. Tom Youle, wife of one of the owners, sat behind the cash register, a formidable woman with red hair who looked with disdain at the collection of dimes, nickels, and even pennies I counted out.

"That stuff's no good here," she said.

"It's legal tender," I insisted.

"Look here, young fellow, if you haven't enough money to pay for your meal, we'll just put it on the cuff."

Defeated, I pulled out my wallet and paid with paper money. But we had one stroke of luck that day. We found a furnished house to rent, a three-room log cabin, owned by Arthur and Eva McGown. Arthur, a quiet Scot, was one of the owners of the Model Cafe. His wife, Eva, exuberantly Irish, was going to spend the winter with relatives on the old sod. For some reason, just spending a few minutes in her warm and joyful presence made us both feel as if Alaska itself had welcomed us with open arms.

The front room of the cabin was dominated by a big Coles air-tight stove and the large kitchen by a wood-burning range. The whole inside was sheathed in heavy canvas painted gunmetal gray and stretched over the ceiling to form what was known as a balloon ceiling.

The cabin was sealed against winter with storm windows and doors and had portholes, six inches in diameter, for ventilation. Little tin doors could be closed in extremely cold weather. There was no running water or sewer connection. We were told to put a card in the window each morning indicating how many buckets of water we would need for the day and the waterman would bring it around,

12

by horse-drawn waterwagon in summer, by sled in winter. Beyond the kitchen was a cold room called a "cache" that would serve as a deep freezer. It also housed a chemical toilet. When sub-zero temperatures arrived, obviously no one was going to linger in there with the Sears Roebuck catalog. Behind the house was a garden, limp now from an early frost.

None of the primitive arrangements bothered Kay in the least. She had already lived in mining camps and had always made them seem like home to me.

While she went down to the Northern Commercial Company store to order groceries (items all quoted in multiples of 25 cents), I set out to explore the town. The homes and stores of Fairbanks clustered along the curving banks of the Chena River. I would start to follow a street and after a few blocks it would end at the riverbanks. In the opposite direction, before long, the street would become a foot trail, an occasional sod roofed cabin hidden away in the trees and brush, until finally the trail itself ended in a tangle of brush. Indians had moved into some of the deserted cabins and their sled dogs, staked out around the cabins, set up a threatening din as I approached. There were probably a dozen Indian families living on the outskirts of Fairbanks. I was very conscious of the wilderness pressing in close. Once I saw a flock of grouse perched on the ridge pole of a cabin. It was no rare thing, I was told, for a moose or black bear to wander into town.

I was anxious to see an Eskimo but when I fell into conversation with some Fairbanks residents, I learned that Eskimos lived only along the shores of the Bering Sea and the Arctic Ocean. The population of the town had dwindled from some ten thousand during the big days of placer mining to fifteen hundred in 1922. Mining, however, was still the chief industry. A dozen small placer gold operations employed about three hundred miners the year around and five or six lode gold mines hired another hundred hard rock miners.

The town was the trading center for a large, thinly populated area of central Alaska. Prospectors, trappers, and Indians came there for their supplies. It was also the terminus of the Alaska Railroad and the hub of the Fourth Judicial district. Federal court officers, law enforcement officers, railroad employees, and some territorial officers lived there. It was very obviously a man's town. At a guess, the men outnumbered the women by three to one.

Accompanied by a chatty old-timer, I walked out Cushman Street, one of the three main business streets of the town. For the first five blocks from the Chena River, the street was faced with frame stores and for the next five blocks with neat homes. After that a gravel road called Richardson Highway branched off to the left and started bravely out toward the little town of Valdez on the coast, three hundred sixty-five miles away.

Going out Cushman we passed the Rickert gardens and greenhouses. As the old-timer explained, about April 1, Rickert would fire up his greenhouses and plant leaf lettuce, tomatoes, cucumbers, and radishes for the local trade. Since shipping time from Seattle was ten to fourteen days, no fresh produce could be shipped in except for occasional oranges and bananas.

"Butter's shipped up in tubs of brine," he said, "and the eggs are pretty gamey. A little catsup helps. After a while you'll get used to them. When you go back to the States, the eggs will all taste flat to you."

Beyond the greenhouses, a rutted wood road extended two miles through the wilderness to the Tanana River. When the river was frozen in winter, dog teams traveled that way, crossing the river to pick up an arrow straight trail

14

stretching due south across the Tanana valley to the foothills of the Alaska Range, ninety miles away.

That afternoon I hiked three and a half miles along the railroad track for my first glimpse of the new college. At the sight of it, I stopped dead in my tracks. There it stood on a birch-clad hill, one bleak, two-story, frame building. So that was the campus of the Alaska Agricultural College & School of Mines! Two thousand miles from home and on the very northernmost fringe of civilization, I faced that unkempt outpost. By any wild miracle could Dr. Bunnell and his staff possibly breathe life into it?

Chapter II

THE "NORTHERN LIGHTS" COLLEGE

WE had neither money nor the whole-hearted support of the community, no proper equipment and, for furniture, only a few second-hand tables, desks, and chairs. But at least we had a view. Our campus was on a low spur of the Yukon Highlands. In Alaska any mountain under six or seven thousand feet is just called "highland," and the summit level of the Yukon's is only four or five thousand feet.

We could stand in front of our building and look straight across the wide valley of the Tanana River, a valley laced with sloughs and covered with a jungle-like growth of brush, birch trees, and gnarled black spruce. It is a swampy jungle because the permanently frozen underground of the valley (which we call "permafrost") forms a perched water table during the warmer months. From a distance we could spot the waterways. Near them the subsoil thaws and there spruce trees reach a height of one hundred feet to parade along the riverbanks.

Ninety miles away rises the huge backdrop of the glacier-clad Alaska Range, stretching for hundreds of miles through Alaska, the great white tower of Mt. McKinley above it all,

20,320 feet tall, the highest point on the continent. So when derogatory remarks were made about our paucity of buildings, we could always say, "Well, anyway, our campus has the most beautiful view of any university on the continent." It was about the only thing we were able to brag about for some time.

For the first few days I was busy unpacking the laboratory supplies that I had ordered for the geology department. Since there was no proper place to put the material, I dragged in packing boxes and laid boards across them to form temporary tables. Kay had been a librarian at Whitman College near Walla Walla, Washington, before our marriage. When we could get a baby-sitter, she would walk the railroad track with me to the campus and spend the day cataloging the few hundred books that were the start of our library.

There were six of us on the faculty. Herbert Bruce had chemistry and physics, Clinton Morgan, agriculture, and Archie Truesdell, civil engineering. Elizabeth Kirkpatrick was to teach home economics—we were coeducational from the start. Earl Pilgrim and I made up the School of Mines, Earl teaching mining engineering and I geology and mineralogy. All of us rated as full professors. Most of us were in our twenties, our teaching experience limited. A good thing—at that point it took the exuberance of youth to be caught up in the dream that fired Dr. Bunnell.

If Dr. Bunnell had doubts, he never let them show.

Dedication Day was September 13. Chuckholes in the dirt road to Fairbanks were filled in; a platform was built in front of our frame building and, on the morning of the dedication, all male members of the faculty and the president scrambled up to the roof and stood in an eager little clump, pulling on a rope to raise our flagpole.

This flagpole had appeared in a mysterious fashion during

17

the night, so mysteriously that W. F. ("Wrong Font")
Thompson, a devil-may-care frontier editor if there ever
was one, broke out with this editorial in the Fairbanks
News-Miner:

A FLAGPOLE FOR THE COLLEGE

Now I ask you, how can a feller run up
a flag when he had no flagpole?

The College had no flagpole and no
money to buy one. They gotta have a flagpole.

M. D. Snodgrass knows where there is a
flagpole. We didn't ask him where it is,
for it's none of our business.

If a feller has a flagpole and hasn't
sense enough or interest to day-herd and
night-herd it—he ought to lose it.

M. D. Snodgrass offered to go out before
daylight this morning and snare it.
Ain't that right?

It must be painted before it is put up—
Some color to prevent the owner from knowing
that it is his flagpole.

President Bunnell knows where some feller
has left half a can of white paint and a brush.

Then we are short handed for raising the pole—
So I promised, if necessary, to go to Bert
Stevens, the U. S. Marshal, and borrow a
murderer and a couple of bootleggers from his
boarding house across the street.

18

At two o'clock in the afternoon we emerged in dignified procession from our building and took seats. Governor Scott Bone and Carl Theil were there to represent the Territory as well as Colonel Frederick Mears, general manager of the new Alaska Railroad. There also were the eight doughty souls, willing to pin their faith to us, who made up the board of trustees. As the ceremony concluded, the Reverend Frederick Scherer rose to give the benediction. He spoke of great mountain peaks and tumbling glaciers and asked God to permit the new institution to rise as a challenge to the mountains and to bring great things to Alaska.

We certainly needed God's help. The captains and the kings departed, as well as the two hundred or so people from Fairbanks who had stood together in the clearing. President Bunnell and his faculty of six filed back into the building and on opening day we were in business, with an enrollment of six students, all from Fairbanks. Well, as we told ourselves, a little wryly, this just balanced the six faculty members. There was no danger that any student was going to be lost in the crowd.

In the next few weeks a few more students came dribbling in, some from other Alaskan towns and some from "outside." We rejoiced over each new student as if he were a gold nugget. One day a telegram, with a request for enrollment, arrived from Montreal, Canada, signed "McCombe." The telegram ended, as if it were an afterthought, with the sentence, "There are two of us." They turned out to be John and Robert McCombe, a husky pair of twins, who seemed to be after adventure as much as education. Within a month they had latched onto a dogteam and a cub bear. The McCombes were followed by three tall brothers from Wisconsin, Jules, Art, and Ted Loftus. So our student body had been boosted by five. Finally we had 21 enrolled, and there

19

was quite a vigorous clumping of boots in the hall during changes of class.

I was pleased (and even a little surprised) to find that students trained in Alaskan high schools were fully as well prepared as those from larger centers in the States. All of the larger towns had excellent grade schools and high schools. In very small settlements, the Territory supplied a teacher or a man and wife team for little one- or two-room schoolhouses attended by a handful of children of grade school age. If a student wanted to go on to high school, arrangements were made for him to live with some family in a larger town.

At that time the more prosperous Alaskan families were sending their children to the States for their college work. Our students were all of limited means and worked during summer months to pay their expenses. About half of them (including our five or six coeds) came from Fairbanks and lived at home, but the out of town boys built themselves cabins around the rim of the campus or fixed up old abandoned cabins within a mile of the college.

In an effort to make the college a part of the community life, in addition to our regular classes, we decided to develop a winter "short course" for miners and prospectors. This was a project that required some unusual innovations in teaching methods.

Most prospectors at the time were devoting much of their attention to the search for placer gold. One aim of the course would be to get them out of the stream bottoms and into the mountains to search for lode mines of various metals, such as silver, copper, lead, and zinc, as well as gold. We also wanted to train them to recognize the nonmetallic minerals that would be of value if they were found in Alaska.

Our first job would be to sharpen them on the sight determination of common rocks and familiarize them with the types of ores that might be associated with the rocks.

I did not think that men from the hills would feel any great enthusiasm sitting in a lecture hall while a professor held up a rock and said, "This is granite. Observe the typical coarse-grained appearance." They would learn much more readily by actually handling specimens of rock and ore minerals.

I racked my brains for several days. The men, I knew, would be of various ages and backgrounds but, as miners, they were almost sure to have one thing in common: a working knowledge of poker. I therefore devised a sort of card game, using rocks (and later some common ore minerals) instead of cards. It bore little resemblance to poker, as a matter of fact. Still there was a certain element there.

Twenty prospectors enrolled in our course, twenty very skeptical prospectors. Some, in fact, looked sheepish about attending class. But as soon as the identification game was explained to them, the atmosphere lightened considerably.

The prospectors were seated around a long table and I, as referee, sat at one end. One side of the table played against the team on the opposite side. Players were dealt a hand of fifteen common rocks, such as granite, gabbro, limestone, dolomite, and so forth, that he kept in a pile in front of him.

The first player might start off by announcing, "I'll open with a granite." Then he would play a specimen of granite and each player in turn would have to ante up with a granite, too. If he had no sample of granite in his hand, he had to sluff another rock and name it. Each specimen was numbered and the highest number won the pot. If a man misplayed or misnamed a rock, the other side could challenge him on it. If the challenger was correct he gained points for his side. If the challenge was not valid, he lost points.

I had not realized what intensity the prospectors would bring to the game. Almost to a man they became deadly serious and competitive. As the game progressed, as the air grew blue with tobacco smoke and tempers flared, there were moments when I had to move fast to break up fights.

Things came to a kind of crisis after we had been playing the game for a week and the prospectors had grown quite proficient in recognizing the rocks. As a new twist I had introduced a few specimens of diorite into the hands.

"Today," I explained, "diorite is a wild card. You can use it to trump in and take the pot."

"What do you say, Prof, if we all ante in a dollar," one of the prospectors sang out.

There was an immediate and approving uproar around the table and money started appearing.

"Now, wait a minute," I cut in. "Do you want me to lose my job?" As a compromise it was finally agreed that the losing side would buy lunch that day for the winners, and for a few minutes the play went on quietly, the men very tense.

Then a prospector called Shorty, at the far end of the table, said in an aggrieved tone of voice, "Hey, Prof, this guy across from me keeps folding his arms all over his cards. I can't see if he reneges."

The player across from him was a man in his sixties, an old-time prospector named Jim. "Renege, hell," he growled. "You couldn't tell if I reneged, even if I shoved the rocks right up your nose."

Shorty, a man with a short-fused temper, stiffened at once. "Why, you—," he began.

"All right, fellows, calm it down," I interrupted hurriedly. "But give your opponents a chance to see your rocks."

Shorty settled back in his chair, but some quite malevolent glances were being passed between the two, I noticed.

After that the game continued without interruption until each man had only four rocks left in his hand. At this point the going always got rough since easily identified rocks had already been played and those remaining were mostly rocks that the men were uncertain about. As it happened, in the next round, Shorty was the apparent winner. He was about to take in the pot when Jim, the last player, said gleefully, "Hold on there. I'm trumping in with a diorite."

"Diorite, hell," Shorty yelled. "If that's a diorite, I'll eat it. You can't get away with a lowdown—"

"What's that you say?" Jim snapped, surging to his feet.

Shorty leaped up too, shoulders swinging. "What I say is you're—"

What Shorty said was drowned out in the general uproar. Someone had grabbed up the rock and it was being passed from hand to hand while noisy arguments broke out all around the table.

"Shorty," I shouted, to be heard above the clamor, "you've challenged, so it's up to you to name the rock."

Dead silence fell while everybody looked at Shorty. "It's a gabbro," he announced.

I began talking fast, explaining what a tough decision it was because of the similarity between diorite and gabbro, mentioning that geologists, when in doubt about a rock, could examine a section under a microscope, but a prospector, who couldn't lug microscopes around in the hills, had to depend on rough sight determination. "Jim," I said, "I agree with you. The rock is a diorite."

I think I held my breath until, reluctantly, Shorty sat down. "Okay, Prof," he said. "If you say it's a diorite, we'll have to go along with you, but it sure as hell looks like a gabbro to me."

So the crisis seemed to be over. But the thought occurred to me that we might have to discontinue our identification

23

games. This had been a close thing. If a real brawl broke out, the good name of our college would not be enhanced. At that moment, to my relief, the noon gong sounded and I began to total up the score.

"Hey, wait a minute," one of the players called out. "Some of these guys are holding back bastard rocks they don't know from Adam and I'm laying for them, see?"

"Yep," another said, "and I've got a piece of diorite here. I'm sure not going to bed with that."

I looked up and down the table. There was not a man there who wanted to stop playing and I thought, these men are learning rocks and learning fast. What's more, they're all having a good time doing it, including Shorty and Jim. Well, I said to myself, there's a risk. But what in life is ever accomplished without some risk?

Most of the men had taken me aside when they enrolled and asked me please, under no circumstances, to let on to their friends in town that they were taking the course. Within a few weeks, they themselves were bragging about the course all over Fairbanks. Excellent promotion for the college. In Alaska the opinion of mining men carries weight. Moreover, prospectors move around. They would spread the word to other towns.

All well and good. But we had our worries. No funds had arrived to pay our salaries. Ours was the last of the land-grant colleges to be formed in the United States and as such we were entitled to receive $50,000 annually in government funds. However, the authorities in Washington, D. C., apparently felt that a college in this faraway place might die aborning and they were reluctant to release funds.

Winter began to close in on us. The birds had started their long migration south, first the swallows (which had a date at Capistrano, California), followed by the twittering hordes of other small birds. By the time the high lakes froze over in early October, the great flocks of ducks, geese, cranes, and swans were in the air.

And still no money arrived. As our savings dwindled, we began tightening our belts. A little gas car, operated by the Alaska Railroad, furnished transportation between Fairbanks and the campus, but the roundtrip fare was fifty cents. The faculty suddenly developed an unusual taste for exercise. We frequently walked the three and a half miles each way to save money.

Every morning I would start out walking the railroad tracks, carrying a .22 rifle. Usually the grouse were out pecking gravel and I could pick off one or two for our dinner before they took to the air. If the grouse did not cooperate, I generally could shoot a rabbit. One day, when word of caribou passing over Cleary Summit spread around town, Earl Pilgrim, Professor of Mining Engineering, and I rented a Model-T Ford, picked up our wives and after ten miles over a deep-rutted dirt road, spotted a small band of stragglers on the hillside. Earl and I both brought down fine young bulls and drove triumphantly home with a caribou on each running board of the car. So we had meat for the winter larder. Grouse or game put into our cold cache in sub-freezing weather would be frozen hard as blocks of wood when we took them out weeks later.

I tried to sell Kay on the idea of tacking strips of the caribou hair onto the seat of our chemical toilet, a device favored by prospectors in their outhouses. Certainly, in that weather, the idea had merit, but Kay refused with indignation.

By that time, winter really had us in its grip. Each day we watched the daylight growing shorter. I would hear people say, "We lost ten minutes today," meaning that there were ten minutes less daylight than on the previous day.

25

The rivers had been frozen over for weeks and small streams were solid ice down to the gravel.

At night, instead of lighted windows, we would see only a feeble beam here and there, shining through the small portholes in the cabins. Sometimes Kay and I would lie in bed and listen to the mournful baying of the huskies, starting with one lonely voice and rising to a chorus, like some wild dirge to the Arctic night.

Whenever I looked out of the window in the morning and saw smoke from neighboring cabins sending a vertical white plume skyward, I did not have to look at the thermometer. I knew we had sub-zero temperatures with the air absolutely still. I would start out from home, bundled up in a coonskin coat, fur hat, and fleece-lined overshoes, and trudge the seven blocks through darkness to the railroad station. The snow underfoot was like dry, white sand.

Presently other bundled up shapes would loom out of the dark—faculty members, students, and a sprinkling of our short course prospectors—all heading in the same direction. Somebody always stopped to glance at the big thermometer fastened to a telephone pole near the Chena River bridge. The red colored tube of mercury often read 20 to 40 degrees below zero. We would hurry across the bridge to the railroad station, the cold air biting our faces and knees, girls wearing fur coats or colorful reindeer parkas, boys in ordinary drill parkas with mukluks on their feet.

Nobody did much talking as the little gas car bounced and swayed along the rails toward the college. We just sat huddled there, thinking our own thoughts or just sitting. When the car halted at the base of College Hill, we plodded single file, lunch sacks in hand, up the narrow snow trail to the lone building on the crest of the hill. Lights would be on in several cabins around the edge of the campus where a few hardy students were toughing out the winter.

26

Then lights would come on in the classrooms and laboratories and the farthest-north college in the world was in session. It was snug enough inside. Our storm windows were all battened down tight to conserve the warmth provided by a wood-fired boiler in the basement.

At midday the little gas car would be back with a dozen Fairbanks housewives who were enrolled in the home economics short course. By early afternoon darkness closed in again. At 5 P.M. we would bundle up and trek down the hill for the return trip to Fairbanks. Lights would go off in the building and it would be left standing there on the hill like a stark gray ghost, enveloped by cold and the Arctic night.

On such days, when I got home from the campus, Kay would glance first at my nose. If there was a white spot on the tip she would jump up, grab my fur hat and rub the frosted spot vigorously to restore circulation, sometimes saying in a chiding voice, "Men with long noses should stay out of the Arctic."

Within a couple of months, we were a closely knit crowd up there at our preposterous college. Classes were small and the faculty young. Only two faculty members were in their thirties. The rest of us were all in our twenties so that, on an average, we were just eight or nine years older than our students.

Our one senior was an agricultural student named Jack Shanley who had studied three years at Cornell before he wandered off to Alaska. When the college opened he had decided to work for his degree. Jack was a devil-may-care sort of fellow in his mid-twenties. He had built two small cabins, one for himself and one that he rented to the McCombe twins.

One night he invited all of the faculty to his cabin for dinner. We arrived in a bob-sled drawn by two big horses,

27

the bed of the sled filled with hay and blankets to ward off the cold during the hour-long ride. The home economics teacher had volunteered to cook the dinner and hurried right into the kitchen. After a few minutes she came out again. "Jack," she said, "I can't find the meat."

"By Gosh," he exclaimed, "I forgot about that!" He jumped up. "Don't worry. I'll run my snares and be right back with some."

When he came in a few minutes later he was carrying four rabbits, frozen stiff. While Jack cleaned and skinned them, the distraught teacher heated up a kettle of water to thaw them. It was late that night before we finally had fried rabbit. But as the professor of agriculture remarked on our way home, "That is a very enterprising young man. A cabin to live in and one to rent. Meat in snares right outside his door."

As faculty members we all discreetly refrained from mentioning a further evidence of enterprise. Those were Prohibition days, but quite obviously Jack had a brew of home-made beer going in one corner of the kitchen.

Washington was still holding off on our money. In my blacker moments I suspected that the money never would arrive. It was hard to put zest into teaching, not knowing if we would have to close our doors. I was particularly concerned for the students who had come from a great distance, the three Loftus brothers from Wisconsin, for example. Having very little money for their first year of college, they had filed on a homestead across the railroad from the campus. As they cleared, they sold the wood at $5 a cord and were doing well at it, too. A sorry thing it would be if the boys had to be sent home.

My own reserves were disappearing fast. When Mrs. Tom Youle from the Model Cafe saw me in town she would wave merrily and call out, "Still carrying that chicken feed around?"

As I waved back I would think that chicken feed may be all we have left before long.

The merchants of Fairbanks had been most generous with credit, but remembering the terrible bills we were running up, I began to feel shamefaced whenever I met one of them in town. Their forebearance was the more remarkable since, in the opinion of most Alaskans, our college had been doomed from the start.

At first friends we had made in town expressed themselves freely on the subject, but as the days darkened and the sorry plight of the professors became obvious, they all dropped the subject—out of a feeling of compassion, no doubt. This was particularly noticeable at dinner parties.

Ice, snow, the Volstead Act, and an absence of fresh fruit and vegetables did not prevent hospitable Alaskans from entertaining. Kay and I would walk across town to a dinner party, snow crunching underfoot, and as our host opened the door a cloud of white fog would roll across the living room floor while we whipped inside as fast as possible. If the temperature outside was, say, minus 40 and the room temperature was 70, the differential would be 110 degrees. I don't know how our respiratory systems could adjust to such a shock. The women would arrive, bundled up until they looked as round and shapeless as polar bears. They would go clumping in their snow boots into the bedroom to shed all manner of garments. Then in a few minutes they would come tripping out in high heeled slippers and low necked evening gowns, as elegant as opening night at the opera.

At our first parties, Kay used to steal curious glances around the dinner table, trying to assay the backgrounds of our companions. In the early years there had been very few women in the area. Even in 1922 the ratio of men to women was one-sided. Each year a new covey of schoolteachers arrived from the States and the single men made a beeline for the depot to look them over. This resulted in a large number of college-trained women who married and cast their lot in the Northland.

Some wives, however, were former dancehall girls and a few even emigrated from the red-light district, a series of drab, small cabins on Fourth Avenue, just off the main street. For the most part they were fine women and we were careful not to go delving into anyone's past, unless the information was volunteered. But we soon discovered that the Alaskans were being just as tactful as we were. They were carefully skirting around any mention of the college and our dismal prospects.

By December 21 we had reached the nadir. At ten-thirty in the morning a counterfeit sun peeped up over the Alaska Range, traversed a low arc to cast a pale light over the land, and by one-thirty fell behind the mountains. But by that time, sun or no sun, our world was bright again. In early December, like manna from Heaven, money from Washington finally arrived.

Nobody even tried to preserve an intellectual detachment. We were weak with relief and did not care who saw it. Professors hurried all over town, from merchant to merchant, paying accumulated debts, shaking hands, and thanking store keepers for the credit that had been extended. Even the *Fairbanks News-Miner* blazed out with our news.

With the arrival of the money, the whole tone of the college changed. Suddenly we were all optimism again, pointing out to each other the great and useful work an agricultural college and school of mines could do in Alaska. Take agriculture, for example. It had become an embryo industry in interior Alaska, with a genesis that dated back to the early prospectors. To ward off scurvy, at the first signs of spring prospectors planted onions, radishes, and lettuce on the sod roofs of their cabins. Warmth from the cabin below kept the roots from freezing. By the time we arrived almost every home in Fairbanks had its big backyard vegetable garden. Sometimes there would be a strawberry patch in one corner and even a little greenhouse for early tomato and cucumber vines. Under the stimulus of long days of summer sunshine, we were told, the gardens would quite literally grow while we slept.

The U. S. Department of Agriculture already had established an experimental station on fields adjoining the campus where they were developing breeds of grain that would mature during the short, intense growing season. Cattle and hogs were being introduced, and small farms had begun to appear on the hillsides and on the valley floor. As agriculture grew, so would the need for an agricultural college. Someday, we told ourselves, the experimental station would be part of the college.

As to the school of mines, no other school in the nation had both lode and placer mines on its very doorstep. Only a few miles beyond the campus was Ester Dome. Ester Creek had yielded several million dollars in placer gold to early miners working by hand methods. The easily won gold was now mostly mined out, but a few plants were still working there. The gold-bearing gravels were covered with a layer of black, frozen muck. Gold, being heavy, had its richest concentration at or near the solid bedrock under the gravel beds. To get at the rich paystreak, miners sank shafts thirty to one hundred feet deep, thawing the frozen ground with steam points, hand driven. From the shaft bottoms, drifts were driven out to follow the paystreak.

It was a natural laboratory, and we decided to exploit it. An exciting business it was, too, the first time I took my freshman mining students down a shaft in a hoisting bucket. The darkness underground was thick with a haze of steam seeping up out of the ground. The carbide lamps on our hats formed only blurred halos in the darkness. As we felt our way along the bedrock drifts, we had to be on the alert to dodge wheelbarrows loaded with gravel being trundled by hurrying men. The pace was set by the leadman, who shoveled the thawed gravel swiftly into his barrow and started off with it at a dog trot to the shaft several hundred feet away, where it was hoisted to the surface. All the other men had to keep up the same pace, to fill their barrows and get to the shaft without holding up the line.

During my student days I had spent my summer vacations working as a mucker in mines where I had worn out a good many shovels. But this drift mining in low tunnels was the most killing work I had ever seen.

Each weekend we took our mining students on Ester Dome to map the geology of the small gold-quartz veins, to study the mining methods being used, and to learn to survey underground.

Among other things, it was a good object lesson on the limitations of manpower. "There are millions of dollars in gold locked up in the Fairbanks area alone," I told the students. "This is true in other parts of Alaska, too. But it's going to require huge capital investment, great and accurate engineering, and powerful machines to win this gold at a profit. Mathematics, physics, chemistry, mechanics, and geology are some of the basic tools you will use to solve your problems. That's why we're cramming the knowledge down your throats."

They got the message, and by spring we were working with a handful of young men who wanted to talk, eat, and sleep mining.

Spring in the south has always been a poetic time. In the

32

Arctic it is sheer, wild drama. Nothing but a great shout of praise can do justice to it. It comes with a rushing of water, a beating of bird wings, and a glorious strengthening sun after the months of darkness. Right after the spring breakup, as soon as the ponds and sloughs were open, the water fowl started coming in. All day we would hear the gabbing of ducks and cranes pushing northward in V-shaped squadrons toward their nesting grounds. The birch trees, which had stood like gray ghosts against the winter sky, were suddenly alive again and all around us nature was in full pulse under the stimulus of daylight around the clock.

So the college had weathered its first winter. Our students were preparing to leave for home. I was rather curious about what reception the McCombe twins might receive in Montreal. They had both proved to be excellent students, but so charged with excess energy that they were never able to keep out of devilment. They had decided to take their dogteam home with them, an expensive undertaking, so they arranged to travel steerage out of Alaska. I wondered how their Canadian parents would react to the sight of all those snarling sled dogs.

Jack Shanley was our one graduate at the first commencement in May. The president and his handful of faculty members must have looked incongruous as we marched into the small assembly hall, shepherding our lone graduate. Mosquitoes, the plague of Alaska in the days before the area was sprayed from the air, were out in force. From the stage we watched the janitor slipping up and down the aisle with tin lard pail lids, each with a little mound of yellow powder called "buhack" on it. As he lighted the mounds and deposited the lids at intervals along the aisle, acrid fumes filled the air until the hall smelled like a joss house.

He should have put one of his offerings on the stage. While the commencement speaker was giving his charge to our graduate, a mosquito started to buzz around my nose. I knew he was preparing to come in for a landing and I did not want to break the solemnity of the occasion by swatting at him, so I gently blew him in the direction of the governor of Alaska, seated beside me. In a moment the mosquito came sailing back. I had a sneaking feeling that he was not traveling entirely under his own power. I tried once more and after a minute, back sailed the pest again. After a few passes he finally gave up and searched elsewhere. I kept wondering if the governor was aware of what had happened. I did not have to wonder very long.

As we marched out he said, "First time I ever played ping-pong with a mosquito. Who won that game?"

Chapter III

GOING TO THE DOGS

O NE day during our first winter in Alaska I fell into conversation with an old-timer at the Model Cafe. "I've seen the ice come on the river and in a few months you can no longer call me a 'chechako'," I said. "When the ice goes out I'll be a sourdough."

"Only a first degree sourdough, son," he replied. "To be a full-fledged sourdough you have to see the ice come and go in the river, shoot a bear, and sleep with a squaw."

"Are you fully qualified?" I asked.

There was a twinkle in his eye as he slapped me on the back and walked away.

Kay and I had come in for a good deal of ribbing about being "chechakos" that winter. I cannot count the number of people who had quoted a verse called "Up In Alaska"—

> If you've lived up in Alaska
>   Where the Arctic breezes blow,
> Till you've seen the autumn ice come,
>   And you've seen the spring ice go,
> And survived one long dark winter,
>   When the mercury ran low
> You can drop the name "Chechako",
>   And become a "Sourdough."
>
> Esther Darling

A catchy rhyme but a little wide of the mark, I discovered. The old-timer in the cafe had done no better. You do not become a sourdough by holing up in a cabin through the long winter or by killing and eating a bear, either. It takes an emotional experience to get the real feel of the country. I believe most Alaskans can remember moments when they suddenly found their perspective had shifted and realized for the first time that they were looking at the country with different eyes. And I believe that these experiences usually occur when a man is away by himself, alone in the great country. Or so it was with me.

I had started early to take the mining students on field trips to the placer and lode mines in the Fairbanks area, but if I were going to be an effective teacher, I had to know more about the mineral deposits and mining methods in other parts of Alaska, too. When summer came I joined three other men on a trip to Livengood, an outlying mining section.

After a week looking around the Livengood camp, I was ready to start home. I could not find anyone headed for Fairbanks so I bought some supplies, stuffed them into my packsack, and set out alone back-packing to Olnes, a fifty-six-mile trip. At Olnes I could catch the narrow gauge railroad to Fairbanks.

The trail was easy to follow and the first two days were uneventful, except for the ravening hordes of mosquitoes and the blazing sun. Occasionally the thought would cross my mind: "Wouldn't it be funny to get sunstroke in Alaska?"

The third day, as I was climbing up Wickersham Dome, I noticed bands of caribou here and there. They did not seem concerned as I slogged by them, but after I had passed timberline and was almost off the summit of the dome, I suddenly heard a thundering of hooves behind me and whirled around. I was being charged by a band of one hundred caribou, all heading straight at me. I had no gun to try to stop the charge and there was not a tree in sight. There was nothing at all to do except stand there and wonder what was going to happen. Well, I thought, who ever heard of anyone being killed by caribou?

Finally I tore off my hat and mosquito veil and started toward them waving it in the air. They came right on until they were about one hundred feet away and then the herd split and cantered up on each side of the trail where they stopped and stood still, looking curiously at me.

I went slogging on past, every now and then glancing uneasily over my shoulder. The caribou were still standing there, staring after me. Then in a few minutes, they all came charging at me again with thundering hooves and tossing antlers, and again the herd split and went cantering by on either side of me, to stop again and stare.

They're playing tag with me, I thought in astonishment. Suddenly I felt like laughing out loud with pleasure. It seemed to me a wonderful thing to be playing on a mountain top with a herd of caribou.

After a time they lost interest in the game and went back to grazing, but as I swung off down the trail I did not feel at all like a chechako. At that moment I felt in tune with the whole country, as much a part of it as the caribou themselves.

That was one of many moments during my early days in the North when I could feel Alaska getting to me. At these unexpected moments I would find myself thinking, "This is my kind of country." The real clincher came on the trail in winter.

In those days, before there were many airplanes in Alaska, you either traveled on snowshoes or used a dog-team if you wanted to get out in the bush in winter. Only a few of the main roads in the area were plowed and those only occasionally, but dogteams were common on the streets of Fairbanks and it was not unusual to look out of my office window and see a team tethered on campus.

I decided to learn to mush dogs. I had hopes of developing some consulting work in the mining field to bring in some extra money, since the high cost of living in Alaska consumed most of a professor's salary. Besides, the gold fever is infectious, and I was at an age when a man dreams easily. If I could get around the country, who knows? I might someday find a new mine or possibly even have a little mine of my own. So I snapped at the chance when a grizzled dog musher invited me to go with him for a trip into the hills one weekend.

"If you're going to drive a dogteam you have to learn to swear all day without losing your temper," he told me.

He was perfectly serious. You control a dogteam entirely by voice, I learned. "Mush" means go, "Gee" means turn right, "Haw" means swing to the left, and a string of profanity means "Stop fooling around and put your back into it." The commands are understood by the lead dog, picked for his temperament and intelligence. Often at a branch in the trails the leader will stop and look back, as much as to say: "Well, which way do you want to go?"

To stop, you clamp down on the brake, suspended between the runners by a coiled spring, and yell "Whoa!" When the dogs feel the steel tongs on the brake biting into the hard-packed snow they seldom pull against it.

All this was explained to me while the musher got ready to harness the dogs. It sounded easy enough. I watched while he fastened the tow line to the sled and then stretched it out in the snow. First he brought up the two wheel dogs that work just in front of the sled. They were powerful big brutes, the heaviest dogs in the team, and they were both excitedly eager to slip their heads through the heavy collar that connected with their harness.

As he was harnessing the other dogs I looked the sled over. Cleats about three inches wide were fastened to the rear end of the sled runner. When I stood on them and grasped the two handlebars, it seemed to me that I was going to have a lot of fun, being transported swiftly down the trail with the wind in my teeth. That was before we started.

The old musher climbed into the basket of the sled and I took the handlebars, yelled "Mush," and we were off. Within fifteen minutes I discovered that it took strong shoulders to keep the sled upright and the runners on the hard packed snow when the dogs were running along a twisting trail. When the trail was soft or steep, as I hurled and twisted the sled, it seemed to me that the musher was just an extra dog.

To add to the general discomfort, the team had noticed a strange voice giving commands and did not work well for me. The leader kept slowing down and glancing back. I began to see the wisdom of the musher's original advice. He would call out their names, in a drill sergeant's voice, damn them and their antecedents, and in a moment we would be back in full motion.

Climbing up a ridge was tough going. I ran along behind the sled, pushing on the handlebars to help the dogs.

"Take it easy, son," the musher cautioned. "Never work up a sweat. When we get on the divide there'll probably be a cold wind blowing and you'll chill fast. Many a man has been frozen on the trail in his own sweat.

"Another thing," he went on, "if you have a bottle of whiskey on the sled and you feel you're getting chilled, don't take a nip. If the temperature is 30 below, the temperature of the liquor will be the same. Think what that would do to your gullet."

39

By that time we had reached the divide and all at once the team took off with gusto. I was not quick enough getting onto the brake and in five seconds the sled was on its side, the old musher had been dumped into a snow bank, and I was being dragged along behind the upset sled, yelling "Whoa" to the team, which was obviously taking advantage of my inexperience. Behind me I could hear the old musher yelling: "Stay with them, son!" and then roaring with laughter as I was skidded along prone over the snow.

We were all straightened away and running smoothly again when one of the dogs became tangled in its harness. He was running with a hind leg over the towline, so I stopped the team and moved forward to get him untangled.

"Wait a minute," the musher ordered. When I stopped he said, "You're asking for trouble. These dogs don't know you. Wrap a dog chain around your left wrist. The dogs respect that. Work from the side and don't get in among them and don't bend over too much. Your hind end would make a mighty tempting target. If one dog jumps you, the others will be on you in a flash."

Gingerly, I obeyed all his instructions, expecting at any minute to feel a dog's fangs tearing into my parka. Wolf blood is bred into the husky to give him the toughness and endurance he needs for his work. But with the wolf strain comes the killer instinct. Each winter children are mauled and sometimes killed by stray dogs. The dogs are particularly dangerous if a child is running or falls.

Sometimes a team will gang up and kill one of their own companions. Later, when I was on the trail with sled dogs and saw another team approaching, I would get the lead dog by the collar and jockey my team into deep snow, to give the approaching team a clear trail. Even then, as the teams passed, the dogs would snarl and lunge at each other, both teams itching for a fight.

At the time I had my first lessons with a dogteam, we were all particularly conscious of the danger. Only a short time before, a newly married couple had borrowed a team from an Indian in Eagle for a drive down the Yukon River on the ice. About a mile below town the dogs tangled in the harness and the young man stepped in among them to unsnarl them. As soon as he bent down they were on him, a pack of killers.

His wife grabbed a club-like stick and ran to his rescue. The pack turned on her, too. She struck at them but at the first blow the stick broke and only a short stump was left in her hand. The dogs, however, had an instinctive fear of a club and hesitated, waiting for the moment to attack.

Calling to her husband, who was badly injured and bleeding, to crawl into the bushes and hide, she started walking backward along the ice toward town, with the dogs stalking her. At the first slip or the slightest stumble, they would have killed her, but she kept her nerve and held them at bay until someone on the riverbank at Eagle saw the tableau, the girl, carefully taking each backward step, and the snarling dogs, with a taste of blood in their mouths, waiting for a moment of weakness or hesitation.

Men from the village grabbed up their guns and ran to her aid; in a few minutes the dogs were stretched out dead on the ice. The husband was flown to Fairbanks and spent several weeks in the hospital. The only thing that had saved him from death was the courage of that girl.

Of course there is another side to the sled dog story, too. Not all teams are killers. As some dog mushers point out, many teams are devoted to their masters and would fight to protect him. I have heard of mushers who have been forced to "siwash" on the trail in bitter cold weather and have toughed out the night with their dogs nested around

41

them. But in my opinion, such dogs are a rare exception to the general type.

I had become fairly proficient handling a team when I made my first trip alone with the dogs. That was during my second winter in the North. I had heard of a new gold quartz discovery some distance from Fairbanks and I wanted to take a look at it and cut some samples for assay. It was three o'clock in the afternoon and the chuckholes in the trail were getting dim in the winter twilight as I swung my team off the trail and into the yard of the roadhouse where I was planning to spend the night.

A man came out of the low, rambling log house to help me unhitch and stake out the dogs for the night. Several teams were in ahead of me, I could see. Over a low fire five-gallon cans of dogfood were simmering, a gooey, smelly compote of oatmeal, tallow, and segments of dried salmon. But to my dogs it was ambrosia. Their last meal had been twenty-four hours before.

When I went inside I found half a dozen men sitting around the stove, waiting for supper. I had just started to pull off my parka when a voice sang out: "Well, if it ain't the Prof! What are you doing out here, Prof?"

It was one of the students from my short course for miners. Then I saw another prospector I knew. As I went around, shaking hands, it was heartening to hear the warmth of their greetings. These were real Alaskans, rugged men who had spent most of their lives in the back country and could cope with most problems that nature and weather could throw their way. I felt a sort of glow at finding myself accepted so casually as one of them. Then I felt diffident, too. In a classroom, discussing geology or mineralogy I could speak with authority. But here, in their environment, I knew I was the rankest sort of amateur.

The stove in the center of the room was made of two

oildrums welded together to hold four-foot logs. The stove pipe went up through a safety collar in the roof and chicken wire was stretched on a frame four feet above the stove. This was festooned with insoles, socks, and woolen mittens, drying out for use the next day and giving off a mild odor of sweat, pungent but not unpleasant. When I had taken off my fur hat and moosehide mitts, the wool mitts I wore inside were hung up with the others to dry, followed a minute later by my insoles and socks. I shoved my feet into a pair of stags and crossed the big room to a series of pole bunks along one wall. There was an empty one, not too close to the stove, so I threw my sleeping bag and packboard there. Blankets and a pillow were on the bed and I was glad to see that the pillowcase was reasonably clean. That night, I would not have to spread my shirt over a grimy pillow, waiting until the lights were out so as not to offend my host.

The roadhouse keeper, who doubled as cook, came rolling out of the kitchen to greet me, wiping his hands on a flour sack tucked into his belt as an apron. "Just the fellow I want to see," he said. "Got some mineral samples over here on the windowsill I want you to identify for me. Could those dark spots be gold tellurides?"

"Here we go again," I thought. It is very difficult to get the true color and lustre of minerals when the only light comes from a gasoline lamp shining down from above. The more common minerals often show cleavage or crystallization and you can check the approximate hardness with a knife blade. Otherwise, good sight determination can be made best in daylight, and I would be on the trail before dawn.

"This is an interesting chunk here," I said. "Let me take it to the college and I'll find out what minerals are there and have it assayed for you."

43

He seemed a little hesitant. "Okay," he said at last. "But don't tell anyone where you got it. I haven't staked the ground yet." As it happened the sample turned out to be worthless.

After supper we sat around the stove toasting our shins while the stratum of pipe smoke thickened above our heads. One fellow sat under a gasoline lamp painstakingly reading a month-old copy of the *Alaska Weekly*. The news was fresh to a man who had been out all winter on his trapline.

Most of the slow, easy talk around the stove had to do with trapping experiences, prospecting trips, stampedes to new gold discoveries or mishaps on the trail, all well larded with humor, even the tales of close brushes with death or with bitter disappointments.

"Well," said one old fellow who had been trying for years to find a rich placer gold deposit, "I've been in the North for twenty years now. When I got here I could put all my worldly goods in a ten-pound oatmeal sack and still have plenty of sack left over to tie a good knot." He scratched his chin through his grizzled beard. "Now I can put all my money in a Bull Durham tobacco sack and the drawstring puckers up real easy."

Another man had broken through an overflow with his dogs while he was coming down the Middle Fork River. "By the time I got the dogs, the sled, and myself back on the ice, I was soaking wet right up to the middle. Did any of you fellows ever have to brush the snow off a log and sit there with a bare hind end, a-shivering and a-shaking, while you wrung the water out of your drawers and pulled them back on?"

There was very little talk of sex and few off-color jokes. They were men without women, physically exhausted at the end of the day. On a trip to town their only woman acquaintance might be a sporting girl. One of their favorites seemed to be the "Oregon Mare," so named because she could whinny like a horse.

"There's a fine woman. Like that time they had the flu epidemic at Nenana and people were dying like flies. She was right in there with her sleeves rolled up nursing the sick. The doctor told her she was the best damn nurse he had and she'd better get some rest before she took sick, too.

" 'Don't worry about me, Doc,' she told him. 'I'm not afraid of any flu bug.'

"Sporting girl, hell. She was an angel during that nightmare."

"Remember the 'Black Bear' used to be on the line at Iditared?" one man asked. "Now there was a gal for you. Built just like a bear except she'd measure an axe-handle across the butt. Sure she would. And she had a coat of hair just like a black bear, too."

The talk had veered off into politics before I finally crawled into my sleeping bag. I felt as if I had been in choice company that night, a company that somehow typified to me the tough heart of Alaska. A remark one of the men had made came back to me: "I can look any man in the eye and tell him to go to hell." He was not being belligerent. He was trying to say that he did not have to defer to any man, not in the environment in which he lived. These men judge you by your ability to adapt to the North country, I thought. I liked this.

The sleeping bag felt good to my tired muscles. The last man in closed the valve on the gasoline lamp. The gauze mantle of the burner faded to a dull glow, flared up in a final flick of light, and after that there was darkness. Through the window I could see bright moonlight on the snow, promising a good day on the trail tomorrow.

The fellow in the bunk next to mine began to snore and

in the yard one of the dogs, feeling the call of his ancestors, pointed his muzzle at the moon and started his mournful wail. He was really putting his heart into it, pulling out all the stops and developing a wavering tremolo. The deep gurgling snores of another sleeper joined the chorus. Clearly there would not be much sleep for me that night.

The next thing I knew my nostrils were twitching at the wonderful smell of bacon frying. Had I been asleep? I wondered. Certainly it could not be morning. But who would be frying bacon in the middle of the night? I raised myself on one elbow and looked at my wrist watch, but I was too groggy to focus on the hands in the darkness. It was pitch black outside. The wind was rattling the stove pipe and a gentle quiet lay over the room. I had just snuggled down to sleep again when a voice roared, "Rise and shine or you'll be burning daylight."

The roadhouse man slammed into the room with a lamp which he hung on a hook suspended by a wire from a pole. As he threw sticks of wood into the stove and opened the draft and damper, men started to climb with protesting grunts from their beds.

After a husky breakfast of oatmeal, sourdough hotcakes, bacon, and coffee, we struggled into our trail clothes. I was wearing two pairs of heavy wool socks in my shoe-pacs but a good many of the men wrapped their feet, mummy-like, with strips of burlap before getting into their foot gear.

Outside it was bedlam, men swearing, dogs barking. I tossed my packsack and sleeping bag into the sled and lashed them down under a canvas tarp. In a canvas pocket on the sled I had an extra pair of mitts and socks, some candy bars, a cheese sandwich and a Thermos of coffee for a quick lunch on the trail. The sandwich would be frozen but the hot coffee would take the curse off of that.

When I had tied the sled to a tree with a slipknot and

brought up the wheel dogs, they seemed glad to get their heads in the collars and have the harness adjusted. But my other dogs were convinced that I was going off without them. They were all at the end of their chains, barking and jumping, saying in dog language, "Hey, don't forget us!"

Some of the drivers, more expert than I, were pulling out, and as each sled left my dogs reared and jerked in the harness trying to pull the sled loose and follow. As soon as they felt me step on the runners, they tightened up the slack on the towline like racers tense on the mark. I reached down and gave a quick jerk on the slipknot, made a grab for the handlebars and we were off down the trail, racing through the dark timber. The cold air made my eyes water and the dry frost bit my nostrils. But the mad dash and the fast maneuvering to keep the sled upright on the turns were exhilarating, too. Within half a mile, I knew, the dogs would have had their morning run and would settle down to a calm pace.

An hour later, just as daylight was breaking, we reached a low saddle that formed the divide between two valleys. All at once I was certain I heard a voice behind me and stepped on the brake to bring the team to a halt. The dogs had been working hard on the upgrade and, glad of the respite, dropped on their bellies, grabbing up mouthfuls of snow. Only the lead dog, with a sense of responsibility, stood upright, looking back at me with a question in his eyes.

There was no one behind me on the trail. I never knew what tricked my ears. I stood looking back over a huge and empty landscape, the whiteness of snow-covered hills broken only by occasional green patches of spruce. Then suddenly I saw it. Mount McKinley stood completely naked of clouds, soaring up to the highest point on the continent, touched by the pink dawn. It was at least eighty miles away but the clear, washed air brought the peak intimately close. I do not know what thoughts rushed into my mind at the sight. I think it was more emotion than thought, something like falling in love.

So this is what Alaska is, I thought after a moment, and all at once I knew I wanted to be part of this country, so magnificent and so full of a great promise.

Finally I turned back to the sled, gave it a shake and called out, "All right, boys. Let's go!" My destination was still fifteen miles away and we had work to do. As the dogs started off toward the small mining camp in the hills (which never did develop into a profitable venture), I took one last look over my shoulder. There it was again, a feeling that the country had reached out toward me and that something in my heart had answered, "I belong here." And that is what it really means to be a sourdough.

Chapter IV

INCHING FORWARD

WHEN college opened for its second year, we had grown a little bit. We now had forty-five regular students plus thirty-six taking special short courses. I wonder how we worked up enough optimism to keep on struggling. The college was still little more than a clearing in the birch forest. We had no funds for lawns but President Bunnell, being a thrifty fellow, contracted a local farmer to put in a hay field on the southern exposure of the campus where permafrost had been driven deep into the earth. So there we sat on our hill with the northern lights playing around, one hundred twenty miles south of the Arctic Circle and fifteen hundred miles from any other college.

At least, we told ourselves encouragingly, two-thirds of our original students had come back to us, including our entire basketball team, which some wag had dubbed the "full house team." The McCombe twins were the pair and the Loftus brothers were three-of-a-kind. Basketball was big in Fairbanks. In addition to the high school team, there were several town teams, one sponsored by the Elks club and another by Fairbanks merchants.

By 1925 we had added a wing to the original frame

49

building and had a full-time enrollment of fifty-nine students. The great majority of these were Alaskans with only a sprinkling of stateside students, some attracted to the college by a sense of adventure and some by an interest in the North. And some came, as they explained, just for the hell of it.

All the fifty-nine seemed to be endowed with boundless energy. They generated enough excitement, from skiing competitions to theatricals, to exhaust a school three times our size. Less than a third of the students were girls. No coeds ever had it so good. They would be dated up for weeks in advance of a college dance, and town girls would be brought in to fill out. Not that attention went to the heads of our coeds. In Alaska women always had been a much sought after minority.

When it came to extra-curricular activities, the youthful faculty were right in there pitching. One of the teachers coached basketball and the head of our new English department put on two plays a year, which always drew packed houses. Plays were a rarity in Fairbanks in those days.

By that time we had had a few other small encouragements, too. The office and laboratories of the U.S. Bureau of Mines were moved to the campus and housed in the basement of our frame building, and our winter short course in mining was thriving. Each year we had veteran prospectors who traveled one hundred miles or more by dog sled to reach the college. At the first hint of spring they would hurriedly say goodbye, impatient to be on the trail and freight the season's supplies into their outlying camps before the breakup.

Encouraged by the success of various short courses on campus, President Bunnell hoped to reach scattered Alaskan communities with extension work in agriculture and home economics, if benefits of the Smith-Lever Act could be extended to Alaska. This would mean that the U.S. Department of Agriculture would match funds provided by the Territory for extension work in farming areas.

The week before he left for Washington, D.C., to confer with the U.S. Department of Agriculture, he called me into his office. "Patty," he said, "I'll be away about a month. I need someone to run things while I'm gone so I have decided to appoint you dean of the faculty and head of the School of Mines. There will be a salary increase of $500 a year."

I was jolted right back on my heels. For a minute I felt the glow of success and then I thought of the responsibility and of the animosity which this might cause among my friends on the faculty, and I began to get panicky.

I stammered out my doubts to him, adding, "I'm only thirty years old. Perhaps if you selected an older man . . ."

The president just swept away my objections, and that evening I hurried home to tell Kay our secret.

The day came for the president's departure and still no formal notice of my appointment had been made. I was too proud to mention it to him. I thought he might have changed his mind. But the next morning, as I walked into the building, I saw a cluster of students and faculty reading a typewritten notice fastened to the wall by the president's office. I peered over their shoulders. Yes, there was the notice of my appointment. Without a word to anyone I slunk down the hall to my office. I had been thrown to the wolves.

There was an ominous silence in the building that morning. By afternoon the dam broke and three of my associates, at different times, came to assure me of their friendship and to tell me how disappointed they were not to have been selected themselves. They told me frankly that they were far better qualified than I for the job. One of these was an older man whom I respected very much. If I had been president, he was the man I would have chosen and it was hard to resist telling him so.

When the tempest died down I received wonderful co-operation, but I also learned that loneliness comes with an executive job. The old free camaraderie with the faculty had vanished overnight.

Dr. Bunnell was successful in his mission to Washington. With funds provided jointly by the U.S. Department of Agriculture and by the Territory, an agricultural extension worker was employed to visit farming areas, introducing new ideas and experimental crops that might be adapted to a northern climate, and a home economist traveled from town to town setting up short courses for Alaskan house-wives.

We seemed to be getting a little on our feet. There were a few additions to our faculty, a few new departments added; hammers sounded as new buildings were put up to take care of a slowly increasing student body. The upper floor of the new wing on Old Main was now a gym. We no longer had to hold basketball games, dances, and plays in Fairbanks. When the second wing was added, it became the largest frame building in Alaska. Finally we got our old boiler out of the basement to a separate power plant; a dormitory was built to house fifty men and had a dining room in its basement.

Up to that time the prospectors had lived in Fairbanks during our winter short course in mining, the prosperous in hotels, the rest in deserted cabins around the town. After the dorm was built, nearly half of the men moved to the campus and I was delighted to see what camaraderie developed between these veteran prospectors and our regular mining students.

We had converted a house on the campus into a temporary girls' dormitory and eight or ten coeds lived there. Most of them came from other Alaskan towns, although there were generally one or two adventurous girls from the States among them. One of these made an indelible impression on the campus. She arrived from California, beautifully suntanned, and refused to wear stockings. Some hefty betting went on among students and prospectors in the men's dorm on when she would be forced to back down. A few quiet bets were even placed among faculty members. Little by little the tan faded and goose pimples appeared. The girl stuck it out into December but when, before Christmas vacation, she finally showed up in the dining room with stockings, from the uproar, anyone would have thought a long shot had come in at Pimlico.

By that time I was doing a little consulting work for mining companies on weekends and one of the jobs was as exciting to me as any search for buried treasure could possibly be. Two brothers, Joel and Don Gustafson, had come to my office, prepared to start an extensive exploration program at the old abandoned Rhoads-Hall mine.

I knew the property well. It was not very far from Fairbanks and I had been taking my students there to study geology and methods of mining a small vein. I also knew its history. It had been developed by Louis Rhoads, who came to Fairbanks in 1906 after making a small fortune in the Klondike and losing it again in a mining venture in Mexico. By that time the best placer ground was already staked, but Rhoads reasoned that there must be rich veins in the hills to have fed gold into Cleary Creek, since a rich paystreak of placer gold was being mined its full length. So he began trenching and panning along the hillsides at the head of the creek and in 1908 discovered a small but rich quartz vein which became the Rhoads-Hall mine.

The production from this rich little vein had totaled

around a million dollars by 1917, when Rhoads found his vein sliced off by a fault. A fault means that there has been a fracture in the rock mass along which slippage has caused displacement. Although Rhoads was sure that his missing vein must be nearby and drove short drifts into both walls, he was unable to find it again.

His wife urged him to give up, pointing out that they had enough money to go to California, buy a ranch, and live comfortably for the rest of their lives. Although Rhoads was a prospector at heart, he was well past middle age and could understand her logic. He finally promised to spend only $50,000 more in the search and to shut the mine down if by then he had not found the vein. His search failed and they bought the ranch.

The Gustafson brothers had raised money from a group of friends in Minneapolis, secured a lease and option from Rhoads, and formed the Cleary Hill Mining Company. Until this time the Gustafsons had been placer mining in Alaska. This was their first venture in underground quartz mining. I think they came to me because it would have been much more expensive to bring in a consulting engineer from the States.

When a fault cuts off and displaces a vein, it frequently leaves a message written in the rock to tell the direction in which the missing ore has been moved. One of the most dependable clues is "drag-ore"—fragments of crushed quartz, ground off when the ore was dragged along the fault. In the fault to the east of the original vein, we found some fragments of crushed gold-bearing quartz. I was confident that the vein had been displaced in that direction. But Rhoads already had driven long crosscuts both east and west without finding ore. This was discouraging until, while mapping the old workings, I found that the crosscut toward the east (made without benefit of a survey) had wandered back across the fault. So now at least we knew where our target should be.

After tunneling one hundred feet, we crossed a small quartz stringer. It was barely an inch wide, but it carried gold. I assumed that the stringer must be running parallel to the vein and we drove ahead with confidence but, after advancing the tunnel-heading another two hundred feet, we were still in barren rock. By this time my clients were running short of funds; we were all discouraged and I felt defeated.

When some additional funds were raised, we began trenching on the surface, several hundred feet ahead of the fault. After days of digging, we began to find chunks of gold-bearing quartz in the hillside mantle, and tracing these down to the bedrock surface, we found rich ore snuggling in the rock. But this was on top of the hill, and several hundred feet from the mine workings. We were going to have to go down the mountainside to the underground workings, find the vein there and connect it, in order to mine from these lower workings. Moreover, this discovery lined up with the little quartz stringer we had seen in our original crosscut. Was it possible that the little knife edge of quartz was really our vein? There was no way of telling. So back we went and drove a tunnel to follow the stringer further into the hill.

The next time I visited the mine the new tunnel had advanced forty feet and we still had only the little, narrow ribbon of quartz. But it was gold-bearing, so we kept on following it. One evening a week later, my phone rang and the excited voice of Gustafson came over the wire. "We have a twelve-inch vein of highgrade ore in the tunnel face!"

So Lady Luck had given us one of her rare and wonderful smiles. There is no excitement like it for a mining man.

Within an hour I was at the mine. I had to see that ore before I could sleep. Eventually over two million dollars of new ore came out of this property before high costs forced the mine to close down.

Beside the immense satisfaction, my only take from the venture was a consulting fee of $50 a day. But $50 a day seemed very good in those days and I continued as consultant for the operation as long as I stayed at the college. I usually spent two Saturdays a month at the mine.

Even before this, Kay and I had decided to cast our lot in Alaska. I had some misgivings about it. Not for myself, the country was already under my skin, but Kay's girlhood had not conditioned her for the rigors of life on a northern frontier and it seemed unfair to ask her to make such sacrifices. A good many wives escaped the long, cold winters by taking vacations in the States. Not a happy arrangement. When I walked into the Model Cafe I would often see their husbands at the counter there. We called it the deserted husbands' club.

The way Kay had responded to life in Alaska made me proud. Her early ancestors had been pioneers and this heritage surfaced quickly. But I did not want to ask too much of her. When I told her so, she just said, "Ernest, if we're going to get ahead, we can't let geography enter into our calculations."

So we bought a home, a three-room log cabin that cost us $500. It had been occupied by a bachelor and the interior was not very inviting. Kay went to work with fresh curtains, paint brush, and deft touches beyond the ken of mere man, and in no time we had a bright, snug home.

When I worried for fear she was working too hard at it, she said, "You should know me better than that by this time. I *like* to build a nest."

56

"Well, yes," I admitted. "If you'd been born a bird you'd be flying around all the time with a straw in your beak."

With fees from the Cleary Hill mine, we built on a bedroom, tore out the canvas that formed the balloon ceiling, and put in a coal furnace. We were very happy.

Ernest Jr. was four years old, high time he had a brother to keep him company. The baby was overdue and our family doctor was leaving for a trip to the States. To hurry things along he prescribed a dose of castor oil and quinine. When even this drastic treatment failed, he left, turning us over to the other doctor in town, J. A. Sutherland, a competent physician but one we did not know well.

At three o'clock the next morning, Kay woke me to announce that the baby was on his way. I leaped out of bed and phoned the doctor. Since it was July, even at that hour the sun was high in the sky as we drove across the bridge to St. Joseph's hospital. From the hospital window I looked across the Chena River to the sleeping town and saw Dr. Sutherland drive up to the Model Cafe and go in for a cup of coffee.

At that moment the nurse said, "Get the doctor here right away. The baby's coming."

I raced to the phone, called the restaurant and was back at the window in time to see the doctor come tearing out of the cafe and leap into his car. He did not make it. The baby arrived before he did and thus, precipitously, in 1926, Stanton Patty came into the world.

With a house of our own, two sons and a car, we were feeling well established. The car was a mixed blessing in winter. I would drive it into the unheated garage, drain the radiator, drain out the crankcase oil, and remove the battery.

If the oil were left in the crankcase overnight in subzero weather, it became too viscous to be drained. When the crankcase plug was removed, it would build up into a tar-like cone under the car.

To start the car again, I would install the battery while pans of water heated on the kitchen stove. Then I would pour several gallons of hot water through the radiator to warm the metal, fill the radiator with more hot water, and cover it with a blanket to hold the heat. Finally I would heat the lubricating oil on the kitchen stove, pour it into the crankcase, pour hot water on the carburetor, hand-crank the car, and pray that it would start.

We generally preferred to walk, if we were only going to some social engagement in town. In those days the most exclusive club in Fairbanks was the Sourdough Dance Club. Its exclusiveness was based not on wealth or social prestige but on your love of dancing. Women came in light dresses and the men shed their coats, because these were vigorous dances. There was a generous sprinkling of people of Scandinavian extraction with their zest for the polka, schottische, Swedish waltz, heel-and-toe polka, skater's waltz, and square-dances. As I tried to thread my way through an intricate square without tangling up the whole thing, or when my partner told me in exasperation that I was getting ahead of the music, I was acutely conscious that our bid to join the club was not because of me.

The big excitement of the year was Ice Pool time in March when we all pitted our hunches against the elements. A tripod, with a rope attached, would be set up on the ice of the Tanana River at Nenana. A coil of slack rope was left at the base of the tripod and the other end of the rope fastened to a clock on shore. When the ice started to float away in late April or early May, it would first take up the slack and then stop the official clock.

Tickets were sold for a dollar apiece and on them you registered the time (month, day, hour, and minute) when you thought the clock would stop. Some people did elaborate mathematical calculations and some relied on dreams. Ice Pool tickets were popular prizes at bridge games, as these were supposed to be particularly lucky. The pool closed in March and in those days it totaled around $60,000, a figure that seared itself into our minds. During our second year we came within one minute of winning. The next year we dug deep into our sock to buy tickets and did not even guess the right month.

At the college we were still fighting to justify our existence. Some people were coming around to the idea that Alaska needed the college. Some thought that it was located in the wrong place. The $50,000 annual federal grant which came to us as a land grant college was used chiefly for salaries. All other funds came from Territorial appropriations. The legislature met at two-year intervals and each of these sessions was a cliff hanger for the college. Many of the legislators were lukewarm about us and some were downright hostile.

One year President Bunnell came back, looking worried, from a meeting of the Territorial legislature at Juneau where he had submitted his request for funds for the next biennium. He had met with a cold reception. The appropriations committee had refused to have him appear before them. Instead he was instructed to return to the college and told that they would in due time decide the appropriation. Later some of our friends in the legislature sent a telegram, warning us that our appropriations might be eliminated.

During this gloomy period, the president's secretary came into my office to say that the president wanted to see me. After one look at her sad face, I decided that the axe had fallen. When I entered the president's office I found him sitting with his feet on his desk and a book in his lap.

"Sit down, Patty," he said. "Put your feet on the desk. I have something here I want to read to you."

I was not about to put my feet on the president's desk and seeing me hesitate, he said, "Relax, Patty. Put your feet up. After all we may not need this desk much longer and a few more scratches won't make any difference."

His book was a racy French novel and he began to read aloud. For a full hour we sat there, the president and his dean, feet on desk, every now and then bursting into loud belly laughs. Once he looked at me with a grin and said, "If that appropriations committee could see us now, we'd be fired on the spot."

At the end of the story he said, "Well, how do you feel now?"

"Wonderful," I answered.

He hauled his feet off the desk and sat up straighter. "You know, Patty," he said. "I think we can lick them yet."

And he did, although it required much horse trading and legerdemain on his part. The funds he requested from the legislature were usually shaved to a bare minimum and there would be grumblings and threats, but after each biennial meeting, Dr. Bunnell would leave with an appropriation that would keep us alive for another two years. This particular year the Territorial appropriation was only $105,000 for the biennium. The staff was reduced, salaries were cut, and we learned the true meaning of austerity. This was the bleakest period in the history of the college.

The students were aware of our life and death struggle and identified with it. Whatever we lacked in equipment, no college could boast of a more loyal student body. Whenever it was necessary to dampen a student escapade, I only had to say, "If the legislature learns of this it is going to be tough on us." The shindigs would stop instantly.

When a visiting legislator arrived on campus, we would

60

ask a student from his district to conduct him about campus. We knew he would be given the full treatment. Frequently I have had the visitor return to my office to say, "You know, I've never been sold on the college, but it's been a revelation to see what goes on here and the fine spirit behind it all." I would glance over his shoulder at the student guide and see a wide grin on his face.

During those early years, the School of Mines was the main prop of the college. People had begun to recognize that our location was remarkably well suited to a mining school. Even in winter, when the big gold dredges were idle, individual miners were busy with small-scale placer drift mining. From my office window I could see plumes of smoke rising from the camps of small gold quartz properties on the surrounding hills. My students and I spent almost as much time underground as in the classroom. The pace was swift and laggards did not last long. Those early students were a rough as well as an eager crew. After one wild tavern brawl, President Bunnell said, in near despair, "Patty, those mining students of yours are going to ruin us yet."

"Don't worry," I told him. "Someday you're going to be proud of those boys."

For once I spoke with the voice of prophecy. One is now chairman of the board of a large mining organization and has his office on Park Avenue in New York. Another is president of a big Eastern technical college, and others of our early mining graduates are among Alaska's leading engineers.

Chapter V

GOLD IN THE BACK COUNTRY

A HOARY old story has been told for years by mining men in Alaska.

When an old prospector knocked at the Pearly Gates, they say, he was told that the prospectors' section of Heaven was too crowded to permit additional entrants.

"If you'll let me in for one day," the old prospector told Saint Peter, "I'll guarantee a big exodus."

Although dubious, Saint Peter decided to let him try the experiment. Sure enough, within a few hours, a large cadre of Alaskan prospectors, packs on their backs, checked out of the Pearly Gates and headed for the nether regions. The old prospector came trudging along at the end of the line.

"How in the world did you accomplish this?" Saint Peter asked.

"Well," the prospector said, "I told them I'd just come from Hell and there had been a big gold strike down there."

As he started to walk away, Saint Peter called out, "Hold on there. You don't have to leave. You've won the right to go back inside."

The old prospector hesitated a moment. Then he shook

his head. "You know, Saint Peter, I've been thinking this over and there just might be something to it, after all. I'll go along with the rest of the boys."

Whenever there is a gold stampede, there is always drama, even if there is not always gold. I have listened, entranced, to stories of all the big stampedes in Alaska and the Yukon, each full of excitement, hardship, tragedy, and sometimes great success. Finally I saw a minor stampede myself.

One winter word filtered into town of a big strike in the Poorman district, some two hundred miles from Fairbanks. Two prospectors, the story ran, had sunk a hole in Beaver Creek and had taken $150 in coarse gold from the bottom of their shaft. One- and two-dollar pans were common, according to the tales.

Prospectors in the Fairbanks area loaded their sleds with steam thawing boilers, steam points, picks, shovels, and grub and took off across the snow with their dogs and their big hopes. A real stampede was on.

The local newspaper played up the story to break the monotony of a long winter. When Associated Press stories were sent out, they were picked up by papers all over the country. The Associated Press wired back for more information. Each day a new release went out over the wires. This alerted a big Eastern mining organization and I was asked to go up there and report back on the facts. Rather reluctantly, President Bunnell consented to let me get away from classwork for a few days, so I gleefully chartered a ski-equipped bush plane and was off in comfort on my first stampede.

When we had passed Tanana and were flying down the Yukon River, I could see dogteams at intervals on the ice, all heading in one direction. As our plane skimmed by overhead, outstripping all that struggle and effort so easily, I found myself feeling guilty.

At Ruby, which was as close to my destination as the plane could land, I rented a dogteam and headed for Poorman, thirty miles across the hills. At noon I pulled in at a small roadhouse, to ask the proprietor if he could feed me.

"Young man," he bellowed, "you're looking at the dirtiest cook in Alaska."

"My friend," I said, "you're looking at the hungriest man in Alaska."

When he brought in a heaping plate of moose meat stew, I was ready to attack with long teeth. When I had gingerly picked a dozen moose hairs out of it, I found that I was not so hungry after all and settled for a cup of coffee. "My friend," I said, as I handed him the two dollars that he asked for his lunch, "you told the truth. You're the dirtiest cook in Alaska."

On that note we parted good friends and I rode off down the trail munching a candy bar.

The next morning I arrived in Poorman and immediately ran into some luck. At the store where I stopped to inquire about the trail to Beaver Creek, I met a little Italian, named Tony, one of the partners who had made the original discovery. He took me into the back room to show me the gold. It was mostly coarse nuggets—beautiful gold.

He also invited me to stay in his cabin, the only cabin on the creek, he told me. All the stampeders were living in tents pitched on the snow. Over his loud protests, I added some canned goods, a ham, a slab of bacon, and several cans of butter to his grocery order. It was the only way I could repay the partners for the luxury of sleeping in a warm, snug cabin. I knew they would never accept money.

In spite of those beautiful nuggets, in a few days it became evident that no placer deposit of a size to interest a

64

large organization could be developed here. Still, there was a second possibility. Another prospector had found gold on a creek eight or ten miles away and I decided to have a look at it.

During my stay with the Italians they had both been the souls of hospitality and yet I had noticed a certain distress in their manner, too. Several times I had walked in on them when they were talking together in earnest, almost tearful Italian.

Finally, just as I was leaving, Tony asked my advice. They were indeed in trouble. They had been busy staking additional claims to protect their original discovery, but a stampeder had jumped a key claim and they did not know what to do.

"Except for your discovery claim," I told them, sounding off at once, like a professor, "you have nothing except snow locations. You won't have a valid mining claim until you sink another hole down to gravel and can pan out some colors of gold. Why doesn't one of you continue with your staking before the other stampeders arrive? In the meantime, the other fellow can move a boiler up to the disputed claim and get started thawing a hole down to gravel."

They brightened up immediately and as I pulled away from the cabin they were busy loading a prospecting boiler into a sled.

I expected no difficulty in finding the second location. The fellow I wanted to see had passed through camp only a few days before. There had been no new snow and his sled tracks should lead me directly to his camp. But after a few miles I found myself on a dome-like summit where the snow and the sweep of the wind had obliterated the sled tracks. There were five creeks heading against the dome, radiating out to form the drainage patterns, and no way of knowing which one to try first. For a while I circled with my team on the glazed snow, only occasionally picking up a short segment of track made by the sled runners. While I was trying to line up these segments to get the man's general direction, I saw a big splotch of tobacco juice staining the crystal snow and, a little further on, another stain. It was better than a row of sign posts.

So my man was a tobacco chewer, one who liked a big mouthful and really worked it over. An hour later we were shaking hands. But again the results of my investigation were disappointing. Nothing there would interest a big mining company. Well, as one philosophical mining friend of mine often says: "It's just like smoking five-cent cigars . . . once in a while you find a good one." And if my first stampede did not provide any gold, at least it had some dramatic moments in store for me.

I got back to Beaver Creek in the late afternoon. When I walked into the murky half light of the cabin I was startled to see my Italian friend sitting shadow-like at the window, watching the trail with his rifle across his knees.

"What's wrong?" I exclaimed.

"I keel heem," Tony cried out, his voice squeaking up into a furious falsetto. "I keel the sonnabeetch. I shoot them both."

From an impassioned flood of words, I managed to disentangle the story. He had followed my advice. He had moved his prospecting steam boiler to the disputed claim and was busy driving a steam point into the frozen ground to make the first thaw of his prospect shaft when the claim jumpers, man and wife, came along the trail with their dogteam. Seeing what he was doing, they ordered him off.

This led to some rough talk and finally the man threw the Italian down in the snow, shouting to his wife to open the blow-off cock on the boiler. The purpose of this was simply to stop the work. However, steam spurted out and scalded the Italian's foot and leg. This unintentional development quickly ended the encounter. But the little Italian was out for vengeance.

I glanced quickly through the window. The trail passed within twenty-five feet of the cabin and the man and his wife could drive along it at any moment. I have never talked harder in my life than I did during the next few minutes. I tried to project a tone of calm reason with my voice, all the time keeping a pretty frantic eye on the trail. Finally Tony regretfully let me take his gun and I hurriedly pumped out the shells. I was just putting them in my pocket when the dogteam appeared up the trail and the two came sailing by the cabin. In my mind's eye I can still see the tassels on the man's fur cap fluttering in the breeze.

This man and his wife are still living in Alaska and both of them are my good friends. I have never told them of the incident.

That night a miners' meeting was called. This is justice in its simplest form. Wherever there have been frontier mining camps, problems have been settled at a miners' meeting. Although I had heard and read about such meetings all my life, I had never expected to sit in on one.

All the men in camp gathered around a big fire. There was none of the usual by-play or joking. This was a serious gathering. After both of the contesting parties had agreed to abide by the decision of the meeting, each man in turn stood up there in the snow and told his side of the story without frills. Afterward a vote was taken. The verdict went in favor of the Italian and was accepted without rancor. I found the whole affair impressive. Incidentally, the claim later proved worthless.

The next morning I hitched up my dogteam and set out on the return trip. The dogs and I were getting well acquainted and they were working well for me. Since they sensed we were heading for home and I had only my pack-sack and sleeping bag in the sled, they hit a good pace. Anyway, it was the sort of glorious spring day when just being alive and on the trail seems wonderful, whether you are a man or a dog.

I was to pick up the plane in Ruby the next day. But Alaska still had another facet of life to show me before I left. In Ruby I was invited to a Saint Patrick's Day dance and dinner celebration at the old Opera House. Everybody in town seemed to be there. Frost action had heaved the building and raised a wavelike hump across the center of the floor, not that the dancers seemed to mind. They would just dance up the hump and then down the other side. A colorful crowd of dancers they were, too. Many of the Indian girls wore print dresses with bright ribbons to accentuate their black hair.

The wife of one business man in town made an entrance wearing a beautiful fur parka with matching mukluks. I watched with awe as she slipped off the parka, for under it she was wearing a beautiful gold evening gown. Then she opened her evening bag and produced matching gold slippers. No one seemed to find this at all incongruous.

During the chicken dinner, my neighbor tapped my knee and passed a bottle of moonshine under the table. I was expected to fill my water glass and then slip the bottle along to my neighbor on the other side, these being Prohibition days.

After a long day on the trail I was sleepy and went back to my hotel as soon as possible. Several times during the night I was wakened by loud talk outside my window and the sound of fists slamming against jaw bones. The next morning at breakfast I noticed several black eyes. "What was all the fighting about last night?" I asked the man seated next to me.

"Oh, the Irish decided to lick all the Swedes."

"What do you have against the Swedes?" I asked.

"Nothing," he said and looked at me as if he thought I was out of my mind. "They were just good friendly fights."

In the next few years, private consulting work for mining companies brought in almost as much money as my university salary. During Christmas vacations and summers, when I was not employed at the college, I traveled all over Alaska to examine mining properties. In the 1920s there were fewer than sixty thousand white people in the whole enormous Territory. As soon as I left Fairbanks I would move into a huge and empty land, seeing only an occasional small Indian village of from twenty to fifty families. The men living there trapped during the winter, brought their furs into Fairbanks by dogteam, and returned with a load of supplies. North of Fairbanks there was not a single settlement of over fifty white people.

Even traveling in summer to places reached by a motor road had its adventurous aspects. In the three hundred and sixty miles from Fairbanks to Valdez on the coast, for example, there was no gasoline pump, no garage, and no settlement of more than ten people. Since the trip by car required two or three days, you carried your own food, camping equipment, shovel, pick, and canvas and always had two five-gallon tins of gasoline lashed on each running board.

Traveling down the Yukon River by boat, I would pass a few small white settlements, seldom of more than fifty white people—just a trading post, a school, and a spread of cabins. A number of Indians lived near these settlements. Along the river I would see their camps and the fish wheels that they operated to provide fish for themselves and salmon to dry for winter dogfood. In winter some cut cord wood that river steamers consumed the following summer.

In the back country there was only wilderness except for

an occasional remote cabin where a prospector or trapper lived. Sometimes I would pack into that back country on foot with a gold pan and a pack sack. It was a quiet summer when I did not wear out two pairs of boots. In winter I went by dogsled or by bush plane.

To any professor who wants a change from the confining routine of the classroom, I recommend a few jaunts with an Alaska bush pilot.

"Want to do a little hunting?" Jerry Jones asked me one evening, as we were flying about four thousand feet above the broad floor of the Tanana valley with the midnight sun shining into the cockpit.

I nodded and we zoomed low over a green meadow where a big bull moose was feeding. After we had made several low passes, herding the moose around the meadow, he saw that he could not escape this huge, pestiferous bird, so he braced his legs like four rigid poles, lowered his huge antlers and prepared himself for final combat.

"There should be lots of game feeding tonight," Jerry said, heading the plane out over the treetops. I glanced back. The moose was still standing there, only now his head was arrogantly raised. No doubt he was telling himself, "Boy, I showed that silly, noisy bird where to get off. Boy! I sure did."

In a few minutes we swooped in over another clearing, caught a black bear completely by surprise, and gave him a good evening workout. Jerry later became a Pan American captain. As he flew the big jets over South American jungles, I'll bet he looked down and thought of the fun he could have with a little bush plane.

The trips were not all unbuttoned fun. The airfield at Fairbanks was thawing out and very muddy one April morning when I took off with Frank Pollack in a little Stinson plane for some mine workings in the Kantishna

70

Hills, a low range of mountains on the northern flank of the Alaska Range. The strip at the mine, we knew, would be unsafe. Our only chance of landing would be on the ice of Wonder Lake some five miles from the mine.

All the other lakes we passed were breaking up, but Wonder Lake, nestled at a higher elevation, we hoped still might be frozen.

The lake was covered with ice when we flew over it, although there were streaks of open water at some points along the shore. The questions were: How thick was the ice? Would it hold the plane? Should we abort the trip and go home? We batted the questions back and forth as we circled the lake, wishing for the miraculous appearance of someone on the lake to signal the depth of ice.

Frank, who was a seasoned bush pilot, finally said, "I'll go down and touch the ice gently with the wheels. You watch over the side and see if any cracks appear."

We dropped down, barely touched the ice, and nosed up again. I could not make out any cracks, even when we skimmed back over the impact point to check.

"This time," Frank said, "I'll give it a good bump and then take off quickly."

Still there were no visible cracks. "I think it's okay," Frank said. "I'll slide it in and you watch over the side."

Soft as a kitten's paw, he eased the wheels down on the ice and we were coasting along.

"Any cracks?" he called.

"No," I said. "But don't cut the switch until I get a better look."

When we finally climbed out of the plane and chopped a hole through the ice, it was six inches thick, perfectly safe for a plane of this weight.

"I don't like to leave the plane here any longer than I have to," Frank said. "You'd better go ahead to the mine

71

and get your work done. I'll cut two small spruce trees so I can tie the plane down."

A few hours later he appeared in the mine tunnel, soaking wet. He had gone ashore to cut the trees and fallen through the ice. Since he was dressed in heavy clothes, he had quite a struggle making it to land.

Late that evening we warmed up the motor and after a quick dash over the ice we were airborne. As we banked we both looked down at the lake and Frank shook his head. "I hope we never have to do that again."

I thoroughly agreed with him, but I couldn't resist saying, "Wonder Lake—well, it certainly made us wonder."

A few years before I had been commissioned by a mining company to examine this property. I knew it was going to be a tough assignment. At that time there was no landing strip for planes, but I was young and had grown used to back-packing on Alaska trails.

I sorted out the things that I felt I should take with me. To my dismay, the accumulation weighed ninety pounds. I have read tales of men carrying packs weighing more than one hundred pounds but I have always taken them with a grain of salt. To carry a pack like that day after day a man would have to have the build of a bull moose. I managed to get my pack down to sixty pounds. It held two nested tin buckets with wire bails, one for cooking and the other for tea; a light frying pan; some dried food; a small slab of bacon; three cans of corned beef; some rye tack; and, as a luxury, two loaves of bread at the top of the pack. These, with a few items of clothing, my notebook, and sample sacks, were all lashed onto a canvas pack board. I left my lightweight summer sleeping bag behind. The summer sun gave us twenty-four-hour daylight. We would travel at night and sleep during the day in relief cabins spaced at intervals along the trail.

72

Albert Wilkerson and I left the Alaska Railroad at McKinley Park station. Albert had just finished his first year as professor of mineralogy at the college and wanted to gain some first-hand knowledge of the geology of the Alaska Range. I was glad of the company during the four or five days it would take to reach our destination, a distance of one hundred miles.

The first part of our trip would be through the park, so we checked in with Harry Karstens, park superintendent. Mount McKinley National Park had only recently been organized and the trail that we were taking was the only means of access. Although Karstens looked askance at the .30-30 saddle gun I was carrying he finally let me keep it when I promised not to shoot in the park.

Late in the afternoon of the second day, we were plodding under our packs upstream on the Sanctuary River. The trail had disappeared on the gravel bars of the river but I expected to pick it up again where Igloo Creek entered the Sanctuary. We were headed into rugged terrain, an unlikely place for a trail, it seemed to me. The country had not yet been mapped. I wondered if we could have passed Igloo Creek. When I glanced back I saw Al, fully half a mile behind me. I decided to push on and make camp, but a few minutes later I heard a noise in back of me and whipped around. Al was right on my heels.

"What happened?" I asked.

"Didn't you see that bear track on the sandbar?" he said. "It's fully twelve inches long and he's heading upstream."

An uncomfortable thought occurred to me—big game animals had not been told that they were in a national park.

The next night, after we left the Igloo and were heading for the Toklat River, we saw a big husky dog ahead of us. He was standing in the trail waving his plume-like tail in friendly greeting. Since his master, no doubt, would be com-

73

ing along the trail soon, we decided to sit down and rest until he arrived. I called to the dog but he would not join us. After fifteen minutes there was still no sign of a man.

I looked at the dog again. "Al," I said suddenly. "Could that be a wolf instead of a dog?"

"A wolf wouldn't stand there and wag his tail," Al said.

We got up and walked to within fifty feet of him. He was a wolf all right. He was standing guard over a young mountain sheep which he had just killed. The wagging tail meant, "Stay away from my dinner."

"Are we going to detour or shoot him?" Al asked.

Although I had promised not to shoot while I was in the park, the park rangers, I knew, were anxious to preserve the bands of mountain sheep. They probably were anything but anxious to preserve the wolves. A well placed shot between the eyes sent the wolf spinning like a top and we dragged the carcass into the brush.

Our next encounter was a sticky one. We had gone on only a short distance when we saw a Toklat grizzly bear feeding in a nearby meadow. More to the point, he also saw us. The Toklat bear is a dangerous animal. This one was a giant of a bear, dirty yellow in color, and so fat that he rolled like a small load of hay as he ambled over to investigate the intruders. All we could do was stand our ground, while I reached in my pocket for extra rifle shells. Not that I wanted to start a fight. My gun was much too light for such an animal.

"Let's try moving to windward," I said. A bear has poor eyesight but if he got our scent he might take off. Moving as quietly as possible, we began to circle. As we came closer, he suddenly started to pick up his feet and put them down slowly. This pussy-footing, I knew, is usually a final maneuver before a headlong charge.

I raised the rifle and drew a bead on a spot just behind

74

a shoulder. For a moment I thought of firing a warning shot over him and quickly dropped the idea. It might precipitate the charge and it would use up one bullet That bullet could mean survival. The bear raised his head, snuffing the air. For a moment he stood motionless, looking us over. Then suddenly he whirled and dashed away like a scared puppy. But for the next few miles we kept looking back over our shoulders.

A few hours later we reached the Toklat River where we planned to camp. I could see an inviting cabin on the opposite bank but the sun had been working on the glaciers at the headwaters and the river separating us from the cabin was starting to boil. I waded in carefully, with a strong stick in one hand to steady myself in the water and my packboard looped over one shoulder, to be free of it if I lost my footing.

Almost at once I was hip deep in water, the current tugging at my legs. With each step I felt ahead with the stick and then anchored it between rocks before taking a second step. I had anchored the stick securely, ready for another step, when I glanced up quickly to see how much further I had to go. My heart skipped a beat. I was standing still but the opposite bank was moving slowly past me. The sand and fine gravel underfoot were in motion.

I eased carefully around and retreated, glad enough to settle for the tent on our bank of the river as sleeping quarters. There were two steel cots inside and each cot had two slab mattresses. Since we were wet and chilled, we slept sandwich style between two mattresses. It's not as bad as it sounds.

By the next night we were on the final lap of our journey, following the trail up into Sable Pass. At the summit we came across a patch of snow perhaps half a mile wide. When we tried to walk on the crust, we kept breaking through and finding ourselves waist deep in snow. Finally we got down on all fours and practically swam our way through the snow, pushing our packs ahead of us. Since the sun on the snow smarted our eyes, we pulled our mosquito veils out of our pockets and tied them over our eyes. Once I took mine off when we stopped to rest for a moment and saw a band of mountain sheep watching us curiously from the cliffs above us.

Beyond Sable Pass, we turned northward to skirt Wonder Lake. Now the mosquitos were at us in full force. They rose from the moss to swarm about us. Some were getting a free ride clustered on our headnets, hats, and the shoulders of our coats. We were trail-weary and their constant buzzing added to our misery. At intervals, Al would take a branch and beat them off and I would run a hundred feet to escape them. In turn, I would give Al the "brush-off" and we would both jog another hundred feet to gain a brief respite. At the end of Wonder Lake the dim trail led us down Moose Creek; after a few more miles we caught sight of some mine workings on the hillside and the Quigley cabins just below them.

The Quigleys, Joe and Fannie, had lived there for years, laboriously developing a silver-lead prospect. I had heard tales about them and was curious to meet the couple. They welcomed us warmly. Joe was a giant of a man, six foot two of bone and muscle, with a Jimmy Durante nose, made more prominent by a great scar across it. Fannie had already become a legend in the North. I had even heard her called "the little witch of Denali." I fault the description. She did indeed live in the shadow of Denali, the Indian name for Mount McKinley. But she neither looked nor acted like a witch.

"Glad to meet you, young fellow," she said, offering me a calloused hand. I found myself looking down into a pair

76

of bright brown eyes, full of humor and wisdom. Her voice and movements were quick and decisive. So this was the legendary Fannie Quigley, I thought. She kept up a correspondence, I knew, with scientists at the Smithsonian Institution and sent them unusual specimens of plant and animal life from her remote area. She was particularly interested in birds and kept a record of those that flew in each spring to nest. She had even discovered and reported on one bird whose nesting habits had never before been known. If Fannie had had the proper education and training, a scientist once told me, "she would have made her mark as a naturalist."

She and Joe assigned us to a cabin adjoining theirs. It was chilly and I had just crumpled up a newspaper to build a fire, when Fannie burst in with some clean towels.

"What are you doing with that newspaper?" she demanded.

"Building a fire," I told her, puzzled.

"Whoever heard of using a newspaper to build a fire?" she snapped. "Don't you know that every paper—each piece of string, even—has to be carried in here by dogsled in winter or on a man's back in summer? How long have you been in Alaska? You must be a chechako. I'll show you how to build a fire." She ran out of the cabin, while I stood chastened and somewhat bewildered by her headlong charges.

In a moment she was back with a big butcher knife. She placed a piece of kindling between the toes of her shoe-pacs and began to burr the end into a tassel of shavings. Then she moved the knife midpoint to the stick. In a jiffy another curl of shavings appeared. When she had turned the stick end for end, she repeated the process, finally holding the stick up for me to see before she broke it into two fuzzy pieces.

"Give me the knife, Fannie," I said. "I can do that."

"Hell no. You'd probably cut off a toe."

"Have you a butter keg?" I asked.

"Now why do you want a butter keg?" she demanded belligerently.

"Well," I told her, "I can stand in the butter keg and not cut my toes off."

She straightened up with a quick grunt, caught the expression on my face, and broke into a big smile. "You and I are going to hit it off, young fellow," she said, slapping me on the shoulder.

Later she confessed, "You know, living like this has made me so thrifty that I won't strike a match unless I have two uses for the flame."

The greater the emergency, I learned later, the crustier Fannie's speech grew. I had already heard the story of the scar on Joe's big nose. The summer before when bush flying had just begun, he had chartered an open cockpit plane to fly him and a few supplies back to camp from Fairbanks. When he described to the pilot a long gravel bar on Moose Creek where he thought a plane could land, he overestimated the length. The pilot cut the switch as soon as the wheels touched gravel, but the propeller was turning over slowly when they reached the end of the bar. It caught the water and the plane nosed down, throwing Joe against the cowling, cutting a deep gash in his nose.

Fannie had watched from the cabin on the hills. Fearing that they might be trapped, she grabbed an axe and started running down the trail. Joe and the pilot met her on the way. Joe was bleeding and holding his big nose in place.

"What are you doing with that axe?" he asked.

"I was just coming down to finish the job," she said gruffly. Back at the cabin, she gave Joe a big drink of whiskey, got out needle and thread and sewed up the wound, while Joe protested and squirmed with pain.

"Stop bellering like a damned baby," she ordered, painting her needlework with a lavish dash of iodine.

But no one could be with her long without discovering what a compassionate heart and what quick sympathy were camouflaged by her gruff façade. Once I was surprised to see tears in her eyes. She wiped them hurriedly away. "God dammit," she said, looking ashamed, "I don't like bawling women."

I used to see her standing just outside the cabin, searching the surrounding hills for the sight of a bear, a moose, or a caribou. If she spotted one, she would reach for the rifle that was always kept on a peg beside the door and head out after it alone. The problem of getting fresh meat was critical and our arrival had made it worse. It would take us two weeks to finish our examination and Fannie could not run to the supermarket for extra supplies.

Our breakfast would be oatmeal, a big stack of hotcakes, and fruit—stewed wild rhubarb, dried peaches or dried apricots, sometimes with a few raisins added. Our lunch, which we carried to the mine, was often made up of bear meat sandwiches and a big piece of cake. We would stop on the mountainside and make a billy of tea to wash it down. Sometimes we would come out on the face of the mountain where we could look down into the valley of Moose Creek. Joe would peer all around. "Yep, Fannie's out fishing this afternoon. Grayling for dinner tonight, boys."

During the day Fannie worked with a bandanna wrapped around her hair, a man's woolen shirt, and overalls tucked into rubber shoe-pacs. But in the evenings her hair would be nicely combed and she would always wear an immaculate house dress. But if you glanced down, you would see the shoe-pacs sticking out below the hem of her skirt.

One evening at supper she proudly put a heaping plate of hot doughnuts on the table. "Dig in," she said. "Bet you've never eaten doughnuts cooked in bear grease before."

Once when I got back to camp I put a log on the sawhorse and started to cut some lengths of stove wood for her.

Within five minutes she came charging out of the cabin. "What do you think you're doing?" she demanded.

"Looks like you're short of stove wood, Fannie," I said.

"Put that saw down. I cut the wood around here. Your job is up on the mountain. My job is running the camp."

I looked at Joe. He nodded his head and I surrendered the saw.

I had come up to the Quigley holdings for Dome Mines Ltd. of eastern Canada. The hill is ribbed with several mineralized veins and Joe had opened these up with shallow pits on the surface and with some short underground tunnels. After I had surveyed the surface of Quigley Hill, plotted the location of the various claim corners and points where different veins were exposed, I set out on the return trip, carrying seventy samples for assay. I was also carrying the conviction that I had never known a more indomitable soul than Fannie Quigley. She had enough energy, courage, and intelligence to supply a dozen women.

Al must have been thinking very much the same thing. "Is there any other woman near here?" he asked, when we turned for a final wave to the couple standing in the cabin door.

"Fannie's nearest woman neighbor is one hundred miles away by trail," I told him.

Dome Mines gave careful consideration to the Quigley property but finally decided not to go ahead, perhaps because the mine was so far from transportation. But the mineralization that I had seen was widespread. I still felt there was a good chance to make a mine there.

Some time later, hearing that Joe Quigley was in the hospital in Fairbanks, I went to see him and found him in traction, festooned with weights and pulleys. This is the story he told me.

He had discovered a new vein of ore four or five miles from their base camp, too far for commuting. Joe set up a tent there and started driving a tunnel into the mountain as a drift on the vein. Each Sunday Fannie would toil her way up the mountain trail, carrying a pack of food supplies for the next week.

One day a big slab of rock on a wall of the tunnel caved. Although it crushed Joe's shoulder and broke his hip, he was able to extricate himself, crawl painfully out of the tunnel and by great effort reach the tent, where he got his body onto the bed.

A few days later Fannie found him there. She hurriedly built a fire in the little Yukon stove and fed him hot soup. Then she dressed his wounds and splinted him as well as she could. Two men who had a dogteam were mining on Eureka Creek eight miles away. With their help, she hoped to move Joe to their base camp where she could nurse him until one of the men could reach the railroad to phone for a plane. Since Joe was chilled, she replenished the fire in the stove before she rushed off for help.

Only a few minutes after she dashed away, the stove exploded, blew open the door and threw hot coals on the dirt floor of the tent. In her excitement, Fannie had grabbed handfuls of shavings from the pile in a corner and had carried them to the stove, leaving a trail of shavings on the floor. As Joe lay there, he saw the hot coals ignite the shavings and the fire slowly follow the trail toward the wood. When it reached the wood, the tent would burn, he knew, but he was too dazed and numb from his injuries to move.

If this was the end, he decided, he would just have to accept it.

In a detached way he kept watching the march of the fire. There was only one gap in the trail of shavings. Once the fire bridged that gap, the tent would be in flames within moments. The fire reached the gap and started to burn itself out. Then the shavings on the opposite side began to smoulder from the heat and one sliver ignited for a moment. The next moment it blinked out.

"Don't ever tell Fannie," he said, looking anxious. "First time I ever saw her lose her head. If she knew about this it would destroy her confidence in herself."

I promised. But the knowledge would not have destroyed her. I am sure of that. She looked at life too squarely to let one failure crush her. Many stalwart women followed their men to pioneer the Northland. I place Fannie well up on the list.

Chapter VI

FATE TAKES A HAND

BECAUSE I was dean of the college, President Bunnell had decided that we should live on campus and an unattractive two-story house was prepared for us. We hated to leave our snug log cabin but when the president insisted we said, "Yes, sir," and moved into it. It was our home for the next seven years.

The college was getting over the hump, gaining prestige and winning friends. It was no longer derisively spoken of as "that Fairbanks College." President Bunnell still had his hay field on campus but back on the hill, where spruce and birch trees had been cleared away and three small faculty residences built, some of us were planting flowers and putting in gardens.

Occasionally, on warm spring days, a faint but unmistakable animal odor hung about our hill. The U.S. Biological Survey had fenced a big corral on campus where they were carrying out experiments with reindeer and musk oxen and the Department of Agriculture had turned over an experimental station to the college, a fact that impressed itself on the minds of the students because of one experiment that did not turn out very well.

An effort was being made to develop a breed of cattle that could forage for itself during the cold winters. With this in mind, several yaks were imported from Tibet and crossed with Galloway cattle. The preposterous hybrid that resulted from the ill-fated mating was called a "galoyak." It had unquestionable foraging ability. Unfortunately the beasts kept breaking loose and foraging in the Patty cabbage patch.

Finally Mother Nature herself put an end to the experiment. The galoyaks did not reproduce and one by one they were slaughtered. To keep down expenses, galoyak meat became a staple article of diet in the student dining hall. Whether it appeared in the form of galoyak ragout or galoyak hash, the result was always the same; a stringy, tasteless concoction. Quite abominable, in fact. When the last galoyak finally made its appearance in the dining hall in the form of a galoyak and onion casserole, the students rose to their feet, cheering wildly.

Another experiment carried on at the college particularly interested me. It gave me my first opportunity to become acquainted with Eskimos. In an effort to help the Eskimos, the government was trying to introduce a reindeer industry into their economy and the U.S. Biological Survey brought five young Eskimos to the campus to be trained as reindeer herders.

They were five very bewildered young men when they arrived. They had just lived through what must have been a most terrifying experience for men only a generation or two removed from the Stone Age. They had been transported through the sky by airplane and had ridden in an automobile for the first time in their lives. To make matters worse, they had passed a puffing, smoke-snorting railroad train, a sight that had filled them with deep horror.

They were housed in a small building near the campus.

Because Eskimos are essentially meat eaters, a reindeer was butchered as the chief item of their diet. However, faculty wives felt sorry for them and came hurrying over with freshly baked bread, puddings, pies, and cakes. As a result, the Survey found themselves with five very sick Eskimos on their hands. When the doctor arrived he ordered all starches and sweet desserts to be withheld and administered heavy doses of castor oil, the taste of which, he reported, the Eskimos found ambrosial.

They were returned to their village after a few months and supplied with a small herd of reindeer, but the experiment was not repeated.

During these years, the faculty at the college had more than tripled; we had added departments of business administration and of education—much needed to train teachers for Alaska. Favorable comments about our School of Mines began to appear in mining journals and as a result an increasing number of students were coming to us from the States. They also arrived from small towns and hamlets throughout Alaska. Some of these young men were of the rough diamond type, decidedly lacking in social polish. "Someday," I told them, "you may be called to New York and invited to lunch in a club. It's important for you to be at ease and to know which fork to pick." Much to their amusement, I had the head of the home economics department give them a lecture on table manners.

I also urged the mining students to drop in at teas given on campus. One day a group, who had just finished drilling a round in a mine tunnel, decided as a joke to appear at the tea in their digging clothes. When the girl brought them dainty white tea napkins, they carefully spread them across the knee of mud-spattered canvas trousers, then looked at me and winked.

In spite of the merriment, the idea did have an effect.

Years later, one of these men said to me, "I've just come back from New York and I thought of you when I was having lunch. Do you remember insisting that we learn social graces because someday we might be invited to lunch in a New York club? That was as important as anything you taught me."

Our students were getting plenty of experience in the rough side of mining. We had developed our own experimental mine on campus and a mining company had given us a small concentrating mill for testing ore in ton lots. All Sophomore mining students were required to take a practical course in mining methods: drilling, blasting, and timbering.

I had a pair of blasters in my own home, I discovered. The campus, after all, was not the best place for two growing boys. When they reached the rock-throwing stage, every time a window was broken on campus, the finger of blame invariably pointed at my sons. Justly, no doubt.

We hoped a little sister might act as a refining influence. A few weeks before our third child was born, a severe staph infection broke out in the hospital and several mothers died. It would be safer, our doctor decided, for Kay to have the baby at home.

One May morning Kay told me to call the doctor. I rushed to the phone but I tried to keep my voice low. There was something that I had not told Kay. During the night high water in Noyes Slough had washed away the only bridge connecting Fairbanks with the campus.

As soon as I had talked to the doctor, I shot out of the house and raced for my car. When I reached the riverbanks, doctor and nurse were standing on the opposite shore, separated from me by fifty feet of rushing water. Gesticulating toward them, rather wildly, I drove upstream, borrowed a rowboat at Bentley's Dairy, and drifted downstream

86

to pick them up. While I pulled frantically for the campus side of the stream, I kept remembering how fast Stanton's birth had been. But we were in plenty of time. It was late afternoon before the baby arrived. Kay endured the long, cruel ordeal without the help of anesthesia; she might just as well have been the wife of a backwoodsman, I thought with self-accusation.

"Well, you have another husky boy," the doctor told me.

As I went back upstairs I wondered what to say to Kay. I knew her heart was set on a girl.

"I'm not disappointed, Ernest," she said, the moment I walked into the room. "He's a beautiful baby. I think nature destined me to be the mother of boys and I like the assignment."

We had discussed only girls' names. Kay suggested "Dean" for our new son. Since I was known as Dean Patty, however, we finally settled for Dale Franklin Patty.

The campus at the time was on an austerity program and the college power plant was shut down each summer until school reopened in September. On Saturdays one boiler was fired lightly to provide hot water for baths and laundry. We could not put in a heating stove of our own because there was no chimney in the house. We cooked over a kerosene stove. During cold, rainy periods we just had to shiver around the house in sweaters. Having a baby to take care of made the problem worse.

One early September as we sat in the chilly darkness I said to Kay, "I think we've had enough of this. I ought to start looking around for a new assignment."

It was not really a spur-of-the-moment decision. Although it looked as if we had an assured future at the college, for some time I had been growing restless, anxious to get back into the mining industry to see if I could still do the things that I had been teaching. The college now had one hundred

87

and forty-four full-time students and the School of Mines had won a prestige rating. I could leave with a clear conscience.

"Don't be too impatient," Kay said. "We can all be together here. That's the most important consideration."

She was thinking of assignments that I had refused because they were in areas too remote for family living.

"Don't worry about it," I told her. "We'll wait until the right thing comes along. But we'd better be on the alert and see what fate has in store for us."

Fate paid no attention to us until 1933, when General A. D. McRae of Vancouver, British Columbia, walked into my office. He was a handsome, big man who looked as if he had force and brains. His life was as remarkable as his looks. When he was a young banker in eastern Canada, he had been sent to Vancouver to liquidate some large timber holdings. As he looked over those holdings and saw the forest resources of the Pacific Northwest, he realized that he was looking at a big industry of the future. Developing it would be far more exciting than banking, he decided, and organized a company to buy the timber and build the Fraser River Mill near Vancouver. At that time it was the largest lumber mill in the world.

When World War I broke out, McRae was sent to Europe as an officer in a Canadian regiment. By the time it ended he had been advanced to Major General, decorated by Marshal Haig, the British commander, and offered a knighthood, which he refused. "After being away seven years," he explained, "I had to go home, roll up my sleeves, and recoup my fortunes. A title would have been an impediment."

He later gravitated to politics and was prominent in masterminding the election of Mackenzie King as Premier. At that time he received a life appointment to the Canadian senate.

88

In 1933, convinced that world affairs would force an increase in the price of gold, he came to Alaska to look for a gold property. When he walked into my office, Ira B. Joralemon was with him. Joralemon I knew to be one of the outstanding mining geologists in the nation. They had come to me because I was familiar with most of the mining districts in Alaska and had examined several of the properties that they had in mind.

It was no new thing for mining engineers on scouting trips in Alaska to ask my opinion of properties. I always gave them any information I had. As dean of the School of Mines, I was vitally interested in the development of Alaska's latent mineral resources, so I brought out my maps and notes and showed them to McRae and Joralemon. For an hour we discussed the properties they planned to visit. As they left my office, McRae paused at the door. "If we find a mine," he said, "I want you to operate it for me."

I did not know at the time how quick McRae was in making decisions. I just thought it an odd way of saying thank you for the information I had given them. But the next summer they were back and this time they employed me to spend a month traveling with them, looking over properties.

It was a high-speed month. We worked long days, trying to cover as much ground as possible, sometimes by car, sometimes by bush plane, and sometimes by chartered boat. During that month we looked over fifty old mines and prospects.

The famous old Cliff mine, near the town of Valdez, caught our interest at once. This mine had a glamorous history. The upper levels of the property had been mined out but a shaft (which we call a winze) had followed the vein downward for an additional three hundred and sixty-five feet. Rich ore there lured the miners into extending one of the drifts out under the sea bottom. As they drilled a round in the face of the tunnel, salt water began to seep in through the drill holes. Foolishly they shot the round and the sea broke in to drown the lower workings.

We talked to the man who, as mine foreman at the time, had examined the break before the workings were flooded. If larger pumps had been available, he said, he could have kept the mine dry and grouted the break with cement. And he told of rich, unmined ore still in the lower workings.

Ore in the bottom of a flooded mine can be enriched by memory, but in this case the records bore out the foreman's story. The vein had averaged one to three feet in width and was valued at about $75 per ton at the present price of gold. Over a five-year period, total production had been $1,070,000, giving an operating profit of $450,000.

Nothing fires the imagination like rich ore just an arm's length away, yet inaccessible. With modern high-capacity pumps, we decided, we should be able to dewater the mine and test those rich lower workings. Since the property was too far away from the college for me to supervise the work, we hired an engineer from San Francisco who had experience with wet mines. He arrived at Valdez with all the necessary pumping equipment, but at the end of two months he reported an input of salt water too heavy to handle and recommended that no more money be spent on the venture.

That was failure number one.

Next we flew from Valdez to Seward, chartered a boat and traveled to Nuka Bay, seventy miles west on the Alaska Peninsula. A little indentation there is called Beauty Bay, a wonderfully idyllic spot where the forest is reflected in quiet, secluded waters. Just at its entrance we found another prospect that appealed to us.

A short prospect tunnel had been driven on a well-mineralized vein and abandoned when assays did not carry enough gold to make commercial ore. After we ran a series of surface cuts ahead of the tunnel and got some very good assays, we contracted two miners to advance the tunnel two hundred feet. This would put us beneath the rich surface showing.

We were still excited about the prospect when a curiously ironic incident occurred. I was on my way to Beauty Bay to have a look at the work in progress. While I was waiting for the boat in Seward, I stopped in at the Van Gilder Hotel to see the proprietor, Joe Badger, an ardent bridge player. The town banker, the merchants, and housewives on their way back from shopping used to drop in for a few hands of bridge with Joe. That day, as usual, he was holding forth at a round table in one corner of the lobby and left his hand with some reluctance when a woman walked up to the desk.

After she was registered and Joe had handed her the key, she looked expectantly at her two suitcases. Joe was not about to take the hint. He had a heart condition and did not carry bags up the stairs.

"Well," she said, "isn't there someone here to take my bags to the room?"

Joe glanced around the lobby and caught my eye. "Boy," he said, "take this woman's bags upstairs."

"Yes, sir," I replied.

On the way up the stairs I tried to remember the proper ritual. I put up the window curtains and turned on the heat. The woman handed me a quarter. I was about to explain the joke when I had a second thought, walked

91

downstairs and slapped the quarter on the bridge table. "Look what I got, Joe," I said.

He made a quick grab for the coin and I jerked it away. "Fifteen cents of that tip goes to the house," Joe said.

Very funny. But my laughter sounded a little hollow later. The twenty-five-cent tip was the total take from that gold mining venture. Yet samples from the new workings had looked good, well mineralized with iron pyrite and some galena. But again, the assays failed to show gold in commercial amounts.

That was failure number two.

Next we tried two small prospects on Ester Dome, where I used to take my students, only a few miles from the college. I thought it offered a chance of making a small mine. A shallow shaft, sunk on a twenty-four-inch vein, had averaged $50 per ton in gold. We deepened this shaft an additional hundred feet in good ore and from the bottom level drifted both ways. After a few hundred feet the vein pinched down and the gold content decreased. Those were failures three and four, although we managed to recover part of our investment by mining out the ore that we had developed and treating it in a nearby stamp mill.

As I told myself, these prospects could only have developed into small mines. There remained the property owned by Joe and Fannie Quigley. I had been impressed by this property at my first visit. It had a chance, I felt, to develop into a large, lowgrade silver mine. The big drawback had been its inaccessibility. This problem no longer existed. A road was being started that would open up the park and end only ten miles from the Quigley property.

General McRae sank $40,000 into the Quigley property. We did over a thousand feet of underground work beside some surface trenching. In one tunnel, the contractors ran into a heavily crushed fault zone. In another, following a quartz vein, we sank a winze and at a deeper horizon found much lower silver values.

At the end of the first year we had been five times at bat and had struck out each time. This is the type of bitter pill that mining men have to swallow sometimes, I knew. As I told myself, failure is a part of every man's life. Not that lecturing myself did much to ease my disappointment. I would wake up in the night and think: I should have stopped the work earlier. Or: if we had run that tunnel another fifty feet. . . .

McRae had spent over $70,000 and had nothing to show for the effort. It was quite embarrassing. I expected him to abandon the project, but he was a tougher man than I realized.

"What else do you have in mind?" he asked.

With some trepidation, I suggested dropping the search for a lode gold mine and trying to find a placer gold property.

In a lode mine the mineral occurs in the earth's crust, as a vein or in some other form. As erosion eats away at these lodes the insoluble and heavy metallics, such as gold and platinum, are concentrated in stream gravels. These are called placer deposits.

I mentioned Coal Creek, a tributary of the Yukon River. Pick and shovel miners had been able to make a scanty living there. By mechanical mining of the gold-bearing gravels, we might develop a profitable venture, I thought.

"Charter a bush plane for morning," McRae said. "Let's go."

We liked what we saw at Coal Creek and optioned several miles of ground from the claim owners. In a few weeks, still haunted by the memory of our five failures, I was back with a drill and crew to prospect and evaluate the gold-bearing gravels. We put down churn drill holes at one-hundred-foot intervals across the floor of Coal Creek valley, the drill lines placed a thousand feet apart, up and downstream. As a check on the drill results, we sank several lines of prospect shafts halfway between the drill lines.

This time the results were encouraging. Then, to top it all, before the prospecting was finished, the price of gold went up from $20.67 to $35 an ounce, just as the general had foreseen. It looked as if our run of bad luck had broken at last.

"This is your baby, Patty," the general told me. "I want you to run the show." He would match my university salary, he said, and give me an interest in the mine, adding (like the good Scot he was), "Of course I want my money back with interest before any dividends are paid."

After talking it over with Kay, I walked into Dr. Bunnell's office with my resignation from the college, effective at the end of the school year. An unhappy session. Dr. Bunnell was very bitter about my leaving. Indeed, it was three years before I could claim him again as a friend.

I had a few second thoughts myself. This was rather an alarming plunge we were taking. The college was now on a firm footing with an enrollment of one hundred and ninety-three credit students. A department of Arts and Letters had been established and we were offering courses in pre-law, pre-medicine, and pre-journalism. By that time all departments were fully accredited and our extension work was booming. We now employed an instructor to travel from town to town to teach the mining short course. The first year he covered six towns and taught three hundred and forty-five students.

For several summers archeological parties from the college had conducted excavations on ancient Eskimo sites on St. Lawrence Island in the Bering Sea. The artifacts recovered had become the nucleus around which a college museum was created. Through a grant from the Rockefeller Foundation, a five-year study of the aurora had been completed. The U.S. Geological Survey had established offices on the campus and the U.S. Department of Agriculture had turned over its experimental stations to us, one at Matanuska and one near Fairbanks. The very year I left, the Alaska Agricultural College and School of Mines became the University of Alaska. We were giving up a secure niche for a venture that might not be successful after all.

We were going to have to make some adjustments, too. When we went to Seattle for a quick visit, General and Mrs. McRae invited us to spend a weekend with them in Vancouver. As we drove to 1489 McRae Avenue, we found that their home, "Hycroft," covered a full city block.

"Drive around the block," Kay said. "I want to collect myself. This is a far cry from our home in Alaska."

We drove around several blocks before pointing our little car up the driveway. As it turned out, our nervousness was groundless. Our visit was thoroughly pleasant. Nor was it difficult to get used to butler and maids smoothing things for us. It was a little harder to adjust my mind to the general's way of doing things. He was accustomed to delegating responsibility. If he once gained a favorable impression of a man, he handed the job over to him, lock, stock, and barrel. He also stood behind whatever decisions were made. I was unused to such sweeping authority. But by that time, I was in it up to my neck. It was sink or swim.

Chapter VII

DREDGING FOR GOLD

O UR supplies arrived at Coal Creek on the first boat down the river in June. I had only a limited knowledge of the type of mining that we were undertaking. There were moments, during the first two weeks, when doubt would assail me. In those moments I would look around at the crew we had assembled, and the sight of their faces never failed to give me a brace. They were good, tough, knowledgeable faces.

The next few months were a turmoil. We erected camp buildings, constructed a road from the Yukon River eight miles upstream to camp, built a two-mile ditch along the hillside to bring gravity water above the mining area for stripping and thawing operations, and prepared the ground for dredging. I worked to the point of exhaustion, caught a few hours sleep, and got up again for breakfast with the crew at six in the morning. After my initial tension wore off, I enjoyed every minute of it.

The frame buildings were mounted on skids so that we would be able to move the camp when the dredge worked its way downstream. Even the large mess hall was built in two sections, so that it, too, could be skidded. There was a series of four-man bunkhouses, a gold room for cleaning the gold, an office, a machine shop, and a tractor repair shop.

Preparation of the ground ahead of the mining is the key to successful dredging operations in the sub-Arctic. First we used bulldozers to strip away the trees, brush, and the mattress of tundra forming an insulating surface blanket. This exposed a shiny black surface of frozen muddy ooze, called "muck," laced with ice seams. The deposit of muck at Coal Creek varied in depth between six and twenty-six feet. Under this was the frozen, gold-bearing gravel that we would thaw and dig with the dredge.

To remove the muck, we spaced hydraulic nozzles called "giants" over the area and used water, piped from the hillside ditch, to sweep away the muck in suspension. The sun thawed about four inches of muck each day, and the water swept away this thawed surface. Before long Coal Creek, below the stripping area, was black with the load of sediments being added to it. It required three or four days to remove the top foot of muck, but within a few weeks patches of the underlying gravel had started to show through.

The gravel was permanently frozen and this permafrost was as resistant to excavation as a mass of reinforced concrete would be. It had to be loosened from the icy grip. As soon as stripping was completed, the crew moved on to a new area and the thawing crew moved in, to set up their lines of hydraulic pipe and prepare for "point" driving. Each point was a ten-foot length of extra-heavy steel pipe, seven-eighths of an inch in diameter, with a chisel bit welded on one end. Water under pressure was led into the top of the pipe and spurted out through two orifices on each face of the chisel bits.

These jets of water worked their way slowly into the

frozen gravel and began the thawing. Ditch water may have a temperature of, say, 45 degrees Fahrenheit, but after contact with the frozen gravel it will emerge on the surface at a temperature of 35 degrees. Thus the water has transferred ten degrees of heat for useful thawing. Obviously, it requires a large volume of water, circulating through the gravel for several weeks, to effect the thaw.

By mid-July we had a substantial area of ground stripped and thawed and were ready for the dredge. McRae and I had gone to San Francisco the winter before to buy a gold dredge. The contract was let to the Walter W. Johnson Co. for a steel dredge with a pontoon hull, a relatively new departure at the time. Each pontoon was like a big steel box. These were bolted together to form the hull on which the dredge machinery floated. Because of our isolated location and the problems of transportation, all of the heavy structures had to be broken down into small pieces and bolted together again at the dredge site.

From San Francisco the dredge parts, which weighed four hundred tons, were shipped by boat to Skagway in Alaska and then loaded on cars of the White Pass and Yukon Route, a narrow-gauge railway built near the site of the famous Chilkoot Pass. We had to get measurements of the tunnels on the White Pass railroad, to make sure none of the pieces would be too big for them.

At Whitehorse in Yukon territory the dredge parts were loaded onto a barge and pushed down the Yukon River by a sternwheeler river boat. Since the steamboat had no equipment for handling such heavy pieces, our unloading problems from the barge to the riverbank at Coal Creek were monstrous.

Finally we were ready to go into production. The construction pond itself was flooded to float the dredge. Its two diesel engines began coughing; the winchman moved the dredge out of the construction pit and the bucket line started to revolve and bite into the gravel.

It was a great moment to hear the thump of the first gravel falling into the hopper. As it cascaded from the hopper into a big revolving screen, I could see the finer gravel, which would be sand and gold, dropping through slots in the screen and onto gold-saving sluices. To catch fine gold that might be swept over the riffles, we added mercury each day to the sluices. Mercury unites with gold to form a silvery amalgam.

The dredge was our "cash register." We had to keep it in around-the-clock operation until late October or early November when sub-zero weather would halt our first season. As the dredge advanced, it gouged out its own pond, sealed at the lower end with sand and gravel. Gravel too coarse to pass through the screen was carried by a conveyor belt, called the stacker, and piled in tall windrows behind the dredge.

After two weeks of dredging we were ready for our first cleanup. General McRae came up for it, because this was the acid test. It would show whether our evaluation of the deposit had been correct or whether we had the wrong pig by the tail.

The dredge stopped digging. The pumps were shut down and the crew started pulling the gold-saving riffles from the sluices. Nobody said a word. We were all too keyed up. I had not felt the same stomach-gripping tension since my college days when I used to wait for a report on final examinations.

When water was turned into the sluices, men with wooden paddles began separating the fine gravel and sand from the amalgam. Little by little, a mound of amalgam built up at the head of the sluice. It looked very promising to me but, as I told myself, I could be wrong. I was not yet experienced in estimating.

After the amalgam was collected and taken to the gold room, it was cleaned again and placed in a retort where heat was applied. The mercury was distilled off and collected for re-use. When the retort was cooled and opened, we could see a large sponge of gold. It was melted in a furnace so we could slag off the impurities and then the molten gold was poured into steel molds to be cast into bars. Finally the gold bars were weighed. We had $27,000 worth and, as we knew, there was still richer ground ahead of the dredge.

That night there was hilarity in camp. As General McRae and I sat in my tent, we could hear the crew outside and there was a lift to the voices and good easy laughter—fine sounds to hear in a mining camp.

I was feeling pretty optimistic myself, confident enough to make a new suggestion to General McRae. Just across a mountain ridge from Coal Creek there is a companion stream valley called Woodchopper Creek, which cuts the same gold-bearing formation. A few individual miners had been working it. I thought we might find another dredging area there and asked McRae's permission to option their claims and move in our prospecting crews. The general slapped me on the shoulder and said, "When you're winning always crowd your luck."

A few days later, before any other mining company could get the same idea, I hiked across the ridge, some ten miles, to Woodchopper Creek and the cabin of an old miner, named Frank Bennett, who owned several mining claims there. When I knocked on his cabin door it swung open and I looked into the bluest eyes I have ever seen. They were merry eyes and his cheeks were as pink as a baby's with only a few wrinkles ironed in. Through a halo of white hair, neatly combed, some pink scalp was showing. All I could think of was a comic strip that I used to read as a boy called "Foxy Grandpa." Here was the same humorous and somehow innocent face. He was wearing a woolen undershirt, well laundered overalls, and heavy wool socks tucked into "stags"—shoe-pacs with the tops cut off to form homemade slippers.

"Come in, young fellow, come in," he said, stepping back.

I glanced beyond him into a neat cabin with well scrubbed floors. Then I looked down at my shoe-pacs, caked with mud from the trail. "I'm not going to muddy up your floor," I told him. "I'll go down to the creek and wash some of this mud from my boots."

"No need. Take off your boots and rest your feet. I'll get you a pair of stags."

I took off my packboard and rested it against the cabin. The stags were much too big but they felt good to my tired feet. As I shuffled into the cabin, I thought, "This is just like being in Japan." It was the first time I had ever taken off my boots before entering a prospector's cabin.

The cabin was sparsely furnished but the whole of it, from the well polished cookstove to the gingham curtaining his dishes, showed a touch as deft as a woman's. Yet I knew there were no women on Woodchopper Creek. I remembered stories I had heard about Frank. Miners said that regularly, every Saturday night, Frank set a washtub in the middle of the floor, heated bath water, and after his bath, got down on his hands and knees with a scrub brush and used the bath water to clean the floor.

While we were brewing a cup of tea, I looked over a shelf of books on the wall. It was full of classics, both prose and poetry. They looked well read, too. I knew Frank had been among a small army of gold seekers who had penetrated the Yukon wilderness about 1890, before the Klondike gold rush. For years he had mined and prospected in the Forty Mile country and had then moved to Woodchopper Creek where he had been living for twenty years when I walked into his cabin. His voice was cultivated and his vocabulary and grammar were not those of the usual man of the hills. But who was he? Not that I even considered prying. In the face of his dignity any impertinent questions about his origins would have stuck in my throat.

While we settled down to our tea, I told Frank that I was there to request a lease and option on his mining claims. "You've been mining and prospecting these claims," I said, when we had agreed on terms. "Can you make an estimate of the gold values per square foot of bedrock?"

"Young fellow," he said, "I have no idea. I can only tell you that I scratch out a bare living. The concentration of gold on the bedrock is very spotty." With a slow, sly grin, he added, "And the good spots are rather far apart."

Such candor was startling to me, after hearing the optimistic tales of some other claim owners. I believe that the affection and respect which eventually I felt toward Frank Bennett began at that moment.

For our preliminary prospecting we decided to sink shafts to bedrock before going to the expense of moving in a drilling outfit. To be ready for an early start in the spring, we freighted in tools and food by dogteam during the winter.

The first few shafts were not encouraging. We found some gold but it began to look as if Frank were right. The good spots were far apart. But before making a final decision, we decided to sink some additional shafts. This meant bringing in more supplies from our main camp at Coal Creek.

102

George Beck, a tractor driver, and I set off across the intervening mountain with several hundred pounds of supplies loaded onto a platform built at the rear of a Caterpillar tractor. After we reached the summit we took an indirect route, following the sinuous ridges that provided good footing for the tractor. I worked ahead, picking a trail, while the tractor plowed its way through the brush.

A few miles from Woodchopper Creek the ridge grew knife-edged and stayed that way for a thousand feet. We stopped to reconnoiter, but there was no alternate route. George finally said, "I think I can make it across by straddling the edge." We both knew the danger of getting the machine stalled on the isolated ridge, or worse, of rolling it over and down the steep mountainside. "I'm willing to give it a try but it's your machine."

"It's not the machine I'm worried about. It's you," I told him.

"If she starts to roll," George said, "I'll unload in a hurry." He carefully nosed the crawler tracks out to straddle the ridge and then slowly edged his way forward while I stood midway on the ridge to give him signals. Halfway across some loose rock, disturbed by the tracks, started to move. There was a brief stop and a quick inspection. We had better keep moving, we decided. I don't believe I breathed until he had covered the next few hundred feet and was on firm ground.

"Lots of atmosphere under us on both sides," he said in a dry voice. Later in the day we would have to cross it again on the return trip. "It's okay," George said. "When we come back I'll just walk her across."

At the Woodchopper camp we unloaded the supplies and after I had looked over the work with our foreman, we were ready to start back. The gasoline starting-motor on the tractor set up its chattering exhaust and I turned to say goodbye to Frank. He was fifty feet away, standing behind a tree. "Sounds to me like the damned thing is going to explode," he said, looking apologetic. It was his first encounter with a tractor.

Later that summer we began to get more encouraging results and moved in a drilling rig, after finding an easier route to the property. On one of my periodic visits, Frank asked for an advance of a few hundred dollars on his option to buy his winter outfit and I gave him a check. He wanted to go to Fairbanks. He had not been there for a good many years.

The sequel was told me later by the crew. Our drill crew felt that they needed a drink because, as they put it, "their skins were growing dry and cracked." So they gave Frank twenty dollars to buy a gallon of whiskey for them.

Frank was gone two weeks and when the river boat pulled in at the mouth of Woodchopper Creek, he came ashore, a bit unsteadily. He had forgotten to buy his winter outfit, but he was clutching the gallon of whiskey to his bosom.

Apparently Jack Welch, who ran the roadhouse at Woodchopper, also had a skin which was getting dry and cracked. "Frank," he said, "it's too hot today to walk up to camp. Better stop over and go up in the cool of the evening."

When the cool of the evening came, the jug was empty. Some days later Frank, empty-handed, arrived back at his cabin. As soon as smoke rose from the chimney the drill crew spotted it. That evening, with great anticipation, they called on Frank. He was the urbane host but made no mention of any whiskey and it was difficult to break through the barrier of his dignity.

The following evening, however, a determined group, with an appointed spokesman, again visited Frank. After due amenities, this spokesman blurted out, "Frank, you

104

remember we gave you twenty dollars to get us a gallon?"

Frank got up and put a stick of wood in the stove, giving himself time to ponder his dilemma. When he straightened up, he turned those innocent blue eyes on his guests and said, "Fellows, I always was a poor hand to send after liquor."

Within the next year we had decided to dredge Woodchopper Creek and the time came to exercise our options and purchase the claims. I had already grown very fond of Frank. He was a courteous man and a kind one. His one weakness was liquor. The sizeable cash payment that we were making to him would be all he would have for his old age and I was worried. Knowing how quickly he could be separated from his money I made an arrangement with an insurance company which would enable Frank to use half of the money for an annuity guaranteeing him $150 a month for life.

I patiently explained the advantages of this to Frank. At first he was skeptical but I finally managed to convince him. Or so I thought. "Income for life," he said, but without great enthusiasm. "Very sensible."

"You'll call on the insurance agent as soon as you get to Fairbanks, won't you?" I urged, still feeling some qualms.

"Right away," he said and left for Fairbanks with the check in his pocket.

A few weeks later I was in Fairbanks myself. At the bank I learned that $5000 of his money had already been spent. Nor had the insurance agent seen him. A gang of hangers-on had him cached in the red-light district. At intervals they would sober him up enough to sign his name and take him in a taxi to the bank where he would scrawl his signature with a trembling hand on a check for a thousand dollars.

"Don't honor the checks," I said to the banker.

He shook his head. "So long as the signature is legible, we can't refuse it."

But the next day the banker called me at the hotel. Frank was making another withdrawal.

"Would you stall until I get there?" I asked. "I'm on my way right now." Fortunately a taxi was idling at the curb. When I stormed into the bank, I saw a disheveled Frank, leaning bewildered and shaky against the counter. A ferret-eyed pimp was holding him by the arm to steady him. It was so pitiful a sight that I could barely resist sinking my fist into the leech's face, an emotion that he must have sensed because when I snapped, "Get out!" he dropped Frank's arm and scuttled through the door.

Leaving Frank propped against the counter, I called a taxi driver whom I knew. "A steamboat's due into Circle City today," I told him, handing him fifty dollars. "Get Frank Bennett to Circle and stay with him until he's on the boat to Woodchopper. When you get back there'll be another $50 for you."

A few days later I went back to camp. Frank was all cleaned up and showed little sign of wear. But he never mentioned the incident and neither did I. Fortunately there was still enough of his money left to provide him with a small income for life.

We were anxious to get Frank's cabin out of the way in order to strip off the muck overburden and prepare the underlying gravels for the dredge, which was advancing ponderously downstream. Frank loved that cabin. He wanted to spend the years remaining to him on Woodchopper Creek, so we fixed up a new cabin on the bench ground overlooking the valley, hauled in a winter's supply of dry wood and were ready to move him.

Each time we suggested the move, Frank had some ingenious excuse to stall for a few days. By that time

106

hydraulic giants were spouting all around the cabin until eventually the house was perched on a mesa-like island above the exposed gravel.

Finally we could wait no longer and I went down with a crew of men. "Frank," I said, "we're going to move you to the other cabin today."

Frank started to protest and then resigned himself. As the load of household goods pulled away, Frank from the top of the load saw a bulldozer standing by. "Please don't knock it down until I get out of sight," he said.

When he had gone, the blade of the dozer nudged into a corner of the cabin, the motor roared and in a moment the cabin was a heap of jumbled logs.

Frank spent a good many more happy years at Woodchopper and was buried there.

He told me once that he came from Boston but he would never discuss his family and I often wondered about his background. He left no papers or letters to give us a clue. Some of his books are in my library now. In his final years I was closer to Frank than anyone and it is still a puzzle to me. How could so good, so kindly, and so likeable a man have passed through this world and leave nothing behind him, not so much as a faded snapshot? Only a shelf of well-read classics.

Chapter VIII

MEN OF THE NORTH

COAL CREEK was only a little stream, easily waded through the better part of the year. During storms it turned into a raging river.

Over eons of time, it had eroded the valley several thousand feet deep, leaving steep sloping sides and sheer cliffs. For three months in the dead of winter, no ray of sunlight entered that deeply incised valley. The sun briefly touched only its upper slopes, lingering a little longer on the snowy summits of the peaks, twenty-five miles away, at the head of the valley.

The floor of the valley averaged two thousand feet in width, a swampy stretch of tundra, dotted with clumps of stunted black spruce and willows. It was a tiring swamp to cross. There, in summer, water lay calf-deep between bunches of nigger-head grass, and there you would feel glare ice under the soles of your boots and mosquitos rising in humming clouds around you. The old-timers, when they traveled the eight miles to the Yukon River for their supplies, built their trails along the hillsides. Our roads followed these old trails.

We wanted our mining camp to look as though someone

loved it. The frame buildings that lined our airstrip—mess hall, recreation room, watchman's log cabin, office and radio room, machine shop, repair shop, and warehouse—were all painted yellow trimmed with white. The mess hall sported window boxes full of flowers.

A log footbridge across the stream led to a group of four-man bunkhouses set in a grove of big spruce trees, a quiet spot for men who worked the night shifts.

The first summer, when Kay and the boys came to Coal Creek, we lived in tents and took our meals in the mess hall with the crew. By the next summer, we had built a primitive cabin, sheathed outside with Celotex and inside with plywood that Kay made attractive with varnish and paint.

Several Indians from the little settlement of Eagle worked at the mine and they usually brought their families with them. As soon as Kay arrived in camp, the Indian women, with their younger children in tow, paid formal calls on her. Since they are by nature reserved and taciturn, I wondered what they found to talk about.

"As soon as I asked about their children, their eyes lit up and they talked freely," Kay told me after their first call. "Ernest, they're worried. There hasn't been a native school at Eagle for several years."

A few days later when I came in from work, I found the cabin piled with textbooks, borrowed from the school at Eagle. "I'm going to try holding summer classes for the Indian children," Kay told me. She looked a little apprehensive, I thought. She had no teaching experience. "I wish I'd taken a few education courses at the University," she added, uneasily.

The morning her school opened, every Indian child in camp was gathered in a timid group outside our front door. "Well, how did it go?" I asked that evening.

Kay looked exhausted but happy. "Ernest, as soon as they get over their shyness, most of them are eager and intelligent. The little ones are so cute I want to pick them up and hug them." She had divided them into age groups and was bearing down hard on the three R's, I gathered, keeping those of kindergarten age busy with crayons and round-pointed scissors. Later she let the older girls stay to watch her prepare our dinner, giving them tips on how to cook and keep a house neat. All the years we spent the summers at Coal Creek, Kay kept on with the school, and during all those summers, every Indian child in camp would be waiting at our door in the mornings.

Kay used to go back to Fairbanks in September, in time for our boys to start school. I would stay until late October. Then, when the ice grew too heavy in the dredge pond, planes would come in to shuttle the crew to Fairbanks and the winter watchman would be left alone with his dogteam to the solitude and the darkening days. After the sun had left the valley, the animals who could not, like the black bear, snooze the winter away in a hillside den, were in for a hard struggle to survive the long cold days and nights. The watchman used to tell me about the mother fox that slipped down from the hills to investigate the quiet camp. She was wary at first when he treated her to a breakfast of hotcakes, but after she had gained confidence she would be back each morning with her pups to share the handout. Sometimes a moose cow would bring her calf close to his cabin as a temporary haven against the wolf pack hunting in the valley.

Kay and I bought an attractive house in Fairbanks for our winter home and I opened an office in town where my accountant and I would handle the paper work. I would place orders for delivery on the first boat down the Yukon in the spring, line up a crew for the next season, and occasionally get out in the field, looking for new properties. Our company at Coal Creek was called Gold Placers Inc. and the one at Woodchopper was Alluvial Golds Inc. I was vice president and general manager.

Sometimes, on a bright winter day, Kay and I would go for a drive. Somehow we always seemed to end up on the university campus. "It draws you like a magnet, doesn't it, Ernest?" Kay asked one day.

"I wouldn't want to go back," I told her. Yet emotionally, as I knew, I was still very deeply involved with the school. Time and again I found myself wishing that it could become a more important force in Alaska.

During the summer months, when I was engrossed with mining operations, its problems would seem remote. But in winter, when the work load eased, I would listen hungrily for news from College Hill. Friends on the faculty often dropped into the office for a visit.

After a few years Dr. Bunnell forgave me for leaving him. He used to invite us to university functions or special lectures and became a frequent guest in our home. Sometimes he, too, would drop into my office unannounced. As soon as I closed the office door he would settle back and talk over his problems. When the winter sun dipped behind the Alaska Range, we would still sit there in the half light, too engrossed to notice. If I got up to snap on the lights, the spell would be broken. He would jump up and say, "I didn't intend to stay so long."

Students in those days used to line up in the office for summer jobs. Our entire engineering staff was composed of young men whom I had trained. Hard driving, trustworthy young fellows they were, too, all on their way up.

We were lucky to start our mines when most of our crew members were old-time Alaskans, a wonderful and colorful breed of men, hard working and fearless, who took pride in their work and expected their co-workers, including the boss, to pull their own weight. The friendships I formed with them have never been broken. We employed forty men at Coal Creek and thirty at Woodchopper.

The crews were flown to camp each April to get the dredge overhauled and to complete preparations for the season. It was always a trying time when the bush pilots were shuttling back and forth between Fairbanks and the mine one hundred and forty miles away. For the next six or seven months, the men would be working seven days a week and had no chance to come to town unless they needed medical attention. Naturally, some of them decided to blast-off with a last minute spree. It was a chore to get them rounded up and poured into the plane. The nondrinkers were helpful. Some of them would stay up all night, keeping a fatherly eye on their pals and getting them safely to the Fairbanks airfield in the morning.

The most difficult to handle were three key men whom I had dubbed "the Three Musketeers." They were skilled and wonderful workers when they were on the job, but they were very high spirited and invariably went on a bender before going to camp. One of them, however, had a great feeling of responsibility. He could always be depended upon to carry out an assignment. One year I tried an experiment. "Harry," I said, "do you remember last spring when your two pals were missing for several days?"

"That was bad," Harry said, shaking his head with a virtuous air.

"You're the only fellow who can control them," I went on. "Will you do me a favor and not drink tonight, but just ride herd on them?"

Harry readily agreed. All the same I kept my fingers crossed.

All night long, at intervals, my telephone would ring and

I would crawl out of bed to answer it. Harry would be reporting in that all was well. By four o'clock in the morning I was getting exasperated.

"Thought you'd want to know, Dean—they're in pretty good shape. I'll have them at the field at seven," he reported.

"How are you doing yourself, Harry?" I asked.

"Glad you brought that up, Dean," he said. "It's been a long, long night. Okay if I have a coupla drinks to see me through?"

"Sure, Harry," I said, sleepily. "No need to call me again tonight. I'll see you at the airport in the morning."

He was there, like a father shepherding along two naughty boys. "Hope you had a good night's sleep?" he asked, looking innocent.

"Why sure, Harry," I told him. "When you're on the job I always know I can sleep like a baby."

More crises usually arrived in October, when snow flurries began and temperatures might get down around zero. As the mining season drew toward a close, the crew would get restless and testy. First they would start complaining about the cook and then their tempers would flare up. You quickly learned to tread lightly and control with only a slender thread.

On one occasion, while I stood nearby, a man was tightening a bolt on the winch when his wrench slipped and he skinned his knuckles. With an oath he threw the wrench into the dredge pond. I could feel my hackles rising, but before I spoke, I had a second thought and pretended not to see the incident. Better to lose a good wrench than a good man.

Whenever I hear the expression, "He's so tough you couldn't kill him with a club," I think of Phil Berail, our hydraulic foreman. He was one of the toughest men I have

113

ever known, completely disdainful of danger or physical discomfort. When the weather turned cold and it was time to dismantle the hydraulic plant, his crew would all be bundled up. Phil would be working with them bare-handed, his shirt open over a mighty chest.

He used to keep his dogteam at the mine. As soon as camp closed he would lash a meager outfit onto the sled and head out alone for the headwaters of Charley River, one of the most remote areas in central Alaska. There he would spend the winter prospecting and trapping.

In the spring we would all wait anxiously for his return and I would hear members of the crew asking each other, "Wonder if Phil made it through the winter?"

Finally Phil would appear in camp, grizzled and weather beaten, but exuberant. When I would see him coming along the trail with his dogteam, he always reminded me of a figure straight out of some Northern myth.

The first year I made the mistake of suggesting that he take a couple of days off to rest up. The disdainful look he gave me would curl your toes, and the next morning he set such a pace at work that his crew, softened by a winter of idleness, could not keep up.

The first time we deducted social security from Phil's paycheck, he came stalking into the office.

"What's this social security monkeyshine?" he demanded.

Patiently we explained the new law to him.

"I don't want it," he said.

When he found that the law demanded the deduction he stormed out, tossing over his shoulder, "We're getting to be a nation of damned softies."

Rugged individualists are a vanished breed, even considered figures of fun, nowadays. All the same, those are the men who conquered the West and Alaska.

To soften the boredom of camp life, we built a recreation

114

hall with pool and card tables and showed movies each week. A good many of the men preferred to spend their off-shift hours fishing for grayling, going hunting, or even borrowing pick and shovel to prospect the mountainsides. Next to a thick steak or a shot of whiskey, the men loved a practical joke. Nor were they respecters of persons.

One morning I was going across the mountains to check on a prospecting crew, drilling on another creek. After I loaded my packsack, I went to the cookhouse to ask the cook for a put-up lunch. At the time, night shift men from the dredge were sitting on the cookhouse steps, waiting for a second breakfast. All unsuspecting, I leaned my packsack against the building before I went inside. A few minutes later, I came out again, put my lunch on top of the pack and slipped into the shoulder straps. As I started down the trail the pack seemed unusually heavy. Besides, something hard was pressing into my back. I kept plodding along until I rounded a bend in the trail and then pulled out three grapefruit-sized rocks from the bottom of the pack.

When I got back the next day, there were some discreet inquiries made about my trip and at dinner that evening one fellow launched into a story about a prospector who carried a heavy pack over mountains until after many years his ears became elongated like a burro's.

I lost one cook when the men discovered his deadly fear of bears. They soaked a pair of canvas gloves in water until they were frozen solid, then put them on sticks and made fake bear tracks in the snow, all around the cookhouse. For a while I expected to lose a good hydraulic man too.

Someone had brought a "lonely hearts" magazine into camp. In the bunkhouse, it was decided, as a prank, that each man should select a woman and answer her advertisement for a husband. They sat there every evening laboring over their letters and roaring with laughter, all except Axel

115

Johnson, one of our hydraulic men. Axel had been schooled in Sweden and would not attempt the difficult chore of writing a letter in English. The others finally excused him providing he signed his name to all the letters.

Each time the mail plane arrived after that, there would be a gathering of the clan. Axel's mail for the next month was heavy. After all the letters had been read aloud and the pictures passed from hand to hand, it was decided to narrow the list down to three. Axel, in his next letter (written by the gang), became a miner with a rich gold claim, but lonely and yearning for a wife who was a good cook and could keep his cabin spotless. She would have to be a woman who loved the out-of-doors, one who would be happy in the solitude of the Alaska mountains.

The first woman bowed out with a nice letter. Always having lived in a big city, she explained, she did not feel capable of adapting to the life that he described, although she would be glad to talk it over with Axel, if he would come to Chicago for a visit.

The other two women were not daunted. They were certain to enjoy life in Alaska, they said. One woman wanted to know if she could bring her dog.

"Well, you've got to pick one of them, Axel," the fellows said. "Which one'll it be?"

Axel simply could not make up his mind. When the men kept pressing him he finally said, "All right. Let's take the woman with the dog. She sounds like a good person."

After that the letters took on a serious tone. The woman wanted Axel's picture, a problem that was solved when one of the men got a blurred image by slipping up behind Axel with a camera while he was directing the hydraulic giant.

I began to feel that the lark was getting out of hand, particularly when one of the men had to go to Fairbanks for dental work and arranged to send Axel a fake telegram.

116

The telegram arrived the next day and our radio operator brought it to me, wondering if it ought to be delivered. It read: "Just couldn't wait any longer to be with you. Paid my way to Fairbanks. Will you come to Fairbanks or can we be married there? Love, Anna."

It is certainly not the business of the vice-president and general manager of a company to hold up a man's telegrams, no matter how ill-advised they may be.

A few minutes later I saw Axel go charging into the bunkhouse. When he came out, shaved and in clean clothes, he marched into the office. He was quitting, he said, and wanted his time.

"You've been with us five years, Axel," I told him. "You're one of the best hydraulic men on the crew. What's wrong?"

"I youst get tired looking at same old hills every day," he said lamely.

"The plane won't be in until tomorrow anyway," I said. "Better go back and finish your shift."

"No, I go now," he insisted, looking very stubborn. "I build me a raft and youst float down river to Circle City."

"Look, Axel," I said. "You trust me, don't you? That's a fake telegram. Driskell sent it from Fairbanks. Don't let those jokers get your goat."

A look of relief and anger washed over his big, honest face. "You sure?"

"Yes, I'm sure. When they ask you about it, just say, 'You can't fool a Swede, not even a dumb Swede.' "

Still he hesitated and I had a feeling that I was about to lose a good hydraulic man. "That damn bunch of yokers," he said at last, with a relieved chuckle. A few minutes later I saw the water turned on again in the stripping area.

The men, I heard later, wrote a nice letter to Anna. The paystreak on Axel's claim had suddenly given out, they reported. He was going off alone into the hills to search again for gold. If he found it he would write, but in the meantime, no mail could reach him.

They were tough men, doing tough work in a tough country, but they were kindly men, too, who would not want their joke to hurt anyone. For all the horsing around, I have never known them to lay for anyone who was really vulnerable. I noticed this particularly in their attitude toward the man with the axe.

He was a hopeless, nameless man, one of the defeated who find their last refuge far away from civilization. I do not know where he came from. He appeared one year along the Yukon River and moved into an old, abandoned cabin on the bank. At intervals during the summer he would walk into our mining camp, driven, I suppose, by hunger. He was always certain of a good meal with us.

He had no apparent skills and was too emaciated and undernourished to stand up to hard toil. If he asked for work, we would hire him to clean up around camp. He would only stay a few days and then trade his paycheck for grub.

Always, wherever he went, he carried an axe, a very light, single-bitted, pole axe. He never used it. When he came to work each morning, he would lay it gently on a log. If he sat down to rest, he would cradle it in his arms as if it were alive.

Sometimes he would take a whetstone from his pocket and gently touch up and shine the blade. Watching him I sometimes thought of the woodsman's expression, "You could shave with his axe." This axe was so delicately honed that the expression might literally have been true. Sometimes he would rub the oiled handle on his sleeve to bring out its fine polish or reach out for a willow branch and slice it across the razor sharp blade. I never saw him plunge the axe into solid wood. Treating it so roughly would have pained him, I am sure. The little axe was his only possession, and in some strange way, I believe, his very sense of identity was tied up with it. I kept thinking of one of my sons who, in his early years, clung to a torn piece of blanket and would not go to sleep without it.

It would have been easy enough for some jokester in the crew to hide the axe. Nobody ever tried it. If any man had been so callous the rest of the crew would not have tolerated it.

The man with the axe finally melted away. I do not know where he went, but if life became too heavy for him and he lay down under a tree for his last sleep, I am certain the axe was by his side.

For more than twenty-five years, the dredges at Coal and Woodchopper Creeks were in profitable operation. As each of our sons reached sixteen, I gave them summer work with the crew, after a stiff lecture about expecting no favors because they were my sons.

After World War II, rapidly rising costs forced many small dredging operations in Alaska to close down. To cut costs we discontinued hydraulic stripping of the muck overburden in favor of ground sluicing—that is, using the creek water to erode the muck. If we stripped the muck away and exposed the gravels one or two years ahead of dredging, the summer heat, we discovered, would thaw the gravels naturally and eliminate the expense of point driving, saving about ten cents a cubic yard. Our gravels yielded about sixty cents in gold per cubic yard, equivalent to only forty cents a ton of material handled. Since we were mining three thousand yards daily, this one development meant a saving of $300 a day. We called it "solar thawing." After we had demonstrated its effectiveness, all of the other small operators copied the development. It was letting nature do the work normally performed by a crew of point-drivers.

Each year, by innovating new techniques, we were able to keep our operation in line with soaring labor and material costs, until at last we reached the endpoint and watched our yearly profit dropping. We had no choice then but to close down the mines.

Chapter IX

HE MISSED TOO MANY BOATS

THE North country has a way of producing a particularly tough and stalwart breed of men who live to a great old age and come out of the wilderness at last, still sound as a dollar, with a sense of humor and a faith in life still intact.

I have been continually amazed at how well the human soul can stand up to hardships and loneliness. But the North can break men, too. These are the men, Alaskans say, who "have missed too many boats."

Before World War I there were between two and three thousand solitary men, trappers, prospectors, and individual miners, scattered over the huge Alaskan wilderness. Perhaps once a year these loners would travel to the nearest settlement for supplies. The rest of the time they were completely isolated from their fellow men. Snowbound in their cabins, they might not hear a human voice for six months.

Battery-powered radios were a wonderful boon when they began to appear in remote cabins during the 1930s. To extend the life of the battery, they would be turned on only a few minutes each day for the news broadcast from Fairbanks. I have often stopped over in these remote cabins. If the battery had grown weak, we would sit with our ears pressed against the cabinet to get snatches of news from the outside world.

Everyone feels the stress of winter in the North, when intense cold grips the world and even the sun has deserted the earth. During the four winter months the highest incidence of insanity and suicide would occur. Inevitably, over the years, I ran into a number of these terrible, stark dramas of the North.

It was December 29 and I was new to Alaska. I had left Fairbanks that morning on the Alaska Railroad and from Healy station walked seven miles up Healy River, over the ice.

A company, prospecting some large coal beds in the Healy River valley, had employed a man whom I shall call Anderson, a Norwegian, to drive a crosscut tunnel through several of the larger beds. I was going to check on his work, measure and sample the coal, and be back in Fairbanks by January 2, when the college would convene after the Christmas holidays.

Anderson's tent was a welcome sight in the gathering darkness. I had been out several hours; it was 40 below and the cold had started to seep through my parka. I had wrapped a woolen scarf around my neck, pulled it up over my mouth and nose and was breathing through it. When the scarf iced up, I would shift it around a few inches to get a fresh surface. By the time I arrived, the entire scarf was stiff with ice.

Anderson turned out to be a big blond man, still quite youthful in appearance, a man of few words but friendly and a good companion. His blue eyes gave very little hint of the thoughts behind them. With his hulking shoulders and his large, capable hands, he exactly fitted my mental picture of a Viking.

122

He had been prospecting for years over the Alaska Range, searching for signs of mineralization, a loner too restless for long-time employment. He had taken this job to earn a grubstake for another summer in the hills.

Anderson and I were going to bunk together. It was my first experience of toughing out a night in such bone-chilling weather. I did not look forward to it with any enjoyment. All we had to protect us from the cruel cold were the thin walls of the tent and a little sheet-iron Yukon camp stove. I left on my wool shirt and trousers and put on a dry pair of socks. As I pulled up the wolfskin robe and settled down for the night, I thought how nice it would be in our snug cabin in Fairbanks. Then I fell to thinking of the pleasant Christmas our family had spent.

I woke a few hours later, chilled by the cold pouring into the tent. The frozen canvas was only a few inches from my nose. Apparently the fire had died down in the stove an arm's length from the bed. Anderson, who was sleeping on the outside, reached out and put in some additional wood. When he had opened the draft, we talked for a few minutes until it was time to close it again. It was amazing how quickly the tent warmed. At two-hour intervals the stove was stoked and we awoke the next morning refreshed.

By the afternoon of the 31st, I had finished my work, and we traveled downstream two miles to the cabin of two trappers, John Fern and Joe Gagnon, who had invited us to spend New Year's Eve with them. Joe, a good cook, had a fine dinner ready for us. Afterward, we settled down for a pleasant evening of talk while the gas lamp sputtered overhead. As midnight approached, Joe brought out several bottles of potent homemade beer for a toast to the new year.

Anderson had been silent all the evening, sitting quietly in the shadows as if he were deep in his own thoughts.

123

This seemed strange. Previously he had been a delightful companion.

"Well," John Fern said, raising his mug, "here's to—"

Suddenly Anderson leaned forward and cut in. "I feel as if you fellows were the best friends I have on earth. I want to ask you an important question. Will you promise to give me an honest answer?"

"Why, sure," we chorused.

"We all like you," Joe said. "If you've got a problem, just ask us. We'll help if we can."

Anderson did not say anything for a moment. Then he blurted out, "All right. Do you think I'm losing my mind?"

There was a stunned silence. Anderson had seemed as sound as any man. But no man asks that question—not with the sort of expression I saw in Anderson's eyes at that moment—unless he really is in deep trouble.

He was searching our faces for an answer and we all started talking at once, trying to soothe his fears.

He was a powerfully built man, just approaching middle age. If he went berserk it would be most difficult to cope with him. I glanced at John Fern. I knew him to be a resourceful fellow and I saw his eyes flick momentarily to the rifles hanging from wall pegs. They were loaded, I knew. If Anderson made a rush for them John would be there first.

Anderson seemed to take heart at our words. After we had talked for a while longer, trying to divert his thoughts, we went to bed. But I did not sleep. The wind had come up and the stove pipe was rattling. Once during the night Anderson moaned and mumbled. I knew the other men in the cabin were awake, too, and ready for trouble. I had slipped my short-handled prospecting pick out of the pack-sack and it was tucked under my pillow.

In the morning Anderson was himself again and no one

124

referred to the tensions of the night. Anderson and I were going on downriver to Healy. Since a strong warm wind was blowing downstream, Anderson suggested that we rig a sail on a dog sled and ride over the glare ice in style. I liked the idea.

Rigging a sail brought back memories to Anderson of his boyhood in Norway and he talked about his days sailing on the fjords.

Before we had completed our task the wind shifted and started blowing upstream, so we could not use the sail after all.

As we were shouldering our packs, John Fern beckoned me into the cabin. "No telling when he'll go off his rocker again. I'll ask you to take my rifle into Fairbanks to get it repaired. You can leave it at Healy."

I showed him the prospecting pick tucked in my belt where I often carried it. Anderson, I reasoned, was a canny fellow. The ploy about the rifle might not fool him.

John shook his head, frowning uneasily. "Keep an eye on him all the time and don't let him get behind you."

As we marched down the ice with the warm Chinook wind bathing our faces, Anderson kept me entertained with tales of Norse history and of his life in the "Old Country," as he called it. Then he went on to talk of his years prospecting in the Alaska Range. At the end of the day, he said, he would try to set up camp in an area where there were ground squirrels. He would pick off three or four of them with a .22 revolver for his meal. As he explained, it was much better than shooting a big animal and wasting meat.

He was in a cheerful mood when I told him goodbye at Healy and I assumed his aberration had passed. But a few weeks later one of his friends in Fairbanks phoned me. He had just had a telephone call from Anderson. "He said he was losing his mind and was going to shoot himself. He

125

asked me to tell you 'goodbye.' I tried to reason with him but the telephone went dead. What do you think?"

I immediately put in a long-distance call to the roadhouse at Healy where I knew Anderson was staying. I could hear the phone ringing.

"Sorry, they do not answer," the operator reported at last.

"This is an emergency!" I insisted. "Keep ringing."

After an agonizing delay, I heard the voice of Jack Singleton, who owned the roadhouse. "Sorry, you're too late. He shot himself ten minutes ago."

When a man recognizes approaching insanity and chooses this escape, I could never think of him as a coward. I remember a message which one man left: "I am losing my mind and am going to end it. Don't call me a coward. If you think it doesn't take nerve to shoot yourself—just try it!"

Sometimes I used to puzzle over what the factors could be that lead to our tragedies. When so many men are strengthened by the hard life of the wilderness, why do others break under long isolation? At first I thought there might be some ethnic trait that made some men unsuited to a loner's life, since so many of our tragedies of this sort involved Finns, Swedes, and other Nordics. Then I realized that there was no validity in the idea—people of Nordic blood predominated in the early days of Alaska.

But if I was never able to pin down an underlying cause, occasionally I have caught a glimpse of the strange ways in which men in the back country keep loneliness at bay. A number of them, like our winter watchman at Coal Creek who used to share his solitary breakfast with a mother fox and her pups, seem to develop a close feeling for the wildlife around them. One of the happiest old men I have ever known was a loner named Frank Slaven. I think that he was able to adjust well to solitude because of a peculiar relationship he had worked up with a pair of ravens.

When I first came to Coal Creek, Frank owned a large block of placer mining claims there which he had been mining in a limited way. I had made the long trek up Coal Creek to discuss his property. We were just sitting down to dinner in his cabin when I heard a loud cawing noise outside.

"Wait a minute," Frank said, jumping up. "My friends are here for supper."

When he had prepared a dish of food I followed him outside and saw a beautiful pair of ravens perched on the woodpile, big birds, three times the size of an ordinary crow, their black feathers iridescent where the evening sun touched them.

Frank talked to them as though they were humans and they chattered right back at him, possibly urging him to hurry up with the food. Frank, however, thought otherwise. He believed they were passing along neighborhood news They allowed him to approach quite close to them as he set down the pan.

After his friends were fed and we were back at the table, I expected to return to our discussion of mining. Instead, Frank wanted to tell about his ravens.

"The male raven was here when I came to Coal Creek years ago. Every night he and his mate used to come to the woodpile and visit me. But one night he flew in alone. He was in a terrible state of excitement and I couldn't figure out what was bothering him until the next day when I found his mate dead in one of my traps.

"Every night after that he would fly in alone and tell me a sad story. He wasn't interested in his food anymore, either. Then a couple of weeks later he showed up and right away I noticed a new note in his voice. That mournful note was gone. I knew he was trying to tell me something but I couldn't make out what he was saying. While I was standing there talking to him, all of a sudden he rose up from his perch, circled the cabin until he was high up in the air and then headed east toward Charley River. That's it, I thought. He's telling me goodbye. He's leaving the country. For two nights he stayed away and I really missed his visits.

"The third afternoon I heard his call again. He sounded very excited so I rushed out the cabin and there he was on the woodpile with a new mate. He wanted me to see her. Pretty cocky he looked too. I think he was trying to make the introductions. But somehow things just didn't work out well for those two. In a few days they were back on the woodpile again. I brought out the food but they didn't eat. That plaintive note was back in his voice. Then they took off, circled, and headed again for Charley River. I guess she just didn't like Coal Creek and he was taking her home. But I knew he'd be back. It didn't take him long either. The very next day he was sitting alone on the woodpile and this time he was really telling a woeful story.

"But after thinking it over for a few days, he regained his appetite and did quite a lot of talking. This time I knew what he was talking about. After he took to the air I watched him heading for the mountains at the head of the creek. I knew he was heading for the Chena River country.

"In a few days he was sitting on the woodpile again and he had a new mate with him. We went through the introductions and this one liked Coal Creek. You saw her tonight."

Frank was not spinning a yarn. To him this was all very real.

During all the years we mined on Coal Creek, the ravens stayed there. There must have been a dozen or more in the flock nesting high in the cliffs above the valley floor. When

128

they would come down onto our airfield and strut around I used to look them over and wonder which pair were Frank's friends.

When my trips to examine mining prospects took me near some remote cabin, I always stopped for a brief visit and volunteered to take any mail into Fairbanks. Sometimes a man would have an order for supplies to be brought in by a passing bush pilot, if there was a nearby gravel bar that could be used as a landing field.

Now and then I could see tragedy building up. The cabin itself, I found, was a reflection of the man's emotional health. Whenever I went into a cabin and found it untidy, a pile of true detective story magazines on the floor, I would find the man himself unkempt and his conversation laden with defeat and pessimism. Then I would want to urge him to leave his mine or his trapline for a while and get into town among people before it was too late. I never did. He would not have taken or welcomed advice. But my words would have lingered in his mind to torment him when the dark winter closed in on him.

Such cabins and such men were rare, though. It was much more usual to find a well kept cabin, even in the remotest spots, to see a thriving vegetable garden nearby, and to be greeted by a cheerful man. There would usually be some project under way. After the evening meal, he would disappear for a while to do his evening chores. I would hear the sound of a hammer, saw, or axe as he got things shipshape. Invariably there would be a neat rick of wood stacked by his cabin door.

A woodpile is always a telltale sign. When a man saws just one stick of wood off a log before starting a fire, trouble is sitting on his shoulder.

One summer I had examined an outcropping of antimony ore on Stampede Creek, a tributary of the Toklat River. As

129

I was on my way to a rendezvous with a bush pilot who was to pick me up, I stopped at an adjacent creek to visit two trappers I knew. They were partners but had separate cabins about one hundred yards apart. Both of them were well past middle age. One was tall and rawboned with a rather truculent manner and the other was a small, colorless fellow.

I have seldom seen messier cabins. When they skinned the animals from their trapline they threw the carcasses out only a few hundred feet from their cabins. A nauseating stench hung over the area. They were living almost like animals themselves, it seemed to me.

Clearly, they were getting on each others' nerves, too. The tall man would snap at his partner and the little man would cringe. Later, when we were alone, he would tell me what a "mean bastard" the big man was.

That winter a bush pilot flew by a forested island in the braided channel of the Toklat River, a few miles below the trappers' camp. The island is more than a mile long but only a few hundred yards wide. The pilot noticed a new, well beaten snow trail circling the island and a tall man striding along the trail.

This was curious. The pilot dropped down for a closer inspection and recognized one of the partners. The figure below paid no attention to the plane circling over his head. On the return trip a few hours later, the pilot flew by again. The trapper was still walking around and around the island.

In Fairbanks, the pilot reported what he had seen and the next day a deputy U.S. Marshal landed nearby. The man was still trudging around the island. As he drew near, the deputy noticed white splotches on the man's nose and cheeks, a sure sign of frostbite.

"Having trouble, partner?" the deputy asked.

"No trouble," the man said. "I shot my partner. Then I

went out and shot down the moon and I shot down a bunch of stars before I ran out of shells. I'm on my way to Fairbanks to get more ammunition."

Just as in the case of the man who shot down the moon, I often have found a terrible, wild poetry in the aberrations of these lost men. I wonder if this is not more true in the Northland than in tamer climates.

Our crews had been flown into Coal Creek a few weeks before. It was early April. The sun was melting the winter snow, and in another ten days the water would be running in the creek. One day a young giant of a man walked into our mining camp, hunting for work.

I looked up into his pale blue eyes and noticed his heavy thatch of red hair. His packsack rested lightly on huge shoulders. "Where in the world did you come from?" I asked.

"Fairbanks," he said. "There are no jobs there, so I caught a ride part way on a truck to Circle City and then walked up the Yukon on the ice."

"We're sixty miles from Circle!" I exclaimed. "And this is the only mining camp in the district."

He did not look worried. If I had no work for him, he seemed perfectly ready to turn around and slog back down the Yukon.

"We're full handed," I told him, "but when a man wants work that badly, I'm not going to turn him away. Find a bed in the bunkhouse and eat at our mess hall. We'll put you to work as soon as possible."

He turned out to be a restless fellow around camp. Each morning he was out watching the crew as they prepared for the opening of actual mining. Some days he would shoulder his pack and walk ten miles over the mountain road to our mining operation on Woodchopper Creek.

One afternoon, about a week after he arrived, I was

131

driving in a pick-up truck back to camp from the Yukon River where I had picked up some supplies. When I saw the new man on the road, I got ready to stop and take him on to camp, but as soon as he saw me, he jumped into the brush. When I drove by I caught a glimpse of him there, hiding like an animal.

This was curious behavior but I did not give it too much thought until I arrived at the office and found the top of my desk almost covered with scrawled notes. At first glance I wondered if someone were playing a practical joke.

But I was not dealing with a joker. The notes were from the new man. The first one which I read announced that he would be back in the evening to broadcast to the world from our radio station. It was signed, "The Devil."

There were others in a similar vein. Then I picked up a letter addressed to his mother. He had been walking over the mountain, he said, when he got very sick and lay down on the ground and died. When he woke up, he found he had become the Devil. He ended the pathetic letter with the words: "I am well and hope you are the same—

Your loving son—now the Devil."

We sent off a radio message at once to the U.S. Marshal at Fairbanks and that evening a plane arrived. By then the red-haired stranger had returned to camp.

As a stratagem to get him quietly aboard the plane, we explained that there was a job for him in Fairbanks. He was docile and did not question us, even when we told him that the air was rough and we would have to tie him securely in his seat.

I patted his shoulder and said goodbye and those blue eyes came up meekly as he thanked me.

Two days later we received word from the marshal's office. He was so violently insane that he had to be restrained in a strait-jacket. As if the Devil really were living inside him.

Whenever I think with sadness of the red-headed young giant, a whole parade of other men troop through my mind. These are the old-timers, loners, too, the stalwart ones whom neither solitude, hardship, nor disappointment could destroy. I know hundreds of such men. They are friends of mine. For the most part they are men who have mined and grubbed for gold. They managed to make a living and led independent lives but the Golden Goddess never smiled on them. I have heard some of their adventures and know the hardships they have lived through and the stark courage it took to survive. It was a memorable day for me when I had completed the long residence requirement and was formally initiated into their fraternity, the Alaska Pioneers.

They are, I believe, as independent a group of old men as ever lived. The State provides two excellent Pioneers' Homes where they could spend their last years in ease. The old-timers will have none of this until they are too infirm to take care of themselves. In each Alaskan settlement you can see their cabins on the outskirts of town. In summer they tend their vegetable gardens. On winter evenings they come into town to warm themselves in the hotel lobbies and visit with their friends. After an hour or so they get to their feet, rather stiffly, and head out into the dark.

During all their years in the back country they led dangerous lives; sickness, injury, and death were daily hazards until at last they have come to treat death with a curious bravado.

In areas where the ground is solidly frozen in winter, digging graves is a hard job. In early days at least, it was the custom of the undertaker to estimate the number of graves that would be required in the Pioneers' plot each winter and to prepare open graves during summer when digging was easy.

Most of the old-timers firmly believe that they are scrutinized and checked off each autumn by the undertaker making his estimates. If he meets one of them on the street or in a hotel lobby and appears to give them a second glance, they will sometimes growl, "Don't look me over, you bastard. You're not going to get me next winter."

It does my heart good just to think about those wonderful old fellows. The courage of the young is a splendid thing. But sometimes I think that it is the courage of the old for which the victory trumpets should blow.

Chapter X

WHEN THE MOUNTAINS FROWN

EVERY wilderness man I know comes to feel, at times, that the primitive areas around him have taken on a distinct personality, sometimes benign, sometimes inimical. Botanists, foresters, trappers, big game hunters, or geologists, we have all known days when the mountains were good companions and other days when the going was tough and the mountains seemed to feel a deep antagonism toward us puny humans.

I can understand why some areas are taboo to Alaskan Indians and why some mountains are believed to be the lairs of demons. I have stretched my tarp in the lee of a cliff and been wakened by the screaming of the wind. As it rose high and then even higher before it changed suddenly to a deep moaning sound, the wind has seemed to be talking to me in malicious, threatening tones. When the rain came beating down there would be a searing flash of lightning, followed instantly by a cannonading of thunder. Then the lightning would strike again, like a clenched fish from the clouds hammering at the mountain peaks above me.

Sometimes, on the trail, I have hauled up short, alert to some unseen hazard. It never pays, in our mountains, to ignore the stirrings of the ancient fears. They are really, I believe, warnings from our subconscious minds, sensing some mantrap that has gone unnoticed by our conscious selves. The subconscious of an experienced wilderness man is his greatest protection against an impersonal nature that can be as cruel and harsh as a demon.

Whenever I went into the mountains I took what precautions I could. In the back of my canvas coat I carried a pound bar of sweet chocolate, never eaten unless I had been hours without food. In the side pocket was a waterproof match case which I never opened and a stub of candle, handy for starting fires or for testing the air in an old prospect tunnel—necessary measures but fruitless if a man's subconscious warning system is asleep on the job.

I knew we were in for a rugged trip when Warren Taylor and I left Valdez in a small boat to examine a gold quartz prospect on a nunatak projecting above Columbia Glacier. A nunatak is a mountain peak surrounded by a glacier. Taylor was interested in a mineral showing there. It was supposed to be a very promising prospect and I wanted to have a look at it, too. We would have to get out on the ice to reach it.

The boat nosed into the dock of the old abandoned Cliff mine, the flooded gold mine that our company, years before, had tried unsuccessfully to bring back into production. We made a date with the boatman to pick us up in four days. Then we shouldered our packs and started out on foot.

Before tackling the nunatak, I wanted to visit another gold quartz property in the area, the Big Four mine, at an elevation of more than five thousand feet. We had been traveling about two hours when our trail left Mineral Creek to switchback up the steep mountainside. The country literally was standing on end. Even the slate beds under our feet were folded into a vertical position.

When we stopped to "take five," I searched the trail ahead. Through overhanging clouds I could make out a cabin notched into the steep cliffs. We were planning to spend the night there. The summit above the cabin, I knew, was covered by a huge ice cap, extending a hundred miles along the crest of the range. The ice cap sent out great tongues of ice to form valley glaciers that were crunching their way down the mountains to the sea.

Toward the west we looked down on the ice fields of Columbia Glacier, one of the mightiest valley glaciers on the continent. We had a date to see it at close range and I hoped the weather would hold. Nearby was Shoup Glacier and to the east we could see the corrugated surface of Valdez Glacier. Far below was the greenish salt water of Valdez Arm merging in the distance with Prince William Sound. It was no country for the inexperienced.

After a comfortable night at the Big Four camp, we got up to find that six inches of snow had fallen while we slept. Our cabin was sporting a white bonnet.

To reach the mine workings, we had to cross a small glacier, only a few hundred yards wide at this elevation. The new snow concealed the crevasses and the surface of the glacier was deceptively smooth. I must have grown careless for a moment, and my subconscious warning system failed to alert me. Suddenly the bottom simply dropped out from under my feet and I was falling. Instinctively I threw out my arms and caught the sides of the crevasse. With a mighty shove, I pulled myself back on the surface.

Behind me, Taylor gasped, "My God, I thought you were a goner!"

It was a small crevasse. I crawled back and looked down. I would have dropped only about fifteen feet to where the crevasse wedged down and veered to one side. But it would have been harrowing to lie there as a prisoner while Taylor went back to camp for a rope.

At the moment I was not unduly shaken. Then, as we plodded on, the reaction set in and I could feel a trembling of my muscles. Presently we approached the mine tunnel and another hazard appeared. When the tunnel had been driven into the mountain many years before, the surface of the glacier was only ten or fifteen feet below it and waste rock from the mine had been dumped out onto the ice. Since then, ablation had melted the ice surface and the portal of the tunnel was now high up on the face of a sheer cliff. The "goat" trail leading to the tunnel had been obliterated by a rock slide. If we lost our footing or if the slide started to move, we would plunge directly down onto the glacier, fifty feet below, its surface ribbed with ominous crevasses.

Ordinarily I would have taken the hazard in stride but my nerve at the moment was badly shaken. "Looks pretty hairy to me, Warren," I said.

He studied it for a moment. "I think we can make it. Let me squeeze past you and I'll give it a try." He balanced and picked his way across the slide like a tightrope performer while I watched in admiration. "It's okay," he called, from the tunnel portal. "Come ahead."

I was not ready. "You'll have to wait a few minutes until my nerves settle down." I filled my pipe, had a smoke and looked out over the country; gradually I could feel confidence returning. Finally I joined him.

We were in the tunnel for an hour cutting samples from the vein; when we came out, the slide area no longer seemed a menace.

That afternoon we hiked off the mountain and spent the night at the Cliff mine. The next day we were going to climb to the mine on the nunatak, a trip that was bound to offer some hardships, we knew.

The most difficult stretch was a long traverse across Anderson Glacier. Before venturing onto the ice we cut long alder branches and sharpened them to a point. Whenever we came to a doubtful area we would probe ahead before we took a step.

Taylor looked at me with a quizzical grin. "You know, I wish we each had a twelve-foot pole. If we slipped into a crevasse, the pole would bridge the gap and we'd have a chance to get out." It sounded like a good idea, but we were then several thousand feet above timberline.

We had passed the point of no return when a dense fog came rolling in from the sea. We could see it advancing toward us and then, quite suddenly, it was swirling around us as it rolled on up the glacier. Warren, who was ahead of me, pointed toward a rocky point on the other side of the glacier, still looming dimly through the fog. "See that promontory? Let's head for that."

As he started on, I whipped out my Brunton compass and took a bearing. In a few minutes, every landmark was completely blotted out. There was nothing to do but plod along carefully through the murk. I kept the compass in my hand and checked Warren's path from time to time. By instinct he was traveling right on course. I have never told him that I had doubts of his ability.

Finally we felt solid ground under our feet, but it would be folly, we knew, to grope around, trying to find the mine cabin in the fog. We spent the next hour cutting green alders for firewood. Alder, I have heard, burns better when it is green than when it is dry. Perhaps so. But it is a difficult job to start a fire with it. Fortunately we had a quart bottle of kerosene in the pack and this solved the problem.

A drizzle of mixed snow and rain was falling and there

139

was no hope of sleep. We crouched there all night, hugging our little fire and nursing it along. You learn a good deal about a man during an experience of that kind. When I first met Warren Taylor, he was operating a cigar store in Cordova. Then he studied law, became a successful attorney in Fairbanks, and was active in state politics. To some people he is a controversial figure. But that night on the glacier I had a real chance to get his measure. He does not whine when the going is tough and he always carries his share of the pack.

A decade later, after I became president of the University of Alaska and appeared before the legislature for university appropriations, Warren was speaker of the House of Representatives. One day, at a committee meeting, when I was having hard sledding, Warren looked at me across the table and winked.

I grinned back at him. In memory we were on the glacier again, caught in the fog.

By four in the morning we had enough light to start on. By the time we reached the mine workings, we were cold and miserable. My fingers were numb and my awkward notes difficult to decipher later. Finally we finished the examination and came out of the tunnel. The cold drizzle had stopped for a time and the swirling clouds had lifted a little, giving us a visibility of perhaps two miles. On each side the tumbled ice surface crowded down toward the sea, only an occasional sharp mountain peak breaking the monotony of white ice.

Our boat was waiting when we got back to the Cliff mine. Warren and I huddled by the engine and as I looked up, tired and wet to the skin, the whole lowering country seemed to be saying, "Man, stay away!" I admit, if the vein I had sampled had shown enough flecks of gold, I would have gone trespassing again. As it was, I had no interest in trying to develop a mining prospect in such an inaccessible setting.

I could remember vividly an occasion several years before when a mountain had rejected me with violence. It happened on a sunny June morning, a happy morning when a man is glad to be out in the hills. Two companions and I were climbing a switchback trail from the little settlement of Hope on the shores of Turnagain Arm to the base camp of the Hershey mine. High above us, just below one of the rugged ridges of the Coast Range, we could see the mine workings and a cluster of small buildings clinging to the mountain. The cliffs above the mine were still heavy with winter snow.

After we had toiled up the steep trail, we spent several hours climbing around in the mine workings and cutting a few samples from the vein for assay. I finally concluded that the property was too small to be of interest to my clients.

The sun was blinding as we came out of the tunnel. Perhaps that blazing warmth sent out its warning to my subconscious. We had started along a trail leading from the tunnel to the waste dump. It was bounded on the uphill side by an icy wall of deep snow and all at once my head jerked up in alarm. I did not know why I was afraid. There was just a sudden sense of danger. It came too late. The next second there was a sharp report like a rifle shot and a mass of ice and snow, triggered by the sun, broke loose and started to move down the slope.

We broke into a run and in a moment I was on the heels of the man ahead of me. He was an older man. The only way to go around him was to jump down onto the dump. I learned later that a blast of air ahead of the slide threw him clear. I was not so lucky. When I had almost cleared the edge of the slide, the frozen face of the avalanche struck me and threw me ahead of it. I was on my feet in an in-

141

stant, trying to leap out of the way. By that time it was gaining momentum and struck again with a brutal force. I was able to make two more leaps toward the side before it crashed into me for the third time.

I felt my body twisting through the air. There was a feeling of numbness and I fought to retain consciousness. I had landed in a sitting position on a rocky knoll and I was dimly aware of the slide thundering by me to spill over a cliff. My scalp and face were gashed. When I tried to wipe the blood out of my eyes, I discovered that my right hand did not respond. I looked around and found it twisted behind me. By gripping the sleeve of my coat with my left hand, I was able to pull the broken right arm gently to my side.

Eventually, I landed in a hospital in Seattle for a bone graft and several months' immobilization in a body cast. There is nothing like a mountain to cut a man down to size. Lying in bed, I sometimes thought of an old prospector I knew. When I had admired the view of the mountain on which his cabin was perched, he gave me a disgusted look from under his struggling white eyebrows. "She's a mean old bitch. Been laying for me over twenty years now." He aimed a vicious kick at the slope where we were standing. "I hate her guts, I do."

"You don't really hate the country that bad," I remonstrated. "If you sold your claims, you would be back here in a few years to prospect again."

"Not on your life," was his emphatic answer.

"Suppose you do sell your claims; where would you go?" I asked.

"Young fellow," he glared at me, "I'd go someplace where I didn't have to wear shoe-pacs and where they don't call dried apples fruit!"

Chapter XI

THE MAN WHO WENT TO SEA

O NE day back in the summer of 1934, a tourist and his wife were standing beside me at the rail of a stern-wheel steamboat on the Yukon River. The boat had just pulled in at the landing near the mouth of Woodchopper Creek, too brief a stop to put out a line. The captain was holding the boat against the current with the wheel.

A twelve-foot plank was run ashore and an Indian deck-hand ran down with a mail sack, followed by a second deckhand balancing a big carton on his shoulder. As they dropped their loads on the river bank, Jack Welch handed them a mail sack too flat to contain more than three or four letters.

The boat was coasting a bit by that time, the shore end of the limber board biting the gravel as it shifted. With a few nimble steps the deckhands were back on board. There was a quick blast of the whistle and the boat nosed out into the current.

"How's it going, Jack?" the captain shouted from the upper deck.

Jack did not answer nor smile. He just raised his hand in salute, picked up the carton and mail sack and started up the trail toward a bluff overlooking the river and a two-story log cabin where a woman stood framed in the doorway.

"I'll bet that fellow doesn't know who's president of the United States," the tourist said to his wife.

I was prompted to tell him how wrong he was. Instead I swallowed my irritation and let the moment pass. After all, the tourist's impression was not illogical. Jack Welch, with his big rawboned frame, his swarthy face, and the cast in one eye which gave him a menacing look would have made an excellent movie heavy. But he could have named the president and probably most of his cabinet. I had seen copies of *Time* and the *National Geographic* on a table in his cabin. More important, he had mastered the rugged environment of the Yukon in a way few other men have done. His story is as touching as any I found in the North.

In winter Jack had a contract to carry the mail from Woodchopper to Eagle. This meant sixty miles of dogteam travel on the treacherous ice of the Yukon, bone chilling cold, blizzards that swept down the river gorge, and the ever-present threat of getting into an overflow.

When the upriver mail team arrived at Woodchopper from Circle City, Jack could not wait for favorable weather. He was expected to take off for Eagle at once. A good many winter travelers perished on the Yukon but year after year Jack had the knowhow and the courage to come through safely.

At breakup time in the spring his dogs would be staked out near the cabin to worry the summer away. Jack, who was a skilled river man, would caulk his shovel nosed river boat and tune up his outboard motors. After the ice run was over he would get his fish wheel into the water. He had an excellent site on a rocky point where a finger of rock stuck

144

out into the channel. The fish wheel gave him salmon to dry and smoke for dogfood, as well as food for his own table.

His wife was a small, quiet, hard-working woman, very proud of Jack. She operated the Post Office, serving a dozen prospectors and trappers, and ran the roadhouse where a traveler on the river could stop for a meal or a bed.

That was their life when I first knew them. But tragedy was setting a dark stage for these two brave people. In the late 1930s, airplanes replaced the dogteam mail contracts. When World War II broke out, most of the people along the river moved to Fairbanks, attracted by the high wages in defense construction. Jack and his wife stayed on. In winter he ran a trapline and in summer picked up some extra money with his boat. Although our two gold-dredging camps were nearby, I saw Jack less frequently. Occasionally we would hire him for an emergency boat trip. Sometimes he would appear in camp with a big king salmon for our mess house.

It was spring of an early year of the war and just about time for ice breakup on the Yukon. We were getting the dredges ready for the operating season. Some supplies had been left on the riverbank during the winter and Jim Mc-Donald and I went down to the mouth of Coal Creek with a tractor to haul them to high ground. That night we slept in a cabin on a high cutback, fully twenty feet above river ice.

At about three o'clock in the morning, loud crashing sounds woke us up and we jumped out of bed. The river had gone wild with the crushing force of the breakup. Normally the Yukon, at this point, is less than a quarter-mile wide. While we slept, the water level had risen fifteen feet. Rushing, swirling ice cakes were flooding the lowland on the opposite bank, crushing the forest of spruce and birch

145

like a giant bulldozer. Before long ice cakes were being rafted up Coal Creek and dumped near our cabin.

It was an awesome and overwhelming sight. We were looking at the brute force of nature on the rampage. "Not many men have seen a spectacle like this," Jim said.

Then at the same moment we both turned and looked at each other. The rapid rise of the river could only come from a gigantic ice dam in Woodchopper Canyon, some five miles downstream. Jack Welch and his wife lived in that canyon. Their cabin must be flooded and probably it had been swept away. There was no way of knowing if they had been warned in time to reach the nearest hill, half a mile from their cabin. No outside help could possibly get to them now.

A few years before I would not have worried so much about Jack. I would have felt sure that he and his wife had reached safety. But Jack and his wife were both getting old. I remembered the last time I had seen him. "The wife is all stove up with rheumatism. Can't hardly get around at all," he had told me. "I'm pretty creaky in the joints myself. We're getting old, I guess."

Those words echoed in my ears as, almost in a daze, we watched the huge ice cakes sweeping in. Unless the ice jam broke soon our own cabin would be flooded. Not that we were in personal danger. We could quickly reach high ground. Ice piled on ice and thundered as if mountains were falling around us.

And then we knew that the jam had broken. The roar climbed to a crescendo and the ice began moving downstream as though sucked by an invisible force. Slowly the water level dropped.

That afternoon I sent two men overland to try and reach the Welches. They told me later what had happened.

The Welches had been awakened by the frenzied howling of their dogs, to find water covering the floor of the cabin.

146

Jack rushed out to cut the dogs loose and they instinctively started for high land. Some made it; others were swept away.

Jack got to his boat and pulled it through the swirling waters to the cabin, planning to take his wife and make a run with the boat for high land. He was too late. Escape was cut off. Water was filling the cabin and ice cakes were swirling and bumping against it. They climbed to the upper floor and Jack fastened his boat by an open window. The lower floor of the cabin was under water by that time and the second floor was awash. As huge blocks of ice smashed against its logs, the whole cabin trembled.

Twice Jack put his wife in the boat and got ready to make a run for it. But each time he hesitated. The ice, he was convinced, would crush his boat. They had less than a fighting chance to escape that way. Better to stay with the cabin, he decided, until water started pouring in the window. Then they would play their last card. He stood by the window with a pike pole, deflecting as much ice as possible away from the boat until at last the water level stopped rising. The jam was breaking.

As it gave way, the clamor increased and ice cakes bombarded the cabin with new speed. The log cabin shuddered but still it held.

Perhaps it would have been more merciful if they had been swept away. The stark terror of the experience deeply scarred both of those aging people. Mrs. Welch became bedfast. Jack took care of her but he was changed, too. People would say to me, "I don't know what's come over Jack. He's getting strange." None of us suspected how strange.

One winter night Jack woke his wife. He was in the grip of an hallucination and shaking all over. The German army, he insisted, was marching down the ice of the Yukon to-

147

ward them. Mrs. Welch tried to calm him but he kept repeating, "If they come, will you protect me?" He was babbling like a child, this man who had always been a tower of strength, a man without fear.

Later in the night he grew silent and she thought that he had gone to sleep. Then she heard his voice in the dark. "I know what's wrong. I'm losing my mind. I'm better off dead. I am going to shoot myself."

In spite of her frantic pleas, he dressed, grabbed up his rifle, and went outdoors. All she could do was to lie there, listening. But there was no sound of a gun. In a few minutes he came back and lay down on the bed. "I can't do it," he said. "I lost my nerve."

Once again she tried to soothe him but at the end of an hour he climbed out of bed again. "I've got my nerve back," he said.

Mrs. Welch forced her crippled body out of the bed and had begun to dress when she heard a shot. A moment later he staggered into the cabin. He had shot himself in the side, but had missed the heart. She helped him to bed, hid the rifle, and then set out for help. With the aid of two canes she hobbled two miles over a winter trail in the cold and darkness to the cabin of their nearest neighbor, George McGregor.

McGregor hitched up his dogs, put Mrs. Welch in the sled, and raced back to the cabin. After giving Jack first aid, he carried him out to the sled and with Mrs. Welch traveled six miles up Woodchopper Creek to our mining camp where our winter watchman sent a radio message to Fairbanks. Within a few hours a plane picked them up and took them to the hospital in Fairbanks.

In a month or so Jack was up and around but the shock had been too much for his wife's tired heart. She lingered on only a little while after Jack left the hospital.

A prospector's cabin notched into the steep cliffs. Near here, the author was caught in an avalanche which he tried to outrun.

The class of 1922 had five coeds and the "full house" team of twins and three brothers.

Ernest and Kay Patty at graduation exercises, with explorers Walter Wood and Sir Hubert Wilkins.

The winter "short course" of miners and prospectors. Dean Patty invented the "rock poker" game to teach identification of rock formations.

In tall timber country, the typical miner's camp includes the dogteam hutch, the cabin, and meat cache built on stilts for protection.

To the left, the college in 1929; by that year both wings were added to "Old Main," the original building of 1922. Above, the University today, with a campus of 2,000 acres; it now accommodates over 2,000 students. The academic buildings are grouped around the mall, with a center pool and fountain. The dormitory complex and faculty residences lie outside the perimeter, the research center on the ridge above. The university also directs six community colleges, "a fur farm, a musk ox herd, a glacier, an archaeological museum, an ice station on the polar cap, two satellite tracking stations."

In the 1920's, no running water. You posted a sign in the window to indicate to the waterman (above) how many buckets of water you needed.

The steel dredges floating on pontoons weigh 400 tons. The bucket line carries gold-bearing gravels inside to screens revolving over the gold-catching sluice.

In the late 1930's, airplanes replaced dogteam mail, and the bush pilot with ski-wheel plane became a new legendary figure of Alaska.

o reach gold-bearing gravels, tundra ust be drilled by "points" of heavy ipe.

Dr. Otto Geist digging tusks of the hairy mammoth uncovered by the dredges.

In the 1920's the dogsled was common on the streets of Fairbanks. Dr. Patty learned the hazards during his first winter: wolf blood is bred into the husky; passing teams lunge at each other, itching for a fight.

Jack refused to believe that his wife was dead. He did not go to her funeral, but just clung to the idea that she was waiting for him in their cabin at Woodchopper. When he did not find her there he cruised along the river bank searching and searching. Finally he walked into our camp. "Have you seen my wife?" he asked me. "I can't find her. She's hiding from me."

I tried to explain, as gently as I could, but it was impossible to reach him. When he went back to the river I sent a radio message to the U.S. Marshal's office at Fairbanks, urging them to take him to the hospital.

But the next day Jack and his boat vanished. Weeks later news started trickling back from small villages along the lower Yukon. People spoke of a mysterious white man sitting in a small boat just drifting down the river. Passing boats had hailed him but he did not answer.

The final word came from some Indians hunting on the Yukon delta. They had seen a white man floating out into the Bering Sea. He was standing in the boat, shading his eyes against the late afternoon sun, looking out to sea.

Still searching for his wife? I believe he found her.

Chapter XII

SOMETHING LOST BEHIND THE RANGES

OCCASIONALLY I have asked mountain climbers why they suffer such great physical hardships and even risk their lives to conquer a difficult mountain. Generally they look at me in a puzzled way because I am not in tune with them. One man shrugged his shoulders and said, "Because it's there."

The present generation probably would say, "He's just doing his thing."

Well, I too have a "thing." I have always thought of it as my secret hobby. Whenever I see a mountain stream I want to follow it to its very head and whenever I see a mountain pass I feel a great urge to explore through it and finally look out over a new wilderness with its endless parade of mountain ridges and its intricate drainage patterns.

I do not know what motivates me. Perhaps I am a throwback to one of my pioneering ancestors. I never was able to explain the feeling in words until I discovered that Rudyard Kipling had said it for me:

Something hidden. Go and find it—
Go and look behind the Ranges—
Something lost behind the Ranges—
Lost and waiting for you. Go.

Frequently in northern Canada and Alaska I have followed my inclination and looked behind the ranges and each time I have brought back a sense of well being and a great contentment.

During the summers our mining organization kept a prospecting crew in the field, drilling the gravels in the valley bottoms to determine the quantity of gold they contained. We were looking for new areas that might be mined profitably with heavy machinery. In each instance we chose stream valleys where early-day miners had found gold and had attempted to mine with pick, shovel, and sluice box.

As part of my job I paid periodic visits to these drilling operations and checked results to see if the work should be continued. If the drill samples showed commercial gold concentrations, I would scout ahead upstream to map the geology and check on probable mining conditions, such as width of valley floor, size of gravels, and water supply.

Generally a well beaten trail would lead me upstream. There would be no use trying to keep dry. The trail would snake back and forth across the valley and the rushing stream had to be waded. I would pass old cabins, their roofs usually caved in by winter snows, and remnants of old prospect shafts or opencuts where some hardy man had attempted to win gold.

When the last cabin had been passed, the trail would fade out and there would be no need to go beyond that point. But looking ahead, I would see a pass at the very head of the valley and the thought would leap into my mind, "What's up there? What does the country on the other side

151

look like?" Then I would feel the old urge to go on. If I am late getting back to camp, I would tell myself, the cook will save supper—but I mustn't be too late or some of the crew will start out to look for me. Well, here we go again.

Sometimes now, when I close my eyes, I can still hear the slipping of some mountain stream, the crunch of my boots on gravel. A scene will "flash upon that inward eye" and I am right there again, above timberline, following a wandering game trail through the heavy buck brush which cloaks the mountain. It is all there in my mind, down to the smallest details. I can see moose signs and I know the moose, hearing my approach, have faded into the bushes, to stand silently watching me as I step across the stream, tumbling among its jagged granite boulders.

Now I have gained the pass and am out in the open. The meadows are brighter than a rainbow with wildflowers and I wish I had some knowledge of botany. How can they thrive in so inhospitable an environment? Is this their natural habitat or do winds, sweeping through the pass, reseed them?

The worn game trail leads by a lake, so small that it is hardly more than a large pond. A mallard is swimming across it, four young ducklings in her wake. She strikes me as being a foolish mother to pick such a vulnerable nesting place. A mink easily could decimate her brood.

A big bird, effortlessly riding the swirling air currents, soars high over me, an eagle perhaps, or a very large hawk. Does he, too, have his eyes on this little family? Will they survive to fly South in the fall?

Before going on through the pass, instinctively I search the hillsides and I do not like what I see. Why didn't I bring a gun? Two hundred yards above the trail a grizzly is digging out a ground squirrel. He is not to be trusted and I do not want to walk under him. Bears have poor eyesight—

152

he might mistake me for a caribou and come down to investigate.

Common sense tells me to go back. But still there is the urge to go on. I stand quietly to watch him. He is not aware of my presence. He has stopped digging and I wonder if the squirrel has escaped or if it was not in its home. The bear is moving slowly up the hill and I decide to eat lunch while keeping a wary eye on him.

As soon as I take the lunch sack out of the back pocket of my field coat, two northern jays, also called camp robbers, appear as if by magic. I should have expected them. They always come out of nowhere when food is evident. Possibly they have been following me all morning. I break off a piece of breadcrust and throw it on the ground ten feet in front of me. The jays jump nervously from branch to branch, edging closer. Then, with a quick swoop, one of the freeloaders claims it.

When I look up, the bear is gone. Startled, I jump to my feet. He was there only a moment ago. As I watch anxiously he ambles out from behind a clump of bushes, still heading uphill. I finish lunch and then, to give him plenty of clearance, I load my pipe and kill time writing my notes before I push on to the other end of the pass.

I find myself on a promontory where a steep cliff below my feet drops off to a long talus slope. I am looking down into the valley of one of the forks of the Klondike River, an uninhabited wilderness; the snow-capped peaks of the Ogilvie Range are beautiful against the horizon. Not many men have passed this way. I am conscious of a feeling of fulfillment and happiness at this minor accomplishment. At least I have had a glimpse behind the ranges.

Then I realize that the trail leading me to this promontory was made by wild game. Many animals have stood on this spot to survey the country below, predators looking for

153

food, the hunted looking for danger before venturing down into the valley.

Did any of these animals, I wonder, feel a joy in their surroundings? Or are they too circumscribed, concerned only with the daily struggle for survival?

Several times in the mountains I have come across a bull moose standing motionless on a crag, gazing out over the country. I would like to know if he is thinking or just standing there, dumbly chewing his cud.

I have always been surprised when I finally open my eyes to discover how short a time I have been traveling in my memory, usually only five minutes. Invariably I have come back to the present feeling rested and able to tackle the job at hand with a fresh mind and a new perspective, as if some vital part of me really had been looking behind the ranges.

Chapter XIII

THE KLONDIKE

IN 1938 we decided to follow an old, sage bit of advice:
"If you're going to hunt bear, go to bear country."

Our dredges at Coal and Woodchopper Creeks were in
routine operation by that time and we had been busy
searching for other dredging areas to expand our operations.
After trying several neighboring creeks on the Alaska side of
the international boundary, without finding anything of interest, we scouted around across the border in the Klondike.

In the mining world, the Klondike is the greatest "bear
country" of them all. Mining men still argue whether it was
Robert Henderson or George Carmack and his Indian companion, Skookum Jim, who first discovered placer gold in
the district which later became the richest and most pro-
ductive placer gold camp on the continent.

In point of fact, Henderson was the first man to find and
mine gold in the Klondike. Carmack and Skookum Jim
were returning from a visit to Henderson's camp on Gold
Bottom Creek when they made their own find of coarse
nuggets in the stream gravels of Rabbit Creek, later known
as Bonanza Creek. It was their discovery that triggered the
stampede.

155

I had cut my eye teeth on tales of the Klondike gold rush. Margins of my copybooks at school in eastern Oregon used to be filled with drawings I had made of gold pans, rockers, and other primitive gold-saving devices. The mining fever must have hit me young. When I went to the Klondike myself, hunting gold, all those stories came rushing back to me. Fine dramatic stories they were, too. Back in 1898, gold seekers by the thousands had fought their way over Indian trails across the forbidding Coast Range, to Lake Bennett and Lake Lindeman, built boats, loaded their scant outfits aboard, and floated into the headwaters of the Lewes River. And still there were plenty of dangers ahead as they were swept through the foaming rapids of Miles Canyon and drifted hundreds of miles downstream until the Lewes River became the Yukon.

I honor the strength and courage of those who finally managed to reach the new settlement of Dawson City, just below the mouth of the Klondike River. They found the stream gravels that contained the golden treasure frozen as hard as concrete and covered with a layer of frozen muck. They had to learn from the old-timers how to use wood fires and hot rocks to burn a hole down to bedrock where the gold was concentrated.

Frozen ground was no mystery to the old-timers, that scattering of adventurous men who had been mining in the Forty Mile and Circle districts in the Yukon basin even before the discovery in the Klondike. As soon as word of Carmack's nuggets filtered in, they had scrambled out of their prospect holes, gathered up their belongings, and headed for the new strike. They were among the first to reach the Klondike and several of them made fortunes.

Finally some ingenious fellow found an easier method of thawing. He attached a hose to one end of a discarded rifle barrel and fastened the other end to a small steam boiler.

Steam escaping through the rifle barrel worked into the frozen ground. That was the beginning of steam thawing and resulted in the development of steam-points six to eight feet long that were hammered slowly into the ground and left overnight to allow escaping steam to sweat the surrounding ground. The next morning the thaw could be excavated. After that a new thaw would be put in, and thus miners would slowly work their way down to bedrock. Thousands of men with picks and shovels were down in the steamy haze of those bedrock drifts and, as they tore into the gravels, they often could see nuggets of gold studded in the gravel face. The supply seemed inexhaustible. Men who had been lucky enough to acquire a rich claim suddenly were richer than their wildest dreams. Pack trains with hundred-pound containers of gold lashed to the backs of mules funneled into the Dawson banks.

There were others who found an easier way to make a fortune than by digging for gold in frozen ground. They staked their claims in Dawson, on Front Street, in saloons and gambling halls; they brought in dancing girls to give the miners a good time and separate them from their pokes. There was Sweet Marie, for example, Klondike Kate, Molly Fewclothes, Ethel the Moose, and Diamond Tooth Gertie, who had a diamond fastened between her two front teeth. One pair of singers, who put on a sister act, were billed as Jacqueline and Rosalinde, but the miners nicknamed them Vaseline and Glycerine.

Some of the miners, who had never before known wealth, lived carefully, took a trip outside to invest with wisdom, and finally, when their claims were worked out, went home to become important men of affairs. But to thousands of others, the gold was hot; they were suddenly bigshots and wanted action. If the gambling tables or a big strand of nuggets for their favorite dance hall girl cleaned them out,

157

it was nothing to worry about. There was plenty more where that cleanup had come from—so back to the diggings.

Raw gold was the common medium of exchange and most of the miners carried a moose-hide poke. If the poke were heavy, he would slap it loudly onto the bar as he ordered drinks for his friends. Yet for all its boisterousness, violence in Dawson was kept to a minimum, thanks to a hardy detachment of Northwest Mounted Police who administered law and justice and whose officers were men of unusual sense and understood men's frailties.

There are names from those bonanza days that are now legendary in the Klondike. One is the name of a holy man, Father William Judge, a thin, frail priest who used to be spoken of as the "saint of the Klondike." Old-timers who still lived in Dawson used to tell me about his makeshift hospital, overflowing with men desperately ill of pneumonia and dysentery. During epidemics, they said, he would give up his own spartan quarters and sleep in a cubbyhole under the stairs, and they said his face was such a one as you see in paintings of saints.

Before Father Judge himself died of pneumonia, a fine modern hospital was started, financed in part by "Big Alex" McDonald, the King of the Klondike. Big Alex was the richest of the men in the area who had dug gold by the bucketsful out of his claims.

When we first came to Dawson, the days of hand mining were long past, and the cream of the gold had been skimmed away. By then the Yukon Consolidated Gold Corporation had acquired all of the important gold-bearing streams in the district and were efficiently reworking the old gravels with eight modern dredges for whatever gold had been left behind.

Since we were late arrivals, we had to take the leavings. First we optioned All Gold Creek and Gold Bottom Creek, where Henderson had made the first discovery in the Klondike. There was nothing golden about them except their names. The only good value we found on All Gold Creek was a limited yardage near the mouth, too small for the scope of our operations. Our drilling results on Gold Bottom were tempting at first, but there again limited yardage and other problems caused us to drop the option. Then we turned to Clear Creek, sixty miles away. This was the creek where Big Alex McDonald had moved, hoping to find another rich pay streak after he lost his fortune. He did not live to test it. His great heart gave out and a visitor found his body in his cabin.

Only a dim trail led into the area. The four or five miners eking out a bare living there moved their supplies in by dogteam in winter and by back-packing during the summer. But William O'Neill, who was in charge of our prospecting, was accustomed to tackling jobs that other people thought impossible. He shipped our tractor-mounted drill up the Stewart River to McQuestin Landing and then walked it forty miles over mountain ridges to the property. This time the drilling was successful. Within another year we had finished a truck road to the property, brought in heavy machinery, and before long had a dredge in operation.

The cabins Big Alex McDonald had built were still there. As we rehabilitated and enlarged the ditch that Big Alex had dug to bring water above his claims, I sometimes thought of the disappointment awaiting him if he had lived. He would not have found a rich paystreak in his last desperate gamble to recoup his fortunes. We had sampled the ground with hundreds of drill holes. The paystreak was thin and could yield a profit only when mined with modern equipment like ours.

Other creeks within a radius of a hundred miles of Dawson had been mined in a small way in early years and we

159

decided on an extensive prospecting program. Some years later we were building two new dredges, one at Thistle Creek and one at Henderson Creek, a tributary of the Yukon River, near the Klondike. This was Jack London country. He once spent a winter in a cabin on Henderson Creek and, I have been told, wrote *The Call of the Wild* during that period.

"As I remember," one of the old-timers told me, "he was kind of a lazy young fellow. I don't believe he sank a single prospect hole all winter long. Most of the time he was just holed up in that cabin."

The first time I made the trip up the Henderson Creek trail from the roadhouse at Stewart, I kept remembering our fourth-grade class in eastern Oregon. Every Friday afternoon, our teacher would read us a few chapters from *The Call of the Wild,* and we would all sit spellbound, willing to stay after school if only she would keep reading. She never did. When the bell rang she would pause in mid-sentence, put a marker in the book, and shove it in a desk drawer. That was in 1904, when the book was new. It was now thirty-five years later, and here I was, directing mining operations on Jack London's creek. I half expected to see the ghost of "Buck" still trotting along the trail I was following.

Nothing of interest remained in Jack London's cabin. The sod roof had fallen in, the logs had rotted, and the interior was a shambles. Nevertheless, when we began muck stripping operations and it became necessary to send a bulldozer downstream to shove the aged cabin logs up against the hillside, I felt as if I were violating a precious boyhood memory. I did not go down the creek to watch.

In all our Klondike camps, the animals had a way of making themselves felt. Our road to the Clear Creek camp broke through uninhabited country and it was not rare to meet a moose or a bear along the road or, occasionally, to

160

see a band of wolves loping off into the brush. One day our truck driver found a new-born moose calf nesting near the road, its mother having either been killed or having abandoned it. The crew fed it warmed milk from a catsup bottle, with the finger cut from a rubber glove serving as a nipple, and it grew up, as tame as a dog, trotting out of the woods when the dinner gong sounded to be first at the mess hall door and then following our master mechanic back to the machine ship after lunch, to stretch out on the floor, undisturbed by the noise of machines or of men walking around it.

Once, when I was spending the night at our Thistle Creek camp, sleeping on a cot in the office, I was wakened by the howling of wolves moving down the valley. The door near the head of my bed was open. I had closed only the screen door. For a while I lay listening to the wolves' hunting calls. They had split into two packs, one pack on each side of the valley. When they reached the camp area they stopped and talked back and forth to each other. Suddenly, just outside my door, a dog started to bark and then stifled the noise in his throat.

"That's a pretty cowardly dog you've got in camp," I said the next morning at breakfast.

"There aren't any dogs in camp," one of the men told me.

Quite literally, I had had a wolf at my door. No doubt he had come into camp to investigate and had started to answer the call of the pack, but at the last minute had decided to play it cool and keep his mouth shut.

On another occasion I was traveling down a frozen river with a dogteam, when suddenly the hair began to bristle on the backs of my dogs. They kept looking across the river, whining, and then glancing back at me.

I could not make out what was disturbing them until I

161

caught sight of five gray forms loping along parallel to us on the opposite bank of the wide valley. For a mile they kept on an even pace with us while I talked to the dogs to reassure them—and myself. It reminded me of the old picture of Russian peasants in a sleigh pursued by a band of wolves. I doubt if such an incident ever occurred. I know my wolves finally just turned and disappeared into the brush of the hillside. In fact I have met many wolves and they always moved away so fast that it would have been hard to get a shot at them.

One experience involving an animal was a little touchier. I was working early one evening in the office of our Henderson Creek camp when I decided to go to the privy, a two-seater located some distance from the office. I had just stepped out of the office door when one of the workmen stopped me to ask a question. We were standing there talking when all at once I heard a fusillade of rifle shots close by and ran around the corner of the building. A wounded black bear was leaning against the privy for support while nearby three of the men were blasting away at him with their rifles. A good many of the bullets were missing the bear and perforating the wall of the privy.

"Hold it!" I shouted. "There may be someone in there."

The men turned flabbergasted faces toward me and one said, "My gosh. We never thought of that."

Except for the interruption, I would have been the one in there. Which poses the question, where would a man hide?

Eventually we decided to move our summer headquarters to Dawson. From a base there I would be able to move back and forth from our Alaskan operations to our properties in the Klondike. William O'Neill, an experienced placer engineer, was made assistant manager and supervised Canadian work directly.

Our three boys were grown by that time and Kay would

spend the summers with me in Dawson. The first time she flew in I was a little apprehensive. Dawson is not everybody's dish of tea, but it had a gallant past. "You'll see the town in a moment now," I told her as we flew down the Yukon and I spotted Moosehead Mountain and the white scar left on a hillside by a giant landslide.

Our plane made three lazy circles over town, the signal that we wanted a car to meet us at the airfield.

"Dawson looks lovely from the air," Kay said, peering down. "All laid out in neat rectangles. Green trees, patches of lawn . . ."

We flew on past and up the Klondike River, over symmetrical waves of gravel tailings left by the dredges as they excavated the valley floor. A huge dredge down there was digging slowly upstream. Then below us we saw Bonanza Creek, a tributary of the Klondike, where the original gold discovery was made. Bonanza and its own tributary, Eldorado Creek, were the two richest creeks in the district. Up on the ridge, the white streaks are called the "White Channel," part of an ancient river system, whose gravels are mostly white quartz, rich in gold. Water had been pumped up for hydraulic mining operations and we could see the tailings spilling down the mountainside. In a recent geologic period the country had been uplifted several hundred feet and new draining patterns were developed. Where the present creeks cut back into the White Channel, they are greatly enriched.

Our plane passed the mouth of Hunker Creek where another dredge was working, and then we were beyond the mining area, circling in the valley. Tree tops skidded by under the plane, and we jolted across the gravel strip in a former hay field that was the rough but adequate airport. An hour later we drove into Dawson City—a sad and tattered

163

town which once had boasted a population of thirty-five thousand and was now reduced to a few hundred people.

Dawson has a more dilapidated appearance than other towns that also have had their days of roaring opulence and have fallen on sorry times. Buildings tilt at crazy angles, as drunken looking as any bonanza-day miner cutting loose after months of digging. Because Dawson is built on frozen ground, seasonal freezing and thawing heave the buildings out of plumb unless they are set on piling. Homes and buildings in use have to be jacked up and leveled at intervals. Most of the buildings are not in use now.

"Look at that abandoned store building," Kay exclaimed. "It looks like the leaning Tower of Pisa!"

"Brace yourself," I told her. "We're going to stay at the Royal Alexandra Hotel until we can find a house and it's royal in name only."

We pulled up in front of a ramshackle, false-fronted frame building and climbed out of the car. Once inside, we seemed to have jumped back to another age. The lobby, in early days, had been the famous Floradora saloon and dancehall. The fluted pillars, once, no doubt, the last word in elegance, still stood and crowded all around were worn Edwardian furniture and a row of heavy black leather chairs.

On one wall, where miners bellying up to the bar could feast their eyes, were two large oil paintings. They were both life-sized nudes of beautiful girls, apparently of French extraction. One was Diana the huntress adorned only with a crescent moon in her hair and a bow held lightly in her hand. Her companion in the other frame expressed her modesty with a wisp of diaphanous scarf strategically placed. These paintings had been carried over the Chilkoot trail, rolled up in canvas, in the early days of the Klondike. The massive gold frames had been cut into two-foot segments

164

for mule-back transportation. I could imagine the belly-laughs as miners pointed out to each other how inadequately dressed the girls were for the cold winter. Or perhaps they were all too impressed even to wonder at the absence of goose pimples in those wonderful skin tones.

In contrast to the nudes there was a big framed photograph of the Floradora girls who had been entertainers during the halcyon days. They all wore heavy, floor-length skirts and tight bodices with leg-of-mutton sleeves. Each girl was topped with a large picture hat.

On our way to the sleeping rooms upstairs we stopped to look at another painting entitled "Suzanna and the Elders." Suzanna was cringing in her nakedness while one of the Elders with a leer on his face pointed upwards. "Where is he telling her to go?" Kay asked. "The poor girls can't go up on the roof."

All of the rooms opened onto a long hall; the single bath and toilets were at one end. Our room had a faded carpet, shiny with wear, and a washstand and pitcher that Kay felt had value as antiques. She stood looking the room over and twisting one of the shiny brass knobs on the iron bedstead. "I see what you mean," she said. "Let's start house-hunting this afternoon."

We found a very comfortable house and in a few days Kay was happily putting plants in the front flowerbeds and vegetables in the large back garden.

Just across the road from us was the cabin where Robert W. Service had lived when he was a clerk for the Canadian Bank of Commerce. The few tourists who filtered down to Dawson took hundreds of photographs of the cabin, its simple furnishings, and the framed copy on the front porch of his poem, "Goodbye Little Cabin."

Other boys in the bank, the old-timers told me, frequently went out on the town but Service was a recluse who spent all of his evenings alone in the cabin, no doubt in his imagination living the fanciful lives of the characters he invented.

It seemed to me that some of the people still living in Dawson were as unusual as any in the Service poems. I was always being astonished by some original twist in the people I met.

One evening when I was staying in the Royal Alexandra before Kay arrived, an old-timer who had just eaten dinner in the adjoining Arcade Cafe walked into the lobby and settled down in one of the black leather chairs behind the stove. After a few minutes he quietly slumped over in his chair and died from a heart attack.

After the doctor had pronounced him dead and his body had been covered with a sheet to await the arrival of the Canadian Mounted Police, one of the other men sitting in the lobby jumped up and stuck his head into the cafe. "Come out here, Harry," he shouted to the proprietor. "You've just poisoned a man with your grub."

When Harry Gleaves came in and saw the covered figure in the chair he sensed a practical joke and jerked the sheet away. "My God!" he gasped. "He really is dead!"

The hotel proprietor arrived as the police were removing the body a few minutes later. "What's happened? What's happened?" he demanded.

From across the lobby, someone piped up, "A man just froze to death sitting behind your stove."

I kept puzzling over this curious episode and wondering what could prompt such macabre jokes. These were kindly men but they were also men whose bets on the wheel of fortune had all turned up blanks. They had seen other men, working alongside of them, gather up rich winnings and return to their homes. In late autumn, when there was a hint of winter in the air, the last boat of the season would cast off its lines and with merry toots of its whistle, start for the trip outside. All the more fortunate men would be on board. Those who stayed behind would trudge back to their cabins to face a long winter of isolation. A few grew morose but the majority seemed to develop an acceptance of life, disasters and all, and a strange, off-beat humor. I found most of them delightful companions.

Once I was eating a moose steak at the counter of the Arcade Cafe when my companion nudged me. "See that fellow sitting at the end of the counter? He once wrote a check for a million dollars."

The man at the end of the counter was dressed in work clothes. He was gaunt and gnarled with age and hard work but he had a fine, determined face.

"It's quite a story," my companion went on.

The man, I learned, had come to the Klondike in the early days of the gold rush but he had never struck rich pay. After several years his wife in Vancouver, B.C., grew tired of waiting, wrote him a "Dear John" letter, and sent him divorce papers to sign. She had fallen in love with another man.

The miner signed the papers and wrote his wife a note wishing her happiness. As a final flourish he told her that he was enclosing a check for $1 million, just to show there were no hard feelings.

"They say his wife and her boy friend showed up at the Canadian Bank of Commerce as soon as it opened in the morning and tried to cash the check."

I looked appreciatively at the gaunt old fellow at the counter. This was one off-beat joke that pleased me. I had a hunch that with one fantastic gesture he had wiped out all of the resentment that might otherwise have embittered him for the rest of his days.

I rather sympathized with the moral dilemma of another

fellow in the Klondike, too. I heard about him one day when I was on the trail to Matson Creek. The path was leading us through a high pass when my trail partner and I were caught in a rainstorm and sheltered in an abandoned trapper's cabin.

I have been in hundreds of cabins but this was the most primitive of them all. It looked as if a gnome had lived there. The door was less than five feet high and the sill was two feet off of the ground. When I crouched down to enter, my packboard caught. I had to back up and try again.

The cabin had a dirt floor. By the dim light slipping through the one small window I could see a galvanized wash-tub in one corner, inverted for a stove, a table made of poles, a single bench and two pole bunks. A sprinkling of rusty spruce boughs were laid over the poles on the bunks. I stretched out on one of them and using my packboard as a pillow, settled down to wait out the storm.

"The trapper who owned this cabin died here one winter," my companion said, leaning back in the opposite bunk. "In fact, he died right on the bunk you're using."

I stirred uneasily and he went on to tell the story. After the trapper's frozen body had been found, the police came with a dogteam to investigate. Since a grave could not be dug in the frozen ground outside, they buried him under the dirt floor in the cabin, not expecting anyone else to use the old place.

But the next summer another trapper decided to take over the cabin as a shelter on his trapline. He did not like the idea of walking over the other man's grave and dug a second grave outside, then shoveled under the cabin until he found the fellow, well preserved in the cold ground. When he had knotted a rope around the body, he lifted it from the hole and started dragging it outside. As the body

168

slipped over the high stoop a skinning knife fell from the pocket of the corpse's overalls.

It was a beautiful knife, just what the trapper needed. But he was an honest man, not one to rob a corpse. He slipped the knife back in the dead man's overalls and slid the body over the ground. The knife slipped out again. This time, when the trapper picked it up, he looked at it longingly. All at once the perfect solution occurred to him. He just pulled out his own old knife, put it into the dead man's overalls, and pocketed the new knife.

A perfectly fair trade, under the circumstances, it seems to me.

Kay would stay in Dawson until mid-September and then fly to our camps in Alaska before proceeding on to Seattle for the winter. When the time came for her to leave, we would send a radio message to Ernest Jr. who was in charge of our two dredges on the Alaska side. The next day we would hear the whine of his engines as he brought his Grumman amphibian plane in for a landing on the Yukon in front of town. Forty minutes after takeoff, we would touch down at Eagle, Alaska, to clear Customs. There would always be a cluster of Indian women on the riverbank, waiting to greet Kay. Many of them had spent summers at Coal Creek where their husbands were employed and several of the children had attended Kay's little school there. The women would show Kay their new babies and the older children would smile at her timidly. When Ernest Jr. came out of the Customs office with clearance papers in his hand, the women would all shake hands formally with Kay, the motors would catch and the plane would wheel out into the current. Thirty minutes later he would be landing at the Woodchopper Creek airport. Ernest Jr.'s wife, Lynne, would be there with our first grandson and soon Kay would have him in her arms.

This was the pattern of our life for several summers and we enjoyed it. After I had put Kay on the plane for Seattle, I would stay in the North until freezeup closed our dredges down for the year. Then the plumber would arrive to close our Dawson home. All the pipes had to be drained and the last drop of water removed from the fixtures. Electricity would be turned off and the porthole ventilators opened to let cold air circulate through the rooms. The first winter we had left them closed and hoar frost formed a deep crust on all interior walls. There was always one last chore. I would bend the raspberry canes and weigh them down with rocks. The snow would insulate them from the intense cold and when I returned in the spring and brushed the snow away there would still be green leaves showing.

Our Clear Creek dredge in the Klondike continued to be a good producer for more than ten years. But soon after building the dredges at Henderson and Thistle Creeks we ran into several summers of unprecedented drought. The dredge at Clear Creek was in the high mountains where there was a plentiful supply of water. The newer operations at Henderson and Thistle Creeks were the ones that caused me concern. Henderson Creek, which had only a limited drainage system, was reduced to a mere trickle of water. We had to build dams ahead of the dredge and hold all of the water to keep the dredge afloat. This left no water for muck stripping and we were fast eating up our reserve of stripped ground. Obviously we would be in a helpless position unless we could secure a normal rainfall. Every day we stared up at the brilliant sky, praying for storm clouds to gather over the mountains. But no rains came.

The next winter we bought cloud-seeding equipment, both ground generators and equipment to be installed in a small airplane. Whenever a favorable cloud formation appeared in the vicinity we would be after it, seeding the cloud with silver iodide crystals. Sometimes to our delight we would see the bottom of the clouds darken and boil into a rainstorm, although we never were certain whether we had really induced this or whether it was a natural downpour. It was also a problem to get the rain to fall within our drainage basins. A large cloud would be drifting by and when we seeded it, a rainstorm would be released ten or fifteen miles distant.

On August 25 we had been busy cloud-seeding all morning while sixty miles away Dawson City was celebrating Discovery Day. A few hours later the celebration was dampened by a heavy rainstorm and we were accused of spoiling the festivities. We never knew whether or not we were guilty. There was no rain over our operations.

Finally, when we were fighting the third successive summer of drought, the dredge consumed the last of the prepared ground. There was nothing to do but suspend mining for a year and use all available water for muck stripping. Nothing like this had ever happened to us in our many successful years of operations at the other properties. It was a humiliating experience and a severe financial drain.

Rainfall was normal the next year and our dredge could go back to work. But the long dry period had seriously crippled the operations both at Henderson and Thistle Creeks.

Through the years, I had kept up, as much as possible, with the university. Its progress had been painfully slow and Territorial funds for new, modern buildings hard to get. Dr. Bunnell, who believed with all his heart in its future, had fought valiantly for his goals, but little by little rebuffs and frustrations began to sap his strength. It was painful to see the fire of energy dimming in his eyes. By 1949 his health no longer permitted him to continue.

171

Dr. Terris Moore, who became the university's second president, was a young man, a graduate of Harvard, with a fine academic background. Here, I told myself, is the rugged type of young fellow who should fit in well in the Northland.

Mountain climbing and flying were his avocations. He flew his own small plane across the continent to take up his new duties in Alaska, and within a year, a number of students were accompanying him on mountain climbing expeditions, tackling higher and higher mountains until finally they took on Mt. McKinley itself, the granddaddy of them all.

In previous years Dr. Moore had been through some brave adventures with Bradford Washburn, the noted climber and photographer. Not long after Dr. Moore became president of the university, Washburn came to Alaska to work on Mt. McKinley. Dr. Moore used to leave his office on a clear day, stow some provisions in his little ski-wheel plane, and take off across the Tanana valley toward the mountain, one hundred and forty miles away.

He would thread his way through glacier-choked valleys, the drum of the engine echoing against the flank of the mountain. When he spotted Washburn's base camp on a glacier at the ten-thousand-foot elevation, he would circle to study the ice and then slide the plane in for a precarious landing. After a few minutes there for a cup of tea with Washburn, he would turn the plane and zoom downhill over the glacier. Within an hour he would be circling over the campus.

"That fellow is going to break his neck!" bush pilots were saying. "He's really asking for it."

But Dr. Moore was a past master of this type of flying. Although I was apprehensive for him, I could understand both what was driving him and his love of high adventure.

Those flights were a release that washed out the tensions and frustrations of his problems at the university. It was a difficult job to fill Dr. Bunnell's shoes, particularly since the close-knit Alaskan community resented him as an outsider. He had taken on a heart-breaking assignment.

Chapter XIV

THE MAN WHO MARRIED
KLONDIKE KATE

DURING the summers, after I had made the circuit of our various camps on the Canadian side, there were days to spend in Dawson. In the evenings, Kay and I liked to explore the town and sometimes wander on beyond the broken and treacherous wooden sidewalks to the outer fringes where there were only trails, where deserted cabins stood waist high in grass and brush and trees crept down from the hillsides to surround them. We would pass an old cemetery, the burial ground of many gold seekers, its headboards and monuments now all tilted crazily by the heaving of the frozen ground.

Government House, where early-day dignitaries were elegantly entertained, still stood, stately and silent. The gaiety of the last party had died away thirty years before but the rich carpets and furniture, we were told, still remained, sad reminders of past grandeur.

Back in town, we would peer through the cobwebby windows of the Red Feather Saloon and try to picture the miners whooping it up at the bar. In later years, the saloon must have been used as a warehouse. It was jammed with ancient mining machinery.

In a side street, a weather-faded sign on a building announced the shop of Mme. Trembay, Paris gowns, and I wondered if she had provided the rustle of silk for Ethel the Moose and Molly Fewclothes.

The Nugget Dance Hall, where many famous entertainers of the day had appeared, was kept in repair for the occasional tourists. We would climb the narrow stairs to the three tiers of boxes surrounding the hall, each box draped and curtained with heavy brocade. Then we would wander down the passageway where waiters used to scurry bringing food and liquor to the elite of the mining fraternity and their girls. If a miner were seeking prestige he would reserve a box in the topmost tier, directly below the ceiling, and pay fancy prices for the champagne.

That was Dawson as we saw it. Because it was so obviously a place empty of everything but dead dreams, I was all the more moved when I found the old dream still shining bright in the heart of Johnny Matson, the man who married Klondike Kate.

Klondike Kate, whose real name was Kate Rockwell, had been the most popular of the entertainers and dancehall girls in the roaring days of the bonanza. Kate was a dark haired, dark eyed beauty, cast in the statuesque mold of Lillian Russell, with an open-hearted warmth that reached out to her audience. She was the toast of the Klondike. I once saw an old picture of a Discovery Day celebration in Dawson and there was Kate, leading the parade in a decorated buggy.

The mining kings of the Klondike vied for her favors. They used to pick out choice nuggets from the cleanups and have them made into strands for bracelets, necklaces and even belts for Kate. She owned more nugget jewelry than

175

any girl could possibly wear at one time. Her problem was to select the right jewelry for the man who might be in town on a particular night.

It was Christmas Eve in 1900. The dancehall girls were throwing a party for the miners, a noisy, boisterous crowd of men they were, too, tossing their pokes of gold dust on the bar when they ordered a round of drinks. If the bartender had nervous fingers and spilled a few grains on a strip of carpet under the scales or if he had long fingernails, no one objected. There was plenty more waiting to be mined. Those miners were far from home and more lonely than they would admit. For that night they wanted to forget the sub-zero cold, their lonely cabins on the creeks, and the daily toil of mining the frozen gravels.

Among the crowd was Johnny Matson, unnoticed in the background, taking no part in the festivities. Johnny was a young Swedish boy, desperately lonely but too shy to speak to the dancehall girls or even to his fellow miners. Johnny had no poke of gold in his pocket. He was working in one of the mines for day wages.

All evening the girls had been putting on song and dance skits to entertain the crowd. Then at the stroke of midnight, the lights in the dancehall dimmed and Kate made a dramatic entrance, dressed in flowing white robes with a crown of candles in her hair. Kate always had a great sense of the dramatic.

"She looked like an angel," Johnny told me, nearly fifty years later. "I always carried that vision in my memory and it made me happy."

Kate was not even aware of Johnny's existence but when I asked her if she remembered the evening, too, she laughed and said, "I remember it perfectly. I had a terrible time getting the candle grease out of my hair."

She could have married any one of a number of rich

176

miners. But at heart she was always Alexander Pantages's girl. Pantages was a young Greek who had come to the Klondike in search of wealth and was working as a waiter in the dancehalls. Kate was completely captivated by him. She was far too open-hearted herself to recognize the calculating nature under his swarthy good looks and charming manners. "We cabined up together for two years," she told me.

About 1901 Kate and Pantages took over the Orpheum Theatre and brought in theatrical stars for plays and variety shows, Marjorie Rambeau and James J. Corbett among them. When the fabulously rich paystreaks of the Klondike began to thin out and Dawson City dwindled, Kate and Pantages pooled their finances, moved to Seattle, and opened a moving-picture theater. Later they opened a second theater where variety acts were interspersed with films and the business prospered. Apparently the theaters were in Pantages's name. Kate trusted him, even though he kept postponing their marriage.

Then, without warning, while Kate was away in Spokane, Washington, Pantages married another girl. The shock and grief were almost too much for Kate and it was several years before she regained her poise. Later she began to appear as a vaudeville performer with various song and dance acts. Kate was a trouper through and through. She loved the work and with the applause, her flamboyant nature bloomed again.

As to Pantages, he established a chain of highly successful vaudeville theaters in the principal cities of the Pacific Coast. They brought him wealth and prestige.

But things did not go so well for Kate. After a few good years, she fell again on sorry times. By 1914 she was living in a weatherbeaten shack on a three-hundred-twenty-acre homestead near Bend, Oregon. Her colorful talk, however, still made good newspaper copy and at intervals stories about her would filter back to Dawson. There Johnny Matson heard about her.

Johnny had stayed in the Dawson area. On a creek, now named after him, he found gold—not a bonanza but rich enough to bring him a comfortable living. Other prospectors stampeded to Matson Creek to check on the discovery but after a few years they found the pay too thin and Johnny was left alone again to mine during the summer and trap for furs in winter.

One lonely night in his cabin he worked up enough courage to write Kate a kindly letter, just to let her know that she was not forgotten. The nearest post office was at Dawson, a hundred miles away. The letter was not mailed until he made his yearly trip there to buy his winter outfit. The next year when he went back to Dawson, several letters from Kate were waiting for him at the post office.

During the following winter, to relieve his loneliness, he wrote her more letters, telling about his life in the isolated cabin. And so, by a strange sequence of letters, their lives touched at yearly intervals. Finally they arranged to meet at the 1933 Sourdough convention in Vancouver, B.C., and a few days after this meeting they were married.

The cynical say that poor Johnny did not know what had happened to him. But I knew them both, and I feel that Johnny had enshrined Kate as the goddess of his youth. Looking out for her gave a purpose to his life. He was a kindly and deeply religious man and Kate always had been his secret love. Kate, too, had a kind heart and her romantic nature responded to his blind worship. She was anxious to make him a good wife.

They came to Dawson on their honeymoon. Kate wanted to spend the approaching winter with Johnny at his camp. But it was no setting for this gregarious woman and Johnny knew it. He arranged that she should return to Oregon and meet him again in Dawson a year later. Eventually, after he had dug up more gold, he planned to give up his mining and retire to her home near Bend.

I first saw them in September 1944. They were an incongruous couple. Johnny had come down the Yukon on the last boat of the season and Kate had met him at the dock. They were walking up Front Street in Dawson, Johnny carrying his battered suitcase with a corner of clothing peeking out; Kate a head taller, looking down with a companionable smile on the weatherbeaten man tagging along beside her.

Two days later the river steamer *Casca* pulled away from the Dawson dock. As she nosed into the swift current of the Yukon, I saw Kate and Johnny standing at the rail. When the *Casca* reached the mouth of the Sixty-Mile River, I knew, she would pull in against the bank. The gangplank would go out and Johnny and his winter outfit would be put ashore. The captain would salute him with the whistle and there would be tears in Kate's eyes as she looked at that diminutive, brave figure standing there with the wilderness around him. For another year he would be alone at his distant camp. Many dramatic tableaux have been staged on the banks of the Yukon but surely this was one of the most mysterious.

Two years later I decided to have a look at Matson Creek and check on its suitability for a dredging operation. Kate was spending the summer in a little cabin in Dawson and one evening I saw her in the Arcade Cafe. She was in her late sixties then but she was still a handsome woman and carried herself well. She must have been a dazzler in her youth. When I offered to carry letters and newspapers to Johnny, her dark eyes, which looked a little sad in repose, lighted up. "You're a thoughtful man," she said. She picked up a menu, scribbled something on it and handed it to me with a smile. "I'm saying thank you." On the menu she had written, "Mush on and smile—Win or lose, a Sourdough never squawks."

Joe and John Sestak, who had trapped in the Matson Creek country and were Johnny's trusted friends, went with me. We traveled in a small boat up the Yukon about fifty miles to the mouth of the Sixty-Mile River. Although water was low in the Sixty-Mile we managed to get upstream ten miles before we started shearing pins on the outboard motor. After that we had to head the boat upstream by manpower. Two of us scrambled along the riverbank, pulling on a long tow rope, while the third stood in the stern shoving it along with a long pole.

That night we camped in an old cabin at the mouth of Twenty-Mile Creek. The next morning we shouldered packs and followed a faint trail over the mountains to Matson Creek. We covered twenty miles that day. As we crossed the last ridge we could see the wide valley. From a distance it looked as if a lush cotton field were growing there but we were too experienced to be fooled. We knew we had a "nigger-head" swamp to cross. "Nigger-heads" are closely spaced clumps of bunch grass whose habitat is frozen ground. At first we tried to step from clump to clump, a tight-rope act, for they swivel under a man's weight and after a few steps we would find ourselves sprawling among them. Finally we just sloshed through them. The water was a foot deep. Through our shoe-pacs we could feel the glare ice on the surface of the frozen ground. This impermeable barrier prevents surface waters from seeping into the earth. Clouds of mosquitos rose to pester us as we sloshed along at a speed of about one mile an hour.

We camped that night at the "store" cabin on the bank of Matson Creek. It had one pole bunk which my companions insisted I take. It proved to be a dubious honor. A large spruce tree had fallen across the roof of the cabin and partly crushed it. I spread my lightweight summer sleeping bag on the bunk and squeezed in under the trunk of the tree. A tight fit—it was difficult to turn over in bed. Certainly this was a fine test for claustrophobia but after our grueling day on the trail no minor discomfort could have kept me awake.

The next morning we traveled seven miles up Matson Creek to Johnny's cabin. We would never have guessed by his friendly greeting that we were the first humans whom he had seen for ten months. I handed him the letter and newspapers that Kate had sent and he put them on the table without opening the letter.

For a few minutes we talked about happenings in the news and then Johnny left the cabin. When he did not come back we began to grow uneasy, wondering if perhaps we were unwelcome.

"Did I say anything to offend him?" I asked Joe.

Joe just shook his head, looking puzzled. We waited a bit longer and when there was still no sign of Johnny we went outside to look around. From the bench above his cabin we could hear the sound of shoveling and climbed up the slope toward it. There was Johnny busily shoveling gravel into his sluice box. Having discharged his obligations as host he had gone back to work, harvesting more gold to take into Dawson. His mining cut had been sluiced down to bedrock. I wanted to take a gold pan and test his workings but since he did not invite me to do so, I hesitated to ask him.

That evening, after the supper dishes were washed, Johnny opened Kate's letter and spent a long time reading and re-reading it. The only sound was the heavy ticking of a big alarm clock on the kitchen table.

When he put the letter down he began to talk about that

181

Christmas Eve when he had seen Kate with the crown of candles in her hair. Listening to him I realized something I had only guessed before. That sight of Kate on Christmas Eve had brightened his whole life, as if it were a vision sent only to him. The vision had never dimmed in almost fifty years.

"Kate is a fine woman," he said. "She's had a hard life. Pantages treated her like a dog. She's been vain and a bit foolish but it is God's will that I should be the one to protect and provide for her."

My heart went out to this simple man. He was happy in his dream.

He got up abruptly, put a clean case on his pillow and announced, "You'll sleep in my bed tonight."

I looked at Joe. He was signaling vigorously, warning me that to refuse would give offense. This was Johnny's gesture of hospitality.

"Before you go to bed," Johnny said, "will you check my calendar? It's easy to lose a day and I don't want to miss the *Casca* when she comes downriver on her last trip."

Each day on the calendar had been crossed off, I saw. I put my finger on a number. "You're right on the button. Today's the tenth."

Johnny took the stub of a pencil and carefully drew a large X across the figure 10.

Two days later, when we left for the return trip to Dawson, I asked him if he wanted to send a letter to Kate.

"No, just tell her I'm getting along O.K. and will be down on the last boat."

I can see him now as he stood at the cabin door to say goodbye, a wizened little man in his seventies. His eyes were bright but his shoulders stooped and the hand he gave me was crusted with calluses. We turned on the trail and looked back to wave. He was still standing at the cabin door. We were the last people he would ever see.

Kate was at the dock at Dawson when the *Casca* arrived. Johnny was not on board. The captain had blown his whistle and pulled in close to shore looking for him but there was no one on the landing.

Kate immediately got in touch with me. I assured her that he probably had missed the boat and would build a raft and float downriver. But my mind flashed back to the calendar in his cabin.

A few days later Joe Sestak and a Royal Canadian Mounted Policeman went to investigate. They found Johnny at the "store" cabin. He had started for the river and had gone to bed in the pole bunk. During the night his tired heart had stopped. His watch was hanging on a nail at the head of the bunk.

As they neared the cabin a wolverine had scurried away into the forest. Johnny's body was half out of the small window where the wolverine had dragged it.

So the man who married Klondike Kate was buried in a crude grave on the creek bearing his name.

The following winter Kate phoned me in my Seattle office, wanting to see me for advice about her mining claims.

"Klondike Kate will be here in a few minutes," I told my secretary.

She could not have been more excited if I had announced the imminent arrival of the President. Nor was Kate a disappointment. She was always the actress and made a grand entrance.

Ten years later, at the age of eighty, she, too, passed away in her sleep.

Chapter XV

THE JAPANESE REACH ALASKA

PROBABLY the vast majority of Americans over forty-five can remember exactly where they were when the Japanese bombed Pearl Harbor, but I doubt very much if many of them can remember where they were when the Japanese bombed Dutch Harbor. Except for the Alaskans.

From the moment war broke out, we had known we were vulnerable. As one fellow put it: "Three Japs with a row-boat and a machine gun could capture any town on the Alaska coast." Not as much of an exaggeration as it sounds. The Territory was wide open to invasion, because the Navy and Coast Guard were too thinly stretched to give our communities more than token protection.

Nobody in those days was betting whether or not the Japanese would try to set up bases in Alaska and use them to harass the North American continent. We were just betting on how soon they would come. When that day arrived, the hundred thousand people scattered over Alaska would be trapped. Boats, plying between Seattle and the coastal towns, were our only lifeline. There are a thousand places along the coast where submarines could lurk and sink our ships.

184

If their base were Dutch Harbor, for example, their bombers would be only six hundred miles from our naval base at Kodiak and only seven hundred and fifty miles from the port of Seward, terminus of the Alaska Railroad. The Alaska Railroad supplies Anchorage and Fairbanks. Without shipping, within a month food and gasoline would vanish.

Fairbanks, at the end of the line, was the most vulnerable of all the towns. Alaskans are used to living close to danger and there was no trace of panic although people were making plans. Some men sent their families outside for the duration. A usual subject of conversation was where to hide silver, jewelry, or personal papers—certainly not in safety deposit boxes in Alaskan banks. People with dirt floors in their basements planned to dig down and cache them there. Others picked a spot in their yards near a tree where they could find them again.

At least Fairbanks did have a military airbase underway. As war clouds began to gather, General H. H. (Hap) Arnold remembered the warnings of General William (Billy) Mitchell who, years before, had recognized the military importance of Alaska in the air age. General Arnold had ordered the construction of Ladd Field, near Fairbanks, and of Elmendorf Field at Anchorage.

When I returned to Fairbanks from Seattle in the early spring, Ladd Field was being rushed to completion and a squadron of fighter pilots were training there to fly under northern conditions.

One day in June, I drove out to the base to keep a luncheon date with one of the officers. As soon as I arrived at the gate I knew from the tenseness and tight security that a military alert was in progress. This was not particularly noteworthy. Such drills were held at frequent intervals. After lunch, when we made a tour of the base, I saw a group of men positioning aircraft markers on a huge map of Alaska in the plotting room. Again the tension in the room was unmistakable. Rifles were placed at intervals along the walls. A sergeant came in, worked the bolt on each rifle and checked to be sure that it was loaded. When he had finished he left without a word. Outside, from time to time, an anti-aircraft gun would speak.

Finally my curiosity got the better of me. "Those sound like anti-aircraft guns," I ventured.

"They are," my host said. "We're keeping them warm."

I chewed on this a moment before I said, "I don't want to pry into military secrets, but could you tell me what this is all about?"

"The Japs are bombing Dutch Harbor right now," he said, in a matter-of-fact voice. "We don't know if they'll try to strike the interior bases or not." After a moment he added, "You'd better not say anything about it when you go back to town."

As we stepped outside, a flight of fighter planes arrived. The tired pilots climbed out and stretched on the floor of the hangar, while mechanics hurriedly refueled and checked the planes. Then the planes took off again, heading westward.

An hour later I was back in Fairbanks, guarding my military secret. I had not walked a block before a friend stopped me. "Have you heard the news? The Japs are bombing Dutch Harbor."

The mukluk telegraph had been at work as usual. The news was all over town. Some people were planning to get into cars and drive out into the hills. If an emergency evacuation were ordered, many of the men had decided to stay behind, fend for themselves, and offer some resistance to the enemy. They would have given a good account of themselves, too. They knew the country; they were resource-

186

ful and good marksmen. "I've got my 30-06 and a good supply of ammunition," I heard one man say. "I'll get myself a few Japs."

There was something very few of us knew. Alaska had an ace up her sleeve after all. Major General Simon Bolivar Buckner, Jr., who held overall command in the Territory, had reasoned that the Japanese, fresh from their early victories across the Pacific, would strike at Alaska soon. As he studied the map, he had put his finger on Dutch Harbor, where a vital naval base was under construction in the Aleutians, that chain of rocky, volcanic islands stretching west toward Japan and the Kamchatka Peninsula of Siberia. His educated guess was correct.

Two airstrips had been built hurriedly, one of them just west of Dutch Harbor on neighboring Umnak island. They were so secret that the construction material and supplies were shipped from Seattle to two mythical salmon canneries.

When the Japanese started pounding Dutch Harbor, our handful of fighter planes rose from those secret bases and came blasting out of the sky. The startled Japanese had no idea how paper thin our defenses were. They retreated to the West and put the troops ashore on Kiska and Attu Islands, near the tip of the Aleutians. For the first time in more than one hundred years an invading army was camped on American soil.

Whatever timetable the Japanese might have had for the invasion of Alaska was upset by the defeat of their forces at Midway and their losses in the South Pacific. The bombing of Dutch Harbor, we learned later, had been a feint for the Battle of Midway. The Japanese task force just stayed marooned on the islands and a sorry time they must have had there, too. Along this chain of islands, the cold air masses from the Bering Sea meet the relatively warm air of the Japanese current in the North Pacific Ocean. As a result the Aleutians are a desolate land of heavy rains and thick fog that hangs for days before it is blown away by "williwaw" winds, often ripping over the islands at more than a hundred miles an hour.

Several months before Dutch Harbor, the military had started punching out the Alcan Highway from Fairbanks to Dawson Creek in British Columbia. The first contingent of U.S. Army Engineers arrived at Dawson Creek in March 1942, while other crews started working from Fairbanks and Whitehorse in Yukon Territory. Construction was so frantic that bulldozers were on the very heels of the survey crews. It was one of the great construction feats of the war. In the short space of eight months they pushed a road through 1,523 miles of wilderness. Then the road was turned over to civilian contractors to widen and gravel. Log bridges and ferries were replaced with steel structures and trucks with supplies began rolling into Fairbanks. All this new construction was behind mountain ranges and relatively safe from enemy attack.

By this time Fairbanks and Anchorage were jumping. Their population doubled, then tripled. Thousands of soldiers and Air Force men were moved into the bases. Within two years, fifty thousand new faces appeared in the area. In Fairbanks, during two of the war years, the military took over several of the university buildings to house and feed personnel, while the university operated on a greatly reduced level.

Millions in government funds were poured into the country to build airfields, military bases, housing, roads, and a dozen auxiliary projects. The contractors arrived with their army of brawny construction workers. Wages skyrocketed. Restaurants and hotels were jammed. You did not ask the desk clerk for a room, just for a bed, and you were lucky to get that.

Behind the construction men came the camp followers, wanting a piece of the action. Vacant store buildings were converted into saloons and amusement parlors. Roadhouses sprang up around the edges of the cities. At times the action was rough and murders became so frequent that one old-timer remarked, "It's cheaper nowadays to kill a man than to shoot a moose out of season."

In spite of the turmoil, heroic construction was being done, as the military threw up a string of airbases westward along the islands, in preparation for an attack on the Japanese forces dug in on Attu and Kiska. On Adak island, for example, a shallow lake was drained and steel mats set on the lake bottom to serve as an airfield.

The Battle of Attu in May 1943 was a heartbreaker for all of us. It lasted nineteen days. More than five hundred young Americans were killed and eleven hundred others wounded. Through a tragic blunder, some of the soldiers had been equipped only with light clothing and footgear for desert warfare. As a result, there were unnecessary casualties from frosted feet and exposure. Although the Japanese were driven back into the hills, they countered with suicidal banzai charges. Of almost twenty-six hundred Japanese on the island, only eleven survived as prisoners.

When American and Canadian troops assembled at Adak in August to storm Kiska, occupied by five thousand Japanese, they expected another bloody battle. Instead the twenty-five thousand Allied soldiers who stormed ashore were met by a puzzling silence, broken only by the crashing of the surf and the howling of wind. In a daring evacuation, the Japanese had slipped away by sea, under cover of a dense fog. Alaska was secure.

A few months later, Kay and I could breathe easily again, too. Ernest Jr. came home on leave after more than one hundred combat missions in the New Guinea area. A few days after Pearl Harbor, he had left the university where he was a senior and entered the Air Force as a cadet. Since he was under age, Kay and I had to sign his enlistment forms. Flying had been an important part of his life. He had made his solo flight at the age of sixteen and at eighteen had won his commercial pilot's license. Commissioned First Lieutenant, he was squadron navigator for the first group of B-25s sent to Australia, and based at Port Moresby in New Guinea.

When he stepped off the train in Seattle, after more than a year of combat, his face was thin and drawn and his body taut. On his blouse were ribbons denoting the Distinguished Flying Cross, the Air Medal, and an oak leaf cluster of Presidential citations. But this uniform was sweat- and oil-stained and jungle dry rot was in the cloth and in the leather of his shoes. After several weeks of rest, he spent the remainder of the war as an instructor.

The government had decided that gold mining was not vital to the war effort and issued Order L-208 which had the effect of closing most of the gold mines in the United States. In Alaska we were allowed to hire men over seventy years of age and Indians. Although many of the dredge camps closed down, we decided to try to operate for at least one more summer. We needed some extra funds for a development that we had in progress on several possible war mineral deposits.

By scratching around we were able to get an elderly skeleton crew together, to operate one of our dredges on a two-shift basis. Fortunately we had always kept our equipment in good repair, our warehouse was well stocked, and we could live off of our fat for at least one more season. We managed to keep water flowing through the ditches and one dredge digging sixteen hours a day, while I put in a full day working wherever I was needed, in the morning per-

190

haps driving points to thaw the gravels ahead of the dredge, in the afternoon trucking supplies over the mountains.

One day while I was sweating it out in the point field an old fellow working near me said, "I thought you were the president of this company?"

I grinned at him and went on working. As a matter of fact, at that time I was still vice president.

"First time I ever drove points with the president," I heard him mumble to himself.

Somehow we finished the season and accumulated some additional funds. The following summer I spent scouting over the hills of Washington, Oregon, and Nevada for strategic war minerals, as I had been spending many of the winter months. We did some preliminary development on showings of mercury and manganese ores and expended a good bit of money opening up and exploring a deposit of nickel ore near Chelan, Washington. But after a time the ore petered out and we had to write it off.

When the war ended we expected the bottom to drop out of Alaska's boom. Nothing like that happened. Military planners had recognized the strategic importance of Alaska as Russia had become a threat. Airfields were improved, highways paved, and an extensive network of early warning radar stations set up like a picket line stretching across the Arctic coastline of Alaska and Canada.

Young military men and some of the construction workers decided that the new land suited them and came back to take up homesteads, open shops, or hunt jobs. The days were gone when it was "good morning" to almost everyone who passed by. New high-rise apartments overshadowed primitive log cabins; a government housing authority moved into Fairbanks, condemned several blocks near the center of the city and demolished the old cabins and buildings, including the former red-light district. The area was covered with modern office buildings and chain stores, ringed with paved parking lots.

The lonely road that had connected Fairbanks and our campus during the university's early years became a paved highway, lined solidly with homes and businesses. The homestead that the Loftus brothers had developed when they were students was turned into a modern subdivision. Other old homesteads on the outskirts of Fairbanks and Anchorage were also subdivided, and hundreds of attractive homes suddenly sprang up.

The pioneers were fast disappearing. A new generation of would-be earth shakers were in the saddle. The country had become a land of young men and their energy and daring were shaping a new Alaska.

Chapter XVI

TRAGEDY

LATE October in Alaska is a time bush pilots dread. Then, when temperatures approach zero, but the Yukon has not yet frozen over, the air is colder than the water, and vapor, drawn upward, creates dangerous ice-fog conditions.

I had seen what it meant to fly in such weather. One day, about the middle of October in 1947, Ernest Jr. and I took off from Woodchopper for Fairbanks. There was clear air under the low-hanging ice fog, until, when we had been in the air for twenty minutes, we found ice fog banked heavily against the mountains and turned to go back. By that time the fog had lowered behind us, too, cutting off our retreat, so we circled and headed for an alternate field at Circle Hot Springs. There was still good visibility in that direction but after a few minutes the fog blanket again started settling down on the tree tops. We were trapped and our only escape was to reach the Yukon River. We were flying just over the trees and in a matter of seconds the windscreen was coated with ice.

"I'll turn the plane from side to side so we can see ahead through the side windows," Ernest Jr. shouted. "Watch for tall trees."

The trees were there. We were just clearing them and ice was building up on the wings. I could see that it was going to be touch and go but we got to the river. There was clear air for about fifty feet over the water. In an emergency, Ernest Jr. would be able to land the amphibian plane on the water. As we skimmed along he opened the side window and used his pocket knife to chip away a small peek hole on the windscreen. We managed to find the mouth of Woodchopper Creek, left the river and sneaked up the creek to a safe landing on our airstrip. As we climbed out to inspect our ice-sheathed plane, the crew all gathered around. There was even a skin of ice on the propellers.

The layer of ice fog had dissipated by the next morning. The day was bright and clear and we made a routine flight to Fairbanks. I was due to leave the next morning for Seattle but the weather turned sour again and the Pan American plane could not land. For three mornings, Ernest Jr. and I drove to the airport and each morning the flight was cancelled. On the fourth morning the storm lifted and I took off for Seattle while Ernest Jr. went back to Woodchopper to finish the few remaining days of the dredging season.

A week later I was enroute to Toronto to attend a directors' meeting and as I changed planes in Chicago I heard my name called over the public address system. Kay was on the phone from Seattle with chilling news. Ernest Jr.'s plane was down. There were no details except that bad weather was preventing a rescue attempt.

There would be no western flight until morning. At the hotel I spent most of the night on the phone and finally reached the pilot in Fairbanks who had reported sighting Ernest Jr.'s plane. He had been flying, fighting to get through a mountain pass, in a severe snowstorm that forced him to treetop level. As he flashed by he caught a glimpse of our red plane among the trees. It appeared intact, but he

194

was in such severe trouble himself that he could not turn to investigate.

On the flight back to Seattle the next day, I kept reliving the flight I had made with Ernest Jr. from Woodchopper. I knew what a skilled and experienced flier he was. If he had control of the airplane, I felt sure, he could get it down in the brush without serious injury.

The family met me at the Seattle airport. There was no news and foul weather was still holding back the rescue attempt. Kay had brought a suitcase packed with my winter field clothes and I took the first flight for Fairbanks, accompanied by Ernest Jr.'s wife, Lynne.

Friends were waiting for us at the airport to take us to their home and the next morning an experienced bush pilot, Frank Pollack, and I took off in a little plane. Although the weather was marginal, we felt that we could sneak up the Chena River to Palmer Creek. There was a little landing strip and some cabins at Palmer Creek which we could use as a base camp. The plane we were hunting was only ten or fifteen miles away on the other side of the mountain.

A rescue helicopter would join us, we were told when we radioed the Air Force squadron at Fairbanks of improving weather conditions.

Two trappers with their dogteam were waiting for us at Palmer Creek. They had heard the news on their battery-powered radio and had traveled to Palmer Creek to volunteer their services. While they started out overland for the wreck, Pollack and I took off again by plane. The fog was lifting and we could get through the pass. I had to have a look at the wreck myself. Ernest Jr. had told me what he would do if he were ever forced down and survived. He would use the canvas engine covers, he had said, to fashion a tent beside the fuselage and would wait for rescue.

195

We flew low over the red plane there among the scrub timber. Except for one crumpled wing it looked as if it would fly again. But there was no one in sight and I looked in vain for the improvised tent.

"Looks pretty good," Pollack said. "Let's make another pass over it."

We came in just over the plane and that time I could see evidence of a fire that had blackened the tail surfaces. I knew then that Ernest Jr. and his passengers had perished. I have never fainted but as the plane pivoted and climbed to regain altitude, I had to fight to retain consciousness.

Pollack circled and flew over a third time. As I looked down at the crippled plane, in place of anguish a feeling of peace flowed over me. It was almost as if Ernest Jr. were there in the cockpit with me saying, "Take it easy, Dad. Everything's all right." That is just the way Ernest Jr. would have spoken if he had been privileged to console me.

Since that moment I have never doubted the real answer to Job's question, "If a man die, shall he live again?"

Ernest Jr. and I had been through a great deal together and there was an unusually close bond between us.

Ours has always been a close knit family. From the time they were little, the boys had taken part in family councils. Around the dinner table we used to talk over the day's activities while they joined in. We even discussed financial investments in their presence and they were encouraged to ask questions. Under Kay's guidance there was a feeling of easy camaraderie about our home life and a great deal of laughter.

With Ernest Jr. gone, we closed ranks and we could sense the boys trying to help us fill the void. Stanton and Dale were both attending the University of Washington. But Kay

196

and I felt the need to be together. Instead of waiting until school was out, Kay decided to go North with me in the spring when mining operations reopened.

The summer was an an ordeal for both of us. Whatever reserve force had carried us through the winter seemed to have drained away. Up to that time, mining—whether it was bringing in a new operation or solving an operating problem—had always been sheer fun. All at once the job was just hard toil. One evening I said to Kay, "I'm tired tonight."

She gave me a startled look. "Ernest, that's the first time I've heard you say you were tired."

Kay was with me a great deal that summer as I made the circuit of the various operations. We would load our sleeping bags into a bush plane or riverboat and take off together. Kay particularly liked to travel on the river by small boat. Twice that summer we traveled two hundred miles down the Yukon from Dawson to our Coal Creek operations. Kay would take her place in the bow with a sleeping bag and a pillow as a windbreak; the outboard motor would start to chatter and we would head out into the current.

Except for a little settlement at Eagle, we had the river to ourselves. Our lunch stop would be at Forty-Mile, a deserted log cabin settlement that had flourished before discovery of gold in the Klondike had siphoned away its people, now a place of silent streets where the cabins were half hidden by encroaching brush and trees.

When we had finished our picnic lunch, we would go back to the boat. Sometimes we would intercept a caribou or moose swimming the river and we would manoeuver in swinging circles around it, while Kay worked the movie camera. Once we herded a black bear, drawing close enough to see the flare of fear in his eyes. Then we speeded away and let him resume his swim. If we got too close, he might panic and try to get into the boat with us.

We were alone with the river, seeing it as it had been when the early explorers found it, and all around us was the primeval wilderness, restful and healing.

Chapter XVII

RETURN TO LEARNING

IN May of 1953, I was invited to deliver the commencement address at the University of Alaska. When Kay and I reached Fairbanks, after a three-hundred-mile drive from Dawson City, we found the Board of Regents engaged in selecting a new president for the university. Five candidates and their wives were on campus for interviews.

It had been eighteen years since I had resigned as dean. During those years there had been growth and much change in Alaska but the university had neither changed nor grown. There it sat, very much as we had known it, a huddle of old frame buildings, squatting on its windy hill. It had been struggling along for more than thirty years and its enrollment still was less than three hundred full-time students.

As we stood looking around us, my own thoughts were mirrored in Kay's discouraged face. It was a sorry thing for both of us to see how little had come of all the fine plans that had meant so much to us when we were young. That night at the hotel we talked it over. Neither of us was ready to admit that the early pessimists had been right after all. The potential was there, we told ourselves. With the proper touch the university still could be developed into a vigorous institution, a vital part of Alaska, with several thousand students crowding the campus.

"I hope the new president is a man of force and gumption," I said, words which echoed ironically in my ears when the commencement exercises were over and the Regents, at an informal meeting, asked me if I would accept the presidency myself.

Very much startled, I said no. As I explained, I was too deeply involved in my mining operations. Since the death of General McRae in 1948, I had been president and general manager of the companies and could not possibly leave at the time.

"Sit down, sit down," one of the regents urged me, as I stood up to leave the meeting. "The university's at a low ebb, as you know. We'd like to hear what you think could be done about it."

This problem was close to my heart and for the next half hour we discussed possible ways of revitalizing the school.

By the following day interviews with the candidates had been completed and in the evening Kay and I went to a farewell dinner given by the Regents for applicants and their wives.

"I think I know which man was chosen," I told Kay later. "I kept studying the faces of people at the dinner."

Kay, it seemed, had been playing detective, too. Our choices, however, did not agree.

In the morning, as we were getting ready to check out of the hotel, the phone rang. One of the regents was on the line, asking if I could come to the campus for another conference.

This was impossible. We had to leave within the hour or we would miss the last ferry into Dawson.

"Could you delay long enough for us to get into town?"

he asked. "We'd meet you in an apartment in the Northward Building."

Only two of the regents were waiting when I arrived. The others came slipping in, one by one. The clandestine arrangements and a certain tension in the air alerted me. This was no mere get-together for additional information.

When they had all arrived, I was told that I had been their unanimous choice for the presidency on the first ballot. I was very flattered and touched, too, particularly since Dr. Bunnell, the first president, who had retired some years before, had strongly urged my appointment, I was told. I myself felt that I lacked the academic qualifications and again explained why I could not accept. The regents were insistent, however, and finally offered to hold the position open for sixty days, if I would think it over.

Kay looked at me suspiciously when I rejoined her. "What was that secret meeting all about?"

"Wait until we get on the highway and I'll tell you the whole story." I had already made a tentative commitment in my heart, but I was not quite ready to admit it. Two months later, with many misgivings, I telegraphed my acceptance to the university and late in the autumn flew to Fairbanks for a few days, to get the feel of the problems I would have to face.

"When do you plan to take over?" the comptroller, Harold Byrd, asked me.

I mentioned two or three months. I had to finish the mining season, get out my annual reports and meet with my directors.

"You should take over immediately," Byrd said. "We've overspent our budget and we'll be out of funds before the next meeting of the legislature."

I managed to make it back to the campus in a month.

The first morning I made an inspection trip with the su-

201

perintendent of buildings and grounds. The situation was even worse than I had realized. The old frame dormitories particularly worried me. Most of our students were housed in firetraps. The girls' dormitory was shocking. Many of the dressers, chairs, and beds had been stolen, and some of the girls were storing their clothes in egg crates.

"The interior of this building is in a deplorable condition," I told the coeds at the meeting I called in the dormitory. "Just as soon as we can obtain funds, we'll remedy the situation."

"Why don't you give us paint and brushes?" one of the girls piped up. "We could paint our own rooms."

I thought of Kay at once, of Kay up on a ladder, brush in hand, painting the cabins where we had lived during our early married life. When she was through with the rooms they had always been bright and charming.

"I like that idea," I told the girls.

"What color do you want them?" another girl asked.

"Pick your own colors but make them gay," I said and was answered with a chorus of delighted squeals.

"You don't know what you're letting us in for," the superintendent told me after the meeting broke up. "They'll never finish the job and they'll have paint spattered over everything."

I was conscious of some misgivings myself but I said, "Well, let's give them a try. It might just work out."

And it did. The rooms were transformed by the darndest assortment of Easter egg colors I have ever seen.

When we inspected the frame dormitories for male students, we found some of the rooms neat. Others were occupied by students who had let down and gone native. In one room we found a dismantled Ford gasoline engine sitting in the center of the floor with smears of grease around it. Nearby were cans of highly flammable solvent in which

202

engine parts were soaking. These frame buildings were bone dry and filled with dust. If a fire started the building would explode into flames with heavy loss of life. This was one situation that had to be corrected immediately.

Another room, occupied by two students majoring in wildlife, was festooned with fresh animal skins mounted on stretch boards. Some of the more odoriferous pelts were hanging outside the window on strings. The students were running a trapline near the campus.

Two boilers in the building supplied heat and power for the entire campus. One boiler was very old and the flues were leaking. The superintendent agreed to shut down the old boiler and roll the flues if the weather did not turn too cold over the weekend.

I wrote in my notebook, "Check with manager of Alaska Railroad. Arrange, in power plant emergency, to have locomotive put on sidetrack at campus for temporary hookup."

During the afternoon I dropped into various faculty offices for informal get-acquainted meetings and felt my courage revive. I had inherited some excellent faculty material, men and women who ranked well in the profession and who were interested in the students and in the university. And the faculty, after all, is the core of any school.

Kay had driven with me to Alaska and was spending a few days before flying back to Seattle to close our house. We had dinner in the dining hall, a murky place in the basement of an old dormitory. The oilcloth on the tables, I noticed, was far from spotless and many of the students who came filing in had not freshened up for dinner. Girls were still in jeans and several wore shoe-pacs. A few of the boys had on white shirts and neckties, but most of them were wearing woolen shirts and spattered canvas trousers.

"You have to do something about this," Kay whispered

to me. "The men in our mining camps are much cleaner when they come in for dinner."

I wrote in my notebook, "Immediately paint kitchen and dining hall a bright color. Talk to students." I slid the notebook over to Kay and she read it with a wan smile.

That evening I had an appointment with the comptroller to go into the financial problems. It had thawed during the day. The gravel streets and paths were dotted with puddles and as I came into the hall of the Eielson Building I found the floor covered with muddy tracks. Outside, students were feeling their way to the library with flashlights.

Someday, I told myself, we would have paved streets and walks and mercury-vapor lighting. Possibly by next spring we might be able to put in some nice lawns and flower beds. But as I went into my office and sat down at my desk, I felt as if all this were just wishful thinking. Facing me was a neat stack of correspondence that my secretary had left for me. At the moment I felt too beaten to glance at it. There I was, president of a university, sitting in the president's chair, and it did not feel very comfortable. I'm like the guy who contracted to eat an elephant, I thought. Which leg am I going to chew on first?

My attempt at a joke did not do much to cheer me. The job ahead was going to demand more strength and wisdom than I possessed and I knew it. I looked out of the window and I believe that the prayer for help which came from my heart at that moment was answered.

"I hate to leave you in this mess," Kay said as I put her on the plane for Seattle.

It was undoubtedly a mess and the days and nights which followed were frantic. But sometimes at night I would see lights in a few of the faculty offices. The sight of those lights cheered me wonderfully. Those men and I are working to-

204

ward the same end, I would tell myself. Together we won't be beaten.

At first I had been critical of my predecessor. With the monkey on my own back I began to appreciate the difficulties he had had to face. However, I had more leverage. I was an Alaskan, well known in the Territory. I had cut my salary in half to accept a position I did not seek, and many people knew it. Besides, this was the honeymoon period, a time when boldness on my part would be forgiven.

The first student meeting would be a critical one, I knew. As I had learned in my early days as dean, young people are perceptive and quick to spot a phony so I gave them my unvarnished rundown on our plans and a timetable for accomplishment. I could feel them warming to the ideas. Then I stepped over onto more dangerous ground. As university men and women, I said, many of them would be going on to positions of great responsibility. A vital part of their university life, I told them, was to learn how to adapt themselves to whatever situation they would meet in the future. When I spoke of the importance of personal grooming and of attention to the social amenities, I could feel a stiffening among some in the group. However, on the whole, I felt, the meeting ended on an enthusiastic note.

The following afternoon, a committee representing a segment of the student body called at my office to probe more deeply into what I had in mind. At the close of the meeting, their spokesman said, "Mr. Patty, you don't seem to understand that many of us came to this university to escape the regimentation of civilization." To soften the statement, he added, "I hope you will not consider me impertinent."

"No, that isn't impertinent," I told him. "I'll be just as frank. All of us feel the restrictions of civilization. That's one of the penalties we pay for living in large groups. Now I'm going to let you in on a secret. Civilization has just

205

caught up with you. Even if you moved to the Arctic coast you would have to buy a license and observe certain restrictions before you could go hunting."

They looked somewhat disgruntled as they went trailing out, but the general appearance of the student body did improve.

The first meeting with the faculty had evangelistic overtones. I discussed plans for making the university the cultural and scientific center of Alaska, speaking optimistically of improving the various departments, adding new ones, and rebuilding the physical plant. "It is my responsibility to secure the added funds necessary to accomplish this," I said, with a good deal more confidence than I was feeling.

The departments of sciences and engineering, I found, were well staffed and offered outstanding training. This could have been anticipated. Alaska, with its engineering problems and unique opportunities in the various disciplines of science, drew excellent people. Our weakness was business administration and the liberal arts, and our offering in the fine arts was almost nonexistent. Yet we wanted a well-balanced university, not just a strong technical school with the rest tacked on.

When Kay came North again, it was a wonderful relief to go home in the evenings and try out my ideas on her. With Kay I always could count on a critical response, not just lip service. When I accepted the presidency I had told the regents that they were getting "two for the price of one." This proved to be true. Many of the innovations credited to me were actually Kay's ideas.

In the spring we took a swing through the larger Alaskan communities to sell our ideas to people and legislators. In each city I spoke before the chamber of commerce and various service clubs. Kay worked the other side of the street, appearing before women's groups. Our first assault was only mildly successful.

Finally it was time to face the legislature and ask for money. I had no political experience and had never previously appeared before the legislature. After all my brave planning it was a nerve-racking situation. Several of the regents went to the capital city of Juneau to lend their prestige and prop me up.

We had made a relief model of the campus. Each building was represented by a small wooden block which was slotted into the model and could be removed. The blocks representing frame buildings were painted red and those representing the very few fireproof buildings were painted blue. We met first with the education committee. As the presentation was made, I walked over to the model, pulled out two red blocks and replaced them with blue blocks representing modern buildings. That was our request to this legislature. Then to show what we planned for the future, I took out all of the red blocks and replaced them with modern symbols.

I told them of old frame structures housing several hundred young men and women, of classes and laboratory equipment similarly housed. As my final punch line, I asked them if they would want their own sons and daughters to live and work in firetraps and how they felt about my encouraging students to come to the university under those conditions.

In a few minutes the entire committee was gathered around the model, pulling out red blocks and inserting blue ones. I glanced across at Elmer Rasmuson of Anchorage, president of the Board of Regents, and he was smiling. At least we had caught the interest of the education committee. But there was still tough work to do behind the scenes and before the steely-eyed members of the finance committee.

One evening one of the legislators, a friend of long standing, called me to his hotel room. "Ernest, your plans for the university are wonderful, but they're too ambitious," he said. "The Territory just doesn't have that kind of money. The best we can do is give you one new building and increase the operations budget by ten percent over the previous biennium. Probably two years hence we may be able to do a little better, but don't get your hopes too high."

I knew he was speaking for the finance committee. Unless I dug in my heels, I was licked before I had really started. "If you're speaking for the committee, let's be honest," I said. "Let's admit that Alaska is unable to support a university. We're operating at a starvation level. If that's the best you can do, why make any appropriation at all? Send me back to board up the windows."

"You know we wouldn't do that," he cut in.

"As your committee knows, unless they give me tools to work with, I'm not going to spend my remaining years trying to shore up a faltering university."

"Keep your shirt on," he admonished. "We're going to try to do the best we can for you."

I kept my shirt on and my fingers crossed and they did the best possible. Not all of our requests were met, but we had a reasonable appropriation and I could return to the university.

In the years ahead, I knew, I would have to return to the legislature and face grueling experiences. But these were future worries. At the moment we had funds to increase faculty salaries and make some small additions to the faculty, buy a new boiler for the power plant, and build one modern fireproof dormitory.

A great source of concern was "Old Main," the largest frame building in Alaska with a history of hairbreadth escapes from small fires. This building housed most of our classrooms as well as the chemistry laboratory, always a potential fire hazard.

As fire chief, I appointed John Hoskins, a faculty man who took his responsibilities seriously. Most of the carbon tetrachloride extinguishers were empty, he discovered upon inspection. Students had used the contents for cleaning clothes. The larger soda-ash types had been employed for student horseplay and both hoses and nozzles were plugged. These were overhauled and refilled. Then we tried a fire drill. But the students were not interested in rushing out into the cold; they simply congregated in the halls until the gong stopped ringing.

"Want to see some fun?" Hoskins asked me one day. "At exactly ten-thirty this morning I'm going to have a fire drill that will jar the campus."

In front of "Old Main" he had placed packing boxes heavily soaked with waste oil. The fire company was standing by to keep matters from getting out of hand. While I watched from my office window, black smoke began billowing across the big frame building nearby; the fire siren sounded at the power plant, and gongs began ringing.

Students burst out of every door of "Old Main." As I stood there laughing, I saw a man rush out of a building, fight his way through emerging students and dash into "Old Main." I recognized him as a graduate student in the wildlife department but I could not imagine what he was up to. In a few minutes he reappeared, with a bundle of papers clasped to his chest—his thesis, on which he had been working for two years. Poor fellow, he must have experienced a nasty shock imagining his work going up in flames.

One of our early moves was to establish a community college at Anchorage, the largest city in Alaska. At that time, community colleges were not well known and this was a pioneering venture. It could be of particular value in

209

Alaska, where cities are widely scattered. Evening classes were to be held in the local high schools. An ambitious student would be able to cover the first two years of certain subjects at the community college and then, if he wished, go on to the university to finish his training. There would also be interest courses for adults. The expense was to be shared jointly by the university and the Anchorage school district, but the university would retain control of teaching and course content.

When we met with the Anchorage school board to draw the contract, we had no precedent to guide us, but we did have mutual trust, and we were able to work out an agreement whose principles have stood up through the years and have been the model used by other community colleges. We opened with a few hundred part-time students. Within four years, the Anchorage Community College had grown to more than a thousand students. Other Alaskan cities applied, and today the six largest cities in Alaska have community colleges to enrich the life of the new state.

During our first summer at the university, Kay and I were invited to attend a workshop for new college presidents and their wives at the Harvard Graduate School of Business. It was financed by the Carnegie Corporation because, as one man expressed it, the attrition of college presidents had been found to exceed that of football coaches.

The wives were given a series of lectures and the fifty new presidents were given intensive training by use of the case method. Every day we wrestled with two or three actual problems that had faced other presidents and which we, too, might have to face in the years ahead.

One of the new presidents had a ready answer for each question directed at him. He would always reply, "I would appoint a committee to deal with that problem."

The third time he gave his stock answer I studied him

askance. Possibly, I thought, my many years in isolated mining camps where decisions had to be made without benefit of committees had left me unqualified to follow academic procedures. Faculty committees, I knew, could take a big load off the president's shoulders. But major problems? No, I told myself. Hiding behind a committee's skirts was no place for a university president.

The president's house on our campus was a small four-room cottage, totally unsuited for social functions. As soon as possible it was replaced by a residence planned for semi-public use. Kay made a beautiful home for us and it became the center of university life. Large student or faculty groups were entertained there and, as we wanted the people of Fairbanks to feel a close tie to the university, they too were invited to many of the receptions, teas, and dinners. Students would crowd into the recreation room for meetings of campus organizations or for student recitals. As the university grew there were usually visiting dignitaries occupying the guest rooms.

Since funds were limited, Kay did much of her own landscaping. On of her joys was the development of an Alaskan garden full of native wildflowers, shrubs, and trees. If I wanted to keep on good terms with my wife, I soon discovered, I must always carry a shovel and axe in the car trunk. On summer evenings, when we drove into the country, Kay might spot some shrub she wanted. As we started into the bush, the mosquitos would rise to meet us. While I dug frantically, muttering in a low key, Kay would spray us with mosquito repellent. On the trip home, branches and tree tops waved in the breeze from our car trunk.

As the next few years raced by, it was evident that the university had come out of the doldrums. Several new departments had been created to round out the curriculum, the faculty had been strengthened, and alumni groups were

211

active again in several cities. Each summer new modern buildings sprang up and there were rolling lawns and a blaze of flowers over our once bleak hill. Above all, there was a new feeling on campus. It was a good, optimistic feeling. Alaskans were growing proud of their university and their sons and daughters were coming to us in greater numbers.

Not that any magic wand was waving over the campus. Sometimes we were rocked back on our heels by discouragement and disappointment. Some of our prize faculty members received offers from larger universities, offers we could not match, and the voids created were difficult to fill.

A number of our students would spend the first two years with us and then transfer to large, stateside universities. They felt the need to work in a larger arena. A good many of these young people would never return to Alaska. We were exporting a latent resource, I felt, and it was a resource needed for the future of Alaska. To offset this drain, about a third of our students were coming to us from other states, adventurous young men and women who wanted to cast their lot on the frontier. This cross fertilization, we concluded, was good.

On the other hand, we encouraged many of our graduates to go on for doctoral studies at prestige universities such as Harvard, Yale, and Stanford. Almost without exception, they made outstanding records. It was heartening to receive letters from their deans congratulating us on the excellence of their basic training.

We had fought a delaying action on the expansion of our own graduate work, feeling that it was important first to develop an outstanding undergraduate university. As the university grew, this resistance was partly erased and slowly we began to develop additional graduate work, particularly in the fields of education, science, and engineering.

By that time our gravel roads had been paved and the

old muddy footpaths had been replaced by concrete side-walks. Students were no longer groping through the dark with flashlights. We now had mercury-vapor street lights. I was very proud of those lights and was nonplussed when a professor of physics, who lived on campus, came to my office to complain.

"One of these lights," he said, "is directly in front of my house. On nights when the aurora puts on a display I like to stand on my front porch in the darkness and watch the colored ribbons play across the sky."

I suggested that he watch from the back porch. He was not happy when he left the office.

A valid complaint came from the Geophysical Institute. Geophysical research had begun on campus as far back as 1929 with a small grant from the Rockefeller Foundation for auroral height measurements. The Institute, established as a department of the university in 1949, had grown through a steadily developing series of basic studies until it included many fields of Arctic and sub-Arctic research. The electrical disturbances on campus were affecting some of their more delicate instruments and they, too, needed darkness to study and photograph the aurora. The difficulty was overcome by setting up an auxiliary observatory at a remote site where there would be no electric motors, transmission lines, or bright lights to interfere.

I had expected the honeymoon period with the Board of Regents to last only a short time. Instead the regents continued to be a wonderful support and exciting to work with. Some of the mistakes I made could have given them cause for criticism, but criticism was never voiced. It was my own conscience that kept carping at me, warning of calamity if I blazed ahead recklessly and, if I back-tracked to safety, muttering because I had chickened out.

Sometimes, when I was planning a new building, I would

find myself thinking, "What else could be expected with an engineer running the show? You're more interested in new buildings than in the faculty. Why don't you use these funds to give a mighty boost to faculty salaries? Wasn't it James Garfield who said the ideal classroom is a log with an inspired teacher on one end of the log and an earnest student on the other end?"

This would always put a stop to my soul searching. It was so easy to imagine the inspired teacher and the earnest student sitting on their log, both frozen stiff in the sub-zero weather.

Chapter XVIII

THE NORTH POLAR BASIN

THE duties of a university president might be called "harmoniously confused," particularly if the university is a small one. My own jobs ranged from digging up funds for some new project to trying to find out why a bright Freshman was raising so much hell on campus.

In 1956, as one of my duties, I attended a meeting of polar scientists and explorers in the Baker Library of Dartmouth College. Concentrated in that one room were most of the men in our country who had an active part in polar exploration. They represented various government departments, scientific societies, and universities.

Across the table from me was Vilhjalmur Stefansson, the venerable dean of them all. He was old at that time and his great, shaggy head was bowed as he listened to new plans. Perhaps he was not always listening. The discussions must have awakened memories of his many rugged years in the Arctic.

At least half the men in the room had braved the Antarctic and there was only a handful whose primary interest was pointed northward. Plans were being made for future polar research. The recommendations would be passed on to the American Academy of Science and the National Science Foundation.

For several days most of the attention had been focused on new expeditions to the Antarctic. A few of us were growing apprehensive. We held a meeting the evening before adjournment and decided to attempt the diversion of some attention to the Arctic. I was selected to be the spokesman, a difficult assignment. I felt unqualified to voice opinions before so distinguished a group. But there were strong arguments to be brought out. No one, for example, questions the importance of expanded weather stations in the north polar regions. The north wind which at that very moment was whipping snow across the campus came down from Canada. It may have been spawned in the Polar Basin. It certainly did not come from the Antarctic.

If we were at war with Russia, Soviet planes and missiles would fly across the polar sea to strike our cities while our planes and missiles would take the shortcut across the Arctic to retaliate. Moreover, world population is concentrated mostly in the Northern hemisphere. Take intercontinental travel—the Great Circle routes are the shortest distances between the Orient and any point in the Northern hemisphere. As one example, the flight from London to Tokyo, via New York and San Francisco, is 12,450 miles. Flying the Polar Basin, with just one refueling stop in Alaska, it is about 8000 miles, a saving of about 4500 miles.

That, in brief, was the general tenor of my plea. It was well accepted and a resolution, calling for greater attention to research in the North Polar Basin, was forwarded, with other recommendations, to the National Academy of Science and the National Science Foundation. We could only hope that it would have an effect.

There was a good reason why my interest in the Polar Basin had been whetted. For many years the Office of Naval

Research has maintained an extensive Arctic Research Laboratory at Point Barrow, Alaska. Point Barrow is the true Arctic, where a sandspit projects into the Arctic Ocean to form the very tip of Alaska. In that land, during summer, the sun never drops below the horizon and during several months of winter, there is continuous darkness. This is Eskimo land. Several hundred Eskimos live at Barrow Village, just a few miles from the laboratory, and other settlements are scattered along the Arctic coast.

Scientists from the United States and from some foreign nations come to Barrow to spend a few months or years studying their disciplines. Some study the plants or animals of the land, others probe the Arctic ionosphere, study the aurora, magnetic storms, or weather, chart the ocean bottom and ocean currents, or probe the polar sea to investigate marine life.

During my first year as president of the University of Alaska, we worked out an agreement with the Office of Naval Research, whereby the university would take over the management of this unusual laboratory.

It was obvious from the first that the only effective way to handle the contract was to give full authority to a director and stand behind his on-the-spot decisions, a plan that has worked out wonderfully well over the years, thanks to the high caliber of the men who have served as directors of the operation.

As first director I appointed Ted Mathews, an engineer who had graduated from the university and had spent many years in the Arctic. At that time the laboratory buildings were heated by coal, imported at heavy expense. Mathews knew of two natural gas wells that had been drilled just a few miles from the laboratory. They were idle because the gas, ascending through a thousand feet of permafrost, was chilled and deposited a residue of paraffin on the walls of the drill holes, forming a plug. Mathews worked out a plan to remedy this problem, piped the gas into the laboratory, and heating costs became unimportant.

The director had full responsibility for the operation of the laboratory with all the logistic details of putting scientific parties in the field, often hundreds of miles from Barrow, keeping them supplied, and providing transportation as well as laboratory and library facilities at home base. Much of the transportation was by weasel, a tracked vehicle that could negotiate both the tundra and the snowswept land of winter. At best this was uncertain transportation for distant parties, so Mathews began to rely more and more on airplane transportation.

The high adventure whipping through the laboratory made a stimulating contrast to the routine duties of a university president. I always looked forward to one or two trips each year to Barrow to check on the program. A few hours after crossing the Yukon River, we would be flying over the Brooks Range, a rugged chain of mountains whose ridge line was at ten thousand feet. From the north side of the range, a gently sloping coastal plain stretched for a hundred miles or more, a dreary landscape with no trees, just a few low bushes and patches of willows marking the course of the rivers on their way to the Arctic Ocean. In early September, when a skiff of snow covered the area, it was difficult to decide where land ended and sea began.

I wanted Kay to see this strange land, and she went with me on one trip. As we stood at the very tip of the point with the waters of the Arctic Ocean lapping at our feet, we could see a dozen heavily loaded cargo ships helplessly imprisoned in the icepack.

Normally, during summer months, the face of the icepack stands several miles offshore and permits uncertain ocean transportation to bring in a year's supply to the DEW

218

Line stations and the few trading posts on the Arctic coast. These ships had tempted fate late in the season, and a sudden storm had ripped down from the polar regions to trap the flotilla.

Small lighters were shuttling back and forth, unloading drums of diesel oil, gasoline, and other freight. Nearby, a huge icebreaker was thrashing about like an imprisoned whale. There were loud, crunching noises as the icebreaker sought to open a channel through the pack so that the freighters could escape southward. The battle had been under way for hours. Finally the icebreaker stopped its surging and lay quietly in the ice, defeated. The flotilla of ships with their valuable and essential cargo were at the complete mercy of the elements. A heavy inshore wind would drive them onto the beach. An offshore wind would push back the icepack and permit their escape.

A few days later we were homeward bound. Our plane headed out of the icepack and an hour later I looked down at two freighters threading their way along a narrow open lead in the ice. They had discharged their cargo at a DEW Line station and now were trying to escape the ice and return to Seattle. The captains, no doubt, had been advised that their ships, too, would be imprisoned if they approached Barrow.

We made a stop at Barter Island, and there a storm suddenly struck us. The little waiting room where we were gathered actually shook under the heavy gusts.

"All right, let's go," the pilot announced.

When we bundled up and went out into the black night, the howling wind bombarded us with snow and sand. As soon as we were airborne, high turbulence began slamming the plane around in the sky, until at seventeen thousand feet the air smoothed out. But the plane was not pressurized and we found ourselves breathing deeply to get enough oxygen. Not a pleasant trip, but all the same that was a blessed gale which had come blasting out of the Brooks Range. It was the offshore wind to force back the icepack and free the ships at Barrow.

I was always particularly fascinated by the ice islands, those mammoth icebergs of fresh water ice which have calved from a glacier ice shelf in the Canadian Archipelago and drift almost to the North Pole. There they complete a circular route until they are near the Greenland Sea, and then move westward past Barrow and the Siberian coast before starting another circuit. Several of them have been found floating with the icepack of the Arctic Ocean, like giant, frozen flattops riding high above the pack ice.

The first was discovered during World War II by military planes flying over the Arctic. It was named Fletcher's Ice Island but now is generally called T-3 (Target 3). It averages about one hundred feet thick and is roughly seven miles long and four miles wide. Coaxed along by ocean currents and wind, it makes an erratic circular traverse through the Polar Sea. Each day the scientists who ride it make solar observations to plot its zig-zag path. Some days it reverses direction but generally it advances five to twenty miles each day. As it travels it rotates slowly clockwise and counter-clockwise.

T-3 was occupied first in 1952. In 1961 it went aground near Barrow and was evacuated but the following year it was rediscovered, back at sea again, and was reoccupied by the Arctic Research Laboratory scientists. It has been in use continuously since then.

A cluster of small, well-insulated huts on the island accommodate a dozen scientists and a few support personnel, mostly Eskimos. Some summers the island may be only a hundred miles offshore and then military icebreakers fight their way through the pack to bring in tons of supplies and equipment. But the camp is chiefly supplied by planes flying from Barrow. At times the flight distance may be eight or nine hundred miles. In winter, planes probe through the Arctic night to home on the island radio beacon and settle down on a 4,100-foot snow runway. From June to September, when the summer sun is trying to warm the top of the world, the runway is too mushy for landing. Then streams form from the melting snow and the insulated buildings stand mushroom-like on icy pedestals. During this period the men in camp are completely marooned from the outside world.

One building with a tower-like cupola is known as a hydrahut and covers a well, extending down through the ice. A powered winch lowers instruments into the depths of the ocean to sample or photograph the ocean floor, or to tow nets at different levels and recover samples of sea life. Some of the instruments measure ocean currents and depths. A submarine mountain range breaks the monotony of the ocean floor and nuclear submarines, which at intervals cruise these waters, want to have this submerged range on their charts.

In 1956 we were looking for a new director of the laboratory and Dr. Max C. Brewer was selected. Brewer, now in his early forties, had gone to the Arctic in 1950 for eight months to do geological studies of permafrost. He is still there.

He was a fortunate choice. Under his skilled direction the scope and effectiveness of the work increased. It is a difficult assignment. Within a single year as many as seventy scientists may be working in and out of the laboratory, some floating around on the Arctic Ocean, others scattered widely over Arctic Alaska. Brewer has the responsibility of transporting them to their field stations in hostile environments, keeping them supplied with food and equipment, and, at the end of the season, getting them safely back home. He has their respect as a scientist in his own right and also as a man whose cool judgment and experience could be relied on in the very real emergencies that sometimes developed.

When Brewer suggested that we buy two light, single-engine planes for use out of Barrow, I was reluctant at first. It seemed simpler to continue chartering planes from one of the small airplane companies in Fairbanks. But after hearing about some of the emergencies that arose when chartered planes were not available on short notice, I was convinced and passed on the suggestion to Dr. Louis Quam and Dr. Max Britton of the Office of Naval Research in Washington, D.C. These men, who had direct jurisdiction over the laboratory for the Navy, understood the problem at once and approved Brewer's plan. We bought two Cessna 180 aircraft, sturdy planes, well tested under bush flying conditions in Alaska, and employed two pilots.

Up to this time most of the research away from land had used small boats during summer months. But the work was restricted by the icepack lying offshore and by other serious hazards. Brewer tried sending planes out over the ice. When the pilots had gained experience, he sent out both planes to practice landing on the icepack, one plane making the landing, the second flying cover.

The pilots discovered smooth areas on the ice where a plane could land safely. After that, when a scientist asked permission to be set down on the ice fifty or one hundred miles from shore, to take readings on ocean depths and currents or to get samples of marine life, he was given the go-ahead. The stay, at first limited to a few hours, was later extended to several days while plane and pilot stood by.

But Brewer had an even more daring plan in his mind. He decided to establish a semi-permanent camp on the ice

222

where a scientific party could live for several months as it drifted in the Arctic Ocean. He himself flew reconnaissance over the icepack, chose a large, unbroken floe some fifty miles offshore, and marked it with dye so that it could be found again in the monotonous white sea.

The next day, several Eskimos were loaded into the two small planes and deposited on the ice. Eskimos, we had found, have excellent manual dexterity. Their very survival in the Arctic depends upon their ability to use their hands and to respond quickly to emergencies. With a little training, they became good carpenters, construction men, mechanics, or tractor drivers.

Shortly after the Eskimos were put down on the ice, a big Air Force freight plane was overhead. On the first trip it discharged parts for a portable shelter, on the next it dumped out a small tractor equipped with bulldozer blade. As the Eskimos watched, the big parachute billowed out and deposited the tractor gently on the ice.

While an Eskimo driver operated the machine to smooth down snow ridges and form a hard-packed landing strip, the others put up a portable shack to afford some protection against the weather. The next day a cargo plane landed on the strip, bringing in the first load of supplies and equipment. Within a few days, portable, well-insulated small buildings, transported in sections, were erected and stocked with food, scientific equipment, diesel oil for heating, and gasoline for the generator that operated the radio station. Then four or five scientists and their gear settled in and the drifting ice station was in business.

Drifting stations on the icepack lack the stability of the ice-islands. They become badly crushed and fragmented and have to be abandoned after a few months. The first drifting station, called Station Alpha, was occupied in 1957, Station Charley in 1958, Arlis I (Arctic Research Labo-

223

ratory Ice Station) in 1960, and Arlis III and IV in 1964 and 1965.

At best, life on a drifting ice station is uncomfortable and frequently hazardous. The pack ice averages only seven to ten feet in thickness, and is shifted by ocean currents. It is not unusual for leads of open water to cut through the floe, isolating one building from the others. If leads start opening through the camp, the tractor can sometimes hook onto the skid-mounted buildings and pull them to a more secure position.

In winter, weather permitting, the stations are visited at intervals from Barrow, but during the hot days of summer the surface of the ice becomes too soft for landings and the men are on their own, locked in, until cold weather comes. If the station is within a few hundred miles of Barrow a helicopter can be sent in an emergency, but often the station is drifting near the Pole, beyond the reach of helicopters. During periods of radio blackouts, the station will be out of touch with the laboratory for a week at a time.

One of the minor nuisances is the polar bear that ranges far and wide over the icepack, frequently followed by the Arctic fox who dines on the leavings of the kill. Since the bears have had no opportunity to develop an instinctive fear of man, they sometimes come into camp to investigate when their keen noses catch the scent of the garbage dump. According to instructions, no one can shoot the bear unless it becomes a menace, but several have had to be killed. One troublesome fellow ambled down the airstrip and battered the landing lights.

I have never ceased to admire the scientists who are willing to accept the dangers and hardships involved in life on an ice station. As I sat in my comfortable office at the university, I would think of those men floating around in the Arctic and of the pilots flying out over the icepack in the total darkness of winter. The thoughts gave me some anxious moments.

One of the scientists who has spent many months on these drifting ice stations is my good friend, Dr. Victor Hessler, a member of our staff at the University of Alaska. Vic is an authority on the aurora and electrical current. From the campus he has taken some of the finest color photographs extant of the aurora, involving hours of vigil in the bone-chilling cold of the sub-Arctic night. Vic is an ingenious fellow. To get more sleep, he rigged up a device that picks up the electrical discharges from the aurora and amplifies them to sound an alarm in his bedroom. When the aurora is at high intensity, the alarm clongs, he dresses hurriedly, grabs his camera, and goes out to get his pictures.

The isolated ice station, floating over deep water, gave him the opportunity he wanted to study the interaction of electrical currents and conductive sea water. The fundamental data that he is securing never before have been recorded.

The Russians were the first to recognize the importance of the Polar Basin. They have been conducting Arctic research on a large scale for a long time. When the Americans and the Russians are working in the same areas, a Russian plane, flying low over a station, will dip its wings in salute. We do the same. Recently American scientists on T-3 saw a Russian plane in flight nearby and concluded that they were using the homing beacon on T-3 for navigational purposes. Later one of our laboratory planes found the Russian station, circled, and landed for a visit. The Russians were extremely cordial. The station was occupied by many men and a variety of aircraft, including bush-type biplanes, large helicopters, and twin-engine aircraft.

"How was the visit to the Russian Station, North 67, arranged?" someone asked Brewer.

"We just landed," he said. "We dropped in for coffee, you might say. When you get out in the Arctic Ocean like that, it's like being out in the boonies. You're just happy to see another human being. You have problems in common. You gripe about the lousy weather, the problems of Arctic flying, and things like that."

I have worried a good deal about Max Brewer. He was continually making flights to check on the stations. Whenever a hazardous flight was to be made, Max usually went along. One day I said to him, "Max, there's always the risk of getting a plane down on the ice. In such an emergency you should be at Barrow to direct the rescue."

A year after I retired from the university, one of the planes from the laboratory did make a forced landing on the ice and Dr. Max Brewer was on the plane. I heard the report on the radio.

The plane had landed at a distant station and one of the wingtanks inadvertently was refueled from a drum of diesel oil. A hundred miles out, on the return journey, when the pilot switched to that tank the motors began to sputter. He sent out a "May Day" call, giving his position, found a comparatively level spot on the ice and skillfully brought the plane in for a forced landing. They rattled and bounced to a stop. Plane and passengers were unhurt. Two days later a search plane found them and brought them to Barrow. The plane was later recovered and flown to its base.

In a letter written later, Max said, "I thought about you when we were stranded on the ice—how you had admonished me about so much flying and I'll bet you were 'chewing me out.' "

Another Arctic drama occurred after my retirement. This one involved an ice island, Arlis II. During the winter of 1964, Arlis II reached its northern apogee, about a hundred miles south of the Pole, and turned southwestward, pointing toward the north face of Greenland. It was expected to turn west again and follow its orbit of previous years.

But by January 1965, currents from the Greenland Sea were flirting with it, trying to coax it away from its usual Arctic path. Lapped by opposing forces, the island followed a hesitant zig-zag path on the chart. Within a few weeks, the Greenland currents had the island firmly in their grasp and it turned eastward, working its way around the northern face of Greenland and down its eastern side. We knew then that the island was doomed. It would be swept into the North Atlantic where warmer waters would destroy it. The scientific party would have to be evacuated. By that time the island had picked up speed and was skimming along at twenty miles a day.

Although rescue planes were readied, it was decided to attempt a rendezvous. The Navy icebreaker *Edisto* set out, trying to intercept the island as it floated between Greenland and Iceland. This proved difficult. The *Edisto* often was hemmed in by the pack ice but on May 6 a helicopter from the icebreaker landed at the camp. Five days later all the men and their equipment had been evacuated, except the two radio homing beacons, left on the island to track its southern journey.

The island had been manned constantly by scientific parties during its last four years. It had journeyed more than four thousand miles and permitted the scientists to record a vast amount of important data. A month later it had broken into a dozen pieces and the camp buildings were at the bottom of the sea. Thus ended the saga of the most important ice station in Arctic history.

Chapter XIX

THE OASIS

SOMETIMES I amuse myself with a daydream that may be common to many geologists. I imagine myself in a spaceship reconnoitering the earth between fifteen and thirty thousand years ago, during the glacial age of the Pleistocene epoch. As we cruise over Asia, Europe, and North America, I look down at the great ice cap stretching over all the northern latitudes. For a time I float above the northern tier of our States, a white, silent world where lobes of ice extend as far south as Kentucky and Missouri. I can even imagine the great migration of animals pushed southward ahead of the slow advance of the glaciers.

When my spaceship turns northward, only the high mountain ranges of western Canada are standing above the ice. These, too, are ice-capped, their flanks choked with valley glaciers. Then a great phenomenon comes into view. In the broad intermontane valleys of the Yukon, Tanana, and Kuskokwim, in the interior of Alaska and Yukon Territory, I look down onto a lush green oasis set in a desert of ice. On the west it is open to the sea, but the other three sides are solidly surrounded by ice. In my spaceship, I always am conscious of wonder and delight at the sight.

When I first arrived in Alaska I had no knowledge of this oasis. In the United States, like other geologists, I had studied the tell-tale debris left on the land as the glaciers retreated, melting. After I began to travel around Alaska, I was confounded to find no evidence of this glaciation in the mountains and valleys of the Fairbanks area. Then as I studied the reports of the U.S. Geological Survey, I found that most of interior Alaska had indeed escaped the Ice Age. During the five distinct periods of ice invasion, much of interior Alaska through tens of thousands of years had remained a sort of Shangri-la. No one knows why this should have been so. A number of theories had been advanced, but each is of doubtful validity.

Since there were interglacial periods throughout the northern hemisphere, when soil built up, vegetation grew again, and some animals returned, it is possible that we may be living in an interglacial period now. Conceivably, another ice invasion could come down from the North within the next thousand years and people would have to leave their homes to retreat southward. Conceivably, too, interior Alaska might again escape glaciation and people could ride out the new ice age, snug in their northern oasis.

Certainly during the Pleistocene epoch an extraordinary number of mammals were crowded into this oasis by the encroaching ice. The deep-freeze of permafrost has preserved their skeletal remains to this day. Tons of bones are exposed each year as placer gold miners strip away the muck overburden to get the gold-bearing gravels. These finds always have been a source of deep interest to me.

Many of them are the bones of animals whose descendants live in Alaska today: caribou, moose, and bear. The musk ox, which today roams the barrens of Arctic Canada, was widespread in Alaska during the glacial age. Most of the small mammals, mice, gophers, weasels and mink, carried on their daily lives much as they do now. But in the oasis there also were animals that have disappeared completely from the earth, leaving nothing behind but fragments of their skeletons.

I would love to have landed my spaceship in the oasis back in Pleistocene times, even if it had meant being confronted by a ponderous hairy mammoth or charged by a super-bison. It would have been a paradise for a hunter with rifle or camera. He might listen to the drumming of small hooves and see a band of horses, the size of Shetland ponies, dash away or hear the slap of a giant beaver's tail as he sent out his alarm signal before diving under the waters of his dam.

The concentration of animal life in the oasis was tremendous. There are thousands of stream valleys in interior Alaska and only a few of them contain enough placer gold to interest miners. In the Fairbanks district, twelve valleys have been mined extensively, and that limited area alone has yielded remains of more than a thousand animals. Sometimes an offensive odor of decaying flesh rises as the muck thaws from an area being stripped, and miners find bits of hide with the hair still intact. According to carbon-14 dating tests, some of these animals lived thirty thousand years ago, preserved ever since by nature's icebox.

The collection of fossils in the museum of the University of Alaska was started during the early days of the college. A great number of the fossils are the finds of my friend, the late Dr. Otto Geist. I first saw Dr. Geist in 1925 when he took our mining short course at the university, a course he later repeated. He was always a student at heart, a short, dark-complexioned man who looked gruff until you noticed the warmth and humor in his eyes. He had done some collecting in his native Germany and had come to Alaska after World War I. When I met him, he had been prospecting in

230

the Koyukuk district, some two hundred miles north of Fairbanks. The next year, President Bunnell sent him to St. Lawrence Island on his first Alaskan collecting expedition. That winter he lived with the Eskimos, ate their food, hunted with them on the ice, and was initiated into their tribe. He brought back a ton of material. In summer he returned with an expedition to excavate old midden piles for ancient artifacts.

The university then worked out a cooperative agreement with Childs Frick of the American Museum of Natural History in New York. Mr. Frick financed the work of Dr. Geist, who for years after that spent his summers moving over the mining areas, examining fresh exposures, and collecting skeletal remains of Pleistocene mammals which miners put aside for him. Sometimes it would be the skull of a super-bison, an animal that had been very numerous. When they are found, frequently the husk is still on the horns. If a leg bone is broken open, the bone marrow may still be intact.

Judging from the number of skulls, huge leg bones, and great ivory tusks—ten feet or more in length—that have been dug up, several hundred hairy mammoths must have roamed the Fairbanks area alone. A tooth from the lower jaw of a mammoth now serves as a bookend in my study. It weighs about four pounds. The interior of the tooth is ivory-like, and the tooth has nine roots. Yet the mammoth had several such teeth in both the upper and lower jaws. Mine has been heavily coated with shellac to preserve it. Its surface is corrugated like an old-fashioned washboard, ideal for grinding the willows upon which these huge animals browsed.

As a paperweight, I use the small hoof of a Pleistocene horse, which I once picked up. His skull often is found perfectly preserved. As we know, the horse developed in

North America and then disappeared from the continent, presumably migrating across the land bridge to Asia. But in Alaska no traces have been found of the early stages of his development—of the little five-toed animal, for example, the size of a small dog, whose fossil bones have been recovered elsewhere on the North American continent in the Cenozoic sediments of some sixty million years ago. Nor of the later three-toed horse. In interior Alaska we find only the frozen bones of the Pleistocene horse, not the fossilized remains from earlier geologic periods. By that time, except for his small size, he looked like a modern horse.

Although the mastodon was plentiful in the United States, apparently he did not flourish in Alaska, although the museum at the university has one well-preserved set of mastodon teeth, discovered by a prospector on a gravel bar in the Yukon River. No doubt an occasional mastodon took refuge in the oasis to escape the ice sheets.

Most of the skeletal remains are found near the base of the muck, or immediately at the junction of gravels and muck, suggesting that these animals were traveling on the gravel bars when they died. Subsequently they must have been covered quickly and preserved as the muck accumulated.

In some places, miners have found veritable boneyards of different animal remains, all in one small patch. This does not necessarily indicate that the animals met death in some isolated catastrophe. More probably, when the valley floors were flooded, and the animals retreated to nearby hills, an occasional animal returned to the water's edge and became bogged down in the muddy ooze. This could explain why bones of so many massive animals, such as the hairy mammoth, musk ox, and bison, have been found and so few of the more agile animals, like caribou, moose, and bear.

One day, while I was walking by a vertical face of muck in the stripping area at Ester Creek, I noticed a tube of clear ice, about six inches across and extending downward to a depth of six feet. There was a rounded ball of ice at the bottom of the tube. It reminded me of a huge thermometer.

After I had dug the bulb out carefully with a pick and chipped away the ice, I was holding in my hands a nest carefully constructed of mammoth hair and the wonderfully soft wool of the musk ox. When I cracked this open, I found the skeletons of two gophers and a handful of seeds that they had stored but had had no chance to use before water invaded their snug home. After that I often saw these circular "ice eyes" as I walked over a surface of muck. When the ice thawed it was possible to work a stick down into the hole and seeds would float to the surface.

It was always exciting, when the muck was stripped away and the gravel exposed, to find ancient beaver dams with teeth marks still engraved on the brush wood, put there twenty or thirty thousand years ago, when the beaver built his dam. Some of the dams are constructed almost entirely of diamond willow, a type of willow no longer common in Alaska.

Once, on a trip East, I visited Childs Frick. He had inherited a fortune and was devoting his life and his funds to the study of early mammals. After he had given me a tour of his Long Island estate, we stopped at his laboratory. At the time he was working on a monograph on the early camel in America and his assistants were carefully chiseling fossil camel bones from the enclosing rocks.

"Camels roamed over most of North America during the Pleistocene," he told me. "They were great migrants, able to adapt to any climate. We know they migrated at an early period across the land bridge from Alaska to Asia and we

233

find their fossils in China and India. Why doesn't Geist find me some camel bones? I want a good camel skull." He sounded quite irascible about it.

Dr. Geist was a sensitive, conscientious man. When I later repeated the conversation to him, he looked hurt. "He keeps asking me the same question in almost every letter. If the camel was here I'll find him. I can't produce one out of thin air."

One day the next summer, he sailed into my office and triumphantly laid a knuckle bone, about four inches long and stained brown, onto my desk. "What do you think of that?"

"Hardly big enough for a soup bone," I commented. "What is it?"

"The toe bone of a camel!" he exclaimed. "I found several of them today." I had never seen him look so proud or so happy. "The skull and the rest of the skeleton should be washed out soon," he went on confidently, carefully gathering up the bone again.

Strangely, no other part of the camel appeared. As the days went by, Geist grew more and more disconsolate. Trying to cheer him up, I suggested that possibly the camel had lost a foot and hobbled off on three legs. Geist would not even smile. When I retired from the university several years later, he was still searching for his camel.

Over the years, however, he made some surprising and exciting discoveries. Once, on Fairbanks Creek, he found the head of a calf mammoth, frozen in the muck, its flesh, skin, and hair intact and one eyeball still in its socket. This specimen was kept frozen and shipped to the American Museum of Natural History, where it created a scientific sensation.

On another good hunting day, he recovered the well-preserved skulls of two lions. Occasionally the skull of a sabertooth tiger had been found in Alaska, but we had no idea that the lion had been on this continent. These skulls, too, were sent to the Natural History Museum. They were placed on a table beside the skull of a modern African lion and were found to match perfectly. No doubt the lion in this habitat carried a heavy coat of hair, and this leads to a conjecture that possibly the mane and flyswatter tail of the African lion are relics of a northern ancestry. Certainly the presence in the oasis of horse, camel, and lion does not suggest that Alaska at the time had a tropical climate. The climate in our oases was just about what it is now. The animals could have adapted to it without difficulty. Even today pack horses, abandoned in the autumn, have turned up in the spring fat and sassy from feeding along the gravel flats of rivers where the pea-vine flourishes.

Dr. Geist retired in 1957. It turned out to be a very active retirement. One day in 1959, we were discussing possible new areas for the university's work in paleontology. I suggested that he might make a study of the distribution of Pleistocene land mammals. Although he was seventy at the time, he accepted the assignment with delight. During the next few years, using the Arctic Research Laboratory at Point Barrow as a base, Dr. Geist and various assistants made a number of expeditions on the Ikpikuk, the Kokolik, and Kuk and the Usuktuk Rivers, sometimes using a canvas folding boat and sometimes a hired umniak, collecting fossils as well as specimens of birds and small mammals for the university's Biological Sciences department and Cooperative Wildlife Research Unit.

The most engrossing question to me concerns ancient man—was *he* here? With the abundance of food in the oasis, his life would have been easy. The skeletal remains of the animals discovered date back to the Wisconsin glacial period, twenty to thirty thousand years ago. No trace of man has yet been found dating earlier than 9000 B.C.

Archaeologists are much in agreement that the North American Indian originated in Asia, entered North America originally by the Bering Sea route to northern Alaska, and migrated gradually southward. The continental platforms of Asia and North America are joined beneath the Bering Sea, and the short voyage in a skin boat presents no physical difficulty today.

The large island of St. Lawrence in the Bering Sea is a natural stepping stone between the two continents. Teams from the University of Alaska excavating there have collected thousands of artifacts used by these early people. The midden piles reveal several ages of culture; curiously enough, the bottom layer, dating back several thousand years, shows the highest stage of culture. Those people carved their ivory tools and weapons with intricate curvilinear designs.

In the early days of the college, when we began to disturb the surface on College Hill, some arrowheads and crude stone tools were uncovered. Later our scientists excavated a site on the brow of the hill where early man had camped, no doubt watching for game on the floor below. At their camp site there were razor-sharp stone microblades and delicate jeweler-like flaking on flint side blades, these as small as the blade of a pocket knife. Since radiocarbon dating had not yet been fully developed, we were uncertain of the age of the sites where they were discovered. They were placed in the museum; visiting scientists found them similar to tools discovered in the Gobi desert and in the Siberian forest.

Perhaps this discovery in our own front yard influenced Louis Giddings, one of our students at the time, to make archaeology his life work. The climax of his discoveries came after many years, working in Greenland, on the shores of the Arctic Ocean and in northern Alaska. He was already known as a world authority on the early men who inhabited the Arctic when some fascinating detective work led him to a treasure house of artifacts at Cape Denbigh in Alaska. Such artifacts had never before been found in America, although they were quite similar to those used by Paleolithic and Mesolithic hunters of the Old World.

In the ancient houses that he excavated, as much as eighteen feet below the surface, he found primitive stone hearths. Carbon-14 dating of the charcoal remains revealed them to be five thousand years old. This is now considered to be the beginning of Eskimo culture in Alaska.

In the past two years, a still more ancient chapter has been added to the history of man in Alaska. Dr. Robert McKennan, a cultural anthropologist from Dartmouth, happened to stop at a homestead near Healy Lake in central Alaska to interview Mrs. Margaret Kirsteatter, the native wife of the homesteader and trapper. During the course of the conversation he was shown a collection of arrowheads which had been found by the son in his father's garden.

Dr. McKennan alerted Dr. John Cook, a former student, now an archaeologist on the faculty of the University of Alaska. Cook's excavations yielded a rich collection of artifacts and charred animal bones around a buried hearth. Charcoal from the hearth yielded the surprising date of eleven thousand years.

This, as far as I know, is the earliest trace of man in Alaska. Yet during the glacial period, even more ancient man could have had land trails from Asia to North America, trails now covered by the Bering Sea, a shallow body of water, seldom more than three hundred feet deep. The vast continental ice sheets were built from water robbed from the sea. During that period the sea was lowered several hundred feet. Early man could have walked across.

What we are looking for now in the oasis area of interior Alaska are the skeletal remains of this early man or his artifacts buried under the muck and preserved by permafrost. Someday I hope we will find them.

Chapter XX

CRISIS

APPEARING for the first time before the legislature to ask for funds is a trying experience for any university president. But it is a mere cupcake compared to facing an angry student body. For one thing, legislators are not apt to be armed with rotten vegetables. With students, one can never be entirely sure.

For years an unwritten law had permitted the drinking of beer in the men's dormitories at the university. Hard liquor was prohibited.

One day during my fourth year as president, the dean of students came in to report trouble in the men's dormitories. Drinking parties were becoming numerous and some of the sessions had been getting out of hand.

A warning was issued and for a few weeks things were quiet. Then one of the dormitories was thrown into an uproar by a wild party. When the proctor tried to break it up, he met with resistance. In an adjoining room he found a Freshman, one of the few Eskimos on campus. The student was sitting precariously on a third-floor window ledge with his feet dangling, howling like a wolf and threatening to jump.

He finally was coaxed from his perch but the next day both he and his belongings had disappeared from his room. In alarm we called the Fairbanks police and they searched for him in town. He had left that morning to return to his village, the police reported when they checked the airport.

I had had enough. I posted a strongly worded notice on each dormitory bulletin board. No liquor of any kind was to be brought into the dormitory. Anyone caught in violation would be dismissed from the dormitory.

The students felt that their rights had been infringed upon and took strong exception. Before long I was besieged by student groups and petitions. At first the tone was cordial. When I went into the Student Union building, the record player immediately blared out the drinking song from *The Student Prince*. All this was amusing fun.

A few nights later a torchlight parade was held on campus. Several hundred students marched to the front of the Student Union and erected a stone monument, on which they inscribed with a welding torch, "Here Lies Tradition." A drama student, dressed in cap and gown, delivered the funeral oration. It was recorded and later I heard a playback. One by one, he recited the things that I had done to break down campus tradition; after each charge he intoned, "But Ernie is an honorable man."

I thought this a healthy way for them to blow off steam. Instead, pressure was building up. Within a week the president of the student body walked into his dormitory with a bottle of whiskey cradled in his arm, making no attempt to hide it from the dormitory proctor. So the gauntlet had been cast at my feet. In less than an hour he was dismissed from the dormitory.

Overnight the carnival atmosphere changed to one of surly resentment. When I walked across campus, students turned aside to avoid speaking. There were secret student meetings. They had reached the boiling point and I knew it.

The next morning, a petition was delivered to me. It was accompanied by pages of signatures, accounting for the majority of the students. It virtually demanded the reinstatement of their president in the dormitory. They asked for a decision within twenty-four hours.

As I had learned through a lifetime, dealing with men in business, in mining camps, and on the campus, you cannot pussyfoot around a confrontation of this kind. It has to be met head on. But if I lost this bout, I also realized, my usefulness as an administrator was over.

One o'clock classes were cancelled and notices issued, calling for a student assembly. As the hour drew near, from my window I watched students crowding into the auditorium. All of the faculty seemed to be on hand as well as a small group of townspeople who had come to see the excitement.

I had made up my mind to use the front entrance instead of easing in through the wings. When the gong sounded, I walked into the auditorium and worked my way down the crowded aisle. It was going to be a long and hazardous walk up that aisle at the end of the meeting, as I knew, but I was determined, no matter what happened, not to lose my nerve and scuttle out the rear exit.

Instead of mounting the platform I stood at a microphone placed at floor level. Some students in the front row clicked on a tape recorder and it started to whirr. My first impulse was to ask them to turn it off, but I dismissed the idea. "I see you are making a tape," I began. "That's good. This is an important meeting and I want a record of it, too."

"When the chips are down and they view all the facts unemotionally," I told them, "I have always found students to be fair and honorable in their attitudes." It took a few

241

minutes to review the incidents leading up to our decisions and to explain our motivation in making the liquor ruling. It took only a few more minutes to remind them of the public nature of the university, that much of the operating cost came out of the pockets of Alaskans in the form of tax dollars, and that to be here was a privilege, not a right.

Finally I said, "You asked for my decision within twenty-four hours. Here it is. The ruling stands in full force and effect and I am not going to debate it with you. Some of you, I understand, may feel that you want to withdraw from the university. If so, go to the registrar's office and your transcript will be released without prejudice. I hope you are with me, but I realize that we could end up with only a dozen students in the university. That would be a disaster for you and for the university and it will be a disaster for me. In such an eventuality I shall resign immediately and let someone else take over who is more amenable to your desires. Thank you for your courteous attention."

The hall was deadly quiet as I started my long walk back up the aisle. After I had gone a few yards I heard a scraping of feet as they all stood up at the same moment, almost as if by command.

It was the moment when I expected the vegetables to start pelting me. I hope they don't have any soft tomatoes, I thought. Then I almost stopped still in my tracks because I heard a great roar. The students were all applauding and cheering. "Why are they doing it after what I just said to them?" I asked myself completely confused. I began to walk a little faster but there were tears in my eyes before I could reach my office.

I barely had time to pull myself together when the student president and other students came in to shake hands and to tell me that the incident was closed. Then the faculty crowded in, offering congratulations.

242

Possibly all this sounds like a tempest in a teapot. But at the time it was a pretty big teapot. Of course the crisis can not be compared to the epidemic of campus rebellions that universities have experienced in the last few years. I was personally acquainted with most of the students on campus, a situation that is impossible at a university with an enrollment of twenty or thirty thousand. I was dealing with angry students, but I had no outside agitators to contend with. Moreover, I could count on the backing of regents and faculty. No, the situations are not to be compared. But I cannot help doing it, just the same.

I feel like an old retired boxer at the ringside, watching a bout, bobbing and weaving, throwing imaginary punches, and urging some pugilist to be more aggressive—quite unaware that rules have changed since his day, that opponents are more wily, and the fighting dirtier.

So when I watch university presidents, many of whom I know and respect as educators, humiliated and defeated and prestigious universities badly damaged, I cannot keep from yelling, "Don't shilly shally! Move in fast and decisively." When an administrator is ready to put his career on the line for the sake of his convictions, the majority of students, I firmly believe, will respond. And if he is defeated, at least he will go out with honor and public opinion will be with him.

From less than three hundred full-time on-campus students, the university had grown, within a few years, to nine hundred students. Our projections indicated that we would have more than two thousand within ten years. For some time the regents had been urging an extensive long-range planning program. It had been included in our budget request to the legislature, but it had been deleted. Finally I took our problem to the Ford Foundation and we were given a grant. At their suggestion, we employed Dr. James MacConnell of the education department of Stanford University to head the study. He in turn employed a team of educators, consulting architects, and a landscape architect.

We submitted copies of our catalog, maps, photographs of the campus, and collateral data. With the planning program in the hands of experts, we expected to sit back, relax, and await their findings. Instead, the consultants sat down and prepared page after page of questions, all of them requiring hours of research to answer. We could not fault their approach. They needed all the background and every scrap of information we could supply.

The questionnaires kept accumulating in my desk drawer until finally the work was parceled out to the entire staff with faculty department heads enlisted to help. Night after night we were in our offices working. Some were tricky questions, such as, "Do you want a pedestrian campus with the road and parking areas around the perimeter?"

We were proud of our paved roads through the campus. To that question we answered, "We approve the concept of a pedestrian campus but please try to leave present paved roads for service uses."

A month later the team of consultants arrived on campus. Most of them were from the San Farncisco Bay area and snow and sub-zero weather were not part of their daily lives. Unfortunately they arrived during a cold snap. By the end of the first day, we could feel their enthusiasm evaporating into the sub-zero atmosphere.

After the landscape architect looked over the campus, a study in white broken only by brightly painted buildings and a background of green spruce trees, he gave me a puzzled look. "Did you mention lawns and flower beds? Is it possible for lawn grass to survive such extreme temperatures?"

244

The insulating blanket of snow, I explained, was protecting the grass. He still looked dubious. They all seemed very glad indeed to shake the snow off their cold feet and return to California.

A few weeks later the architects sent preliminary sketches. They visualized a central complex of closely spaced new buildings connected by heated walkways, an idea that had merit but it was not what we had in mind. As we explained, we who lived on campus did not object to getting out into the fresh air and we saw no reason to keep our students under glass.

The president's residence was about one-quarter mile from my office and I found it stimulating to walk this distance several times a day. We urged them not to freeze their concept of the campus until they paid us a second visit in the summer.

When they returned in June, the midnight sun was working around the clock. The slender birches had leafed out, lawns were green, and flowers were in full bloom. Their astonishment was a delight to see. "I can't believe it's the same place we saw last winter," one of the men told me. I could almost see new ideas taking shape in their minds. Academic consultants were busy with interviews; architects started sketching; the landscape architect was pacing around the campus making notes and inquiring about the suitability of local material for planting.

Several of them, at various times, said to me, "You should put more emphasis on summer sessions."

It took another year before all the details had been worked out. Many of the recommendations from the academic consultants were adopted. Their organization chart called for regrouping into six colleges, each administered by a dean. In addition each department would have an administrative head. This is the approved organization for a large university. In a small university it created too many chiefs and not enough Indians. I much preferred our streamlined and economical organization. In a few years, however, the university would be large enough for the plan they proposed.

Finally the architects arrived to submit their completed plans for the approval of the regents. They had grouped most of the present and future academic buildings around a central mall with a fountain in the middle. Some distance beyond this was an area for a new dormitory complex. On a ridge above the campus they had outlined a future research center, one which we knew would start to take shape within a few years. On the north side of the campus an area was to be developed for faculty residences. One sketch suggested how the campus would look some ten years hence with two to three thousand students in attendance.

After a good many questions, I could see the regents settling back in their chairs. They were as pleased as I was with the final results. We were going to have one of the most beautiful and best-planned campuses in the nation. For an instant my mind flashed back to the moment in 1922 when I had stood looking up at our one frame building perched on the hill and had wondered despondently if it could possibly have any future. In the sketches before me now I could see what the future of the university was going to be, and it was a great one.

Chapter XXI

THE FIGHT FOR A STATE

BY 1953, the year I returned to the university, Alaskans were fed up to the teeth with territorial status. They were tired of bureaucratic control from Washington, and irritated by the frequent fumbling decisions of men who had no real grasp of our problems.

The question most frequently asked in those days was, "How do you stand on statehood?" The question was discussed, often heatedly, wherever people gathered, in bars, restaurants, homes, or street corners. A group of solid citizens, responsible business and professional men, were spearheading the thrust for statehood and the issue was being kept red hot in the eyes of the public by newspaper publishers—by Robert B. Atwood of the *Anchorage Daily Times,* for example, and C. W. Snedden of *The Fairbanks Daily News-Miner.*

Obviously others were in the campaign for selfish reasons and for the opportunities that statehood would open to them.

Before I had been president of the university a month, leaders of the movement wanted to know if I was with them. I was uncertain at the time. Every Alaskan wanted state-

247

hood eventually, but some men questioned whether Alaska's economic base was strong enough to support it. It was hard to know if we were leading from the heart or from the head. My uncertainty did not last long. When I decided in favor of statehood, each passing month strengthened the decision. I saw first hand what it meant to be a second-class citizen under territorial status.

The university had requested a large grant of land from the public domain, expecting it in future years to bring added income to the university. The federal government at that time owned ninety-nine percent of the land in Alaska.

Our bill had passed the U.S. House of Representatives and had gone to the Senate where Senator Clinton Anderson of New Mexico took exception to it. It was due to be considered by the Senate committee of which Anderson was a powerful member. When I went to Washington and attempted to talk with Senator Anderson, he refused to give me an appointment.

Alaska's only representative in Congress was Delegate E. L. (Bob) Bartlett and, as a delegate, he had no vote. For three hours Bartlett, B. Frank Heintzleman, Alaska's appointed governor, and I sat in an anteroom, hoping to appear before the committee. Finally at noon a clerk came out to inform us that we would not be heard.

As we walked dejectedly down the corridor, I heard Bob Bartlett sigh. "Ernest," he said, "if I were Senator Bartlett from the State of Alaska, we would have had a hearing."

During that same trip, I stopped in New York City and was invited to lunch by a group from the Wilderness Society. They wanted my support for their plan to carve out great chunks of Alaska for a wilderness area, an area that would be held in perpetuity in its primitive state, where there would be no development of natural resources and no entry roads.

248

As I told them, Alaska could not lock up its natural resources. Although I had no objection to wilderness areas, they would have to permit multiple uses of the land. The natural resources, I explained, could be exploited under stringent regulations to prevent despoiling the region's natural beauty. One of the areas they were discussing might have potentials for petroleum development. When I asked if they would permit drilling for oil, they looked horrified. "Oh no!" one of them gasped. "Hauling in the drilling rigs by tractor would deface the area."

"I'm sorry, gentlemen," I had to tell them. "You've wasted a lunch."

As the group began to break up one of the men said to me, "Recently I was talking with President Eisenhower and he asked me what I thought about statehood for Alaska. I told the President, 'Why turn over such a vast country for the benefit of two hundred thousand people? It should be held in its natural state as a great recreation area for future generations.'

"What do you think of that?" he demanded.

"Don't ever go to Alaska and make such a remark," I told him. "You'd never get out alive."

I have no quarrel with wilderness proponents. I have found them to be sincere, dedicated people, but like many of us who believe deeply in a cause or an idea, zeal sometimes marches ahead of common sense.

The Wilderness Society was only one of many groups that, for various reasons, opposed statehood, and their voices often were heard in Congress. Clearly, dramatic action would be required to keep the issue alive. The people of Alaska already had voted overwhelmingly for statehood. Then the territorial legislature appropriated funds to hold a constitutional convention where Alaskans would draft the constitution for their proposed state.

The university, we all felt, should have a part in what surely would be an historic occasion. At the time we were just finishing the Student Union building, a facility badly needed on campus and one that would make an excellent meeting place for the convention. Before issuing an invitation, I asked the students if they were willing to forgo use of the building for a few months and they readily voted approval of the idea. The building contractor agreed to rush construction and the last-minute touches were completed just as the delegates arrived.

Fifty-five men and women assembled on November 8, 1955, joined by a small group of experts in state government, who had been employed as consultants. A good many of the delegates came from distant points in Alaska and had never been on campus before. Since they were going to live with us for seventy-five days and see the university in action, the impression they took home would be important to the university. The students were aware of this and it warmed my heart to see what fine hosts they made, with as lively a sense of responsibility as faculty or administration.

The lack of personal ambition shown on this occasion by the group of Alaskans assembled for the convention was wonderful to watch. There was no jockeying for political advantage. The delegates came from all walks of life but had only one goal. They were determined to draft the best state constitution possible, and in this they succeeded. I believe that the Alaska State Constitution will be used as a model when older states re-draft their own constitutions that have become outdated.

Territorial Governor Heintzleman presided at the first session and William A. Egan, who operated a grocery store in the little coastal town of Valdez, was chosen president of the convention. In the next few weeks, unsuspected qualities became apparent in a number of men, one of whom was

250

Egan. Although the debates on the floor sometimes grew heated, Egan never permitted them to get out of hand. But it was not only his skill in guiding the group and keeping the program on schedule that impressed the delegates. It was the quiet strength that everyone felt as they listened to him.

"There's the man who's going to be the first governor of the State of Alaska," I heard a delegate say. As it happened, he spoke prophetically.

Another surprise was a New Orleans businessman named George Lehleitner who had showed up at the convention. At first nobody could figure out what he was doing there. He said he had made the trip to put in a plea for a so-called "Tennessee Plan"—a program for statehood for both Alaska and Hawaii. The delegates took this with a grain of salt.

One of them remarked to me, "It sounds pretty funny, coming all the way up from Louisiana because he's got this big personal interest in statehood. What's the guy's angle?"

It was generally suspected that he must have an axe to grind. Somewhat reluctantly, he was given time to address the convention. He had not talked more than a few moments before the mood of the delegates began to change from skepticism to respect. As he explained, his interest stemmed from his experiences in Hawaii during World War II. Those experiences had made him realize that Americans under territorial status were treated unjustly. No one listening to him could continue to doubt his honesty. Here, quite clearly, was a man who cared so deeply about a cause that he was willing to give his time and resources to further it. Moreover, as he described it, the Tennessee Plan made good sense and it was adopted.

After seventy-five days of intense work, the constitution had been completed and engrossed. The delegates' job was

251

done, and they were emotionally and physically exhausted. I stood in the back of the room, listening to farewell speeches and watching the presentation of an oil painting to the president, Bill Egan. It was an emotion-charged session. I heard voices break during the talks and I saw tears in the eyes of many delegates. I began looking around for one of them, Mr. "Muktuk" Marston.

"If Marston is crying," I thought, "I've seen everything." Finally I found him, a robust man with angles to his face that look as if they had been chiseled from granite. Tears were trickling from the corners of his eyes and he was picking them off, one by one, and throwing them on the floor. They were husky tears and I wondered if they bounced.

The formal signing of the constitution, a thirteen-thousand-word document, took place the next day. One by one, as each name was called, the delegates went up to the stage and affixed their signatures.

My thoughts raced back almost two hundred years when a similar group of men signed their names to a constitution destined to serve a great purpose. On that day, I was convinced, there must have been the same hush and sense of dedication as I felt in the university's new Constitution Hall.

After the convention had finished its work, the people of Alaska went to the polls and elected William A. Egan and Ernest Gruening as senators and Ralph J. Rivers as a representative. These men opened an office in Washington, D.C., and called on each member of Congress to plead for favorable action on the Alaska statehood bill. As a dramatic gesture they knocked on the doors of both Senate and House, presented their credentials as duly elected representatives of the people of Alaska, and requested to be seated. This plan had been used effectively in 1796, the year Tennessee sought statehood.

The plan proved as effective as Lehleitner had foretold.

The spotlight of publicity was on our representatives. Members of Congress who previously had only a casual interest in the statehood bill or who felt that it was something to consider for the future, were made aware of how intensely the people of Alaska desired to be part of the brotherhood of states.

In the meantime Lehleitner, from his office in New Orleans, was carrying on a one-man crusade for statehood, turning out thousands of letters to service clubs, members of Congress, and other influential people, as well as making frequent trips to Washington to confer and map strategy with the Alaskan delegation. At intervals, groups from Alaska arrived in Washington to add their weight to the efforts.

A number of antagonists were fighting back. Some honestly believed that Alaska was not yet ready for statehood. Others, both in industry and government, felt that statehood for Alaska would endanger their vested interests. And so the debate went on. We were nearer to victory than we knew.

On July 7, 1958, President Eisenhower signed the Alaska statehood bill and on January 3, 1959, Alaska formally entered the Union as the 49th state.

After the bill was signed, elections were held. Gruening and Bartlett, who had been Alaska's nonvoting delegate to Congress, were elected senators and Rivers was elected to the House of Representatives. Egan became Alaska's first elected governor.

Chapter XXII

CLOSING THE RING

APPROACHING the age of sixty-five and facing retirement is generally, I believe, a traumatic experience for an executive. I had a year of grace before the depressing time arrived to brief my successor, clean out my desk, and find myself, the next day, only a spectator.

Originally I had told the regents that I would serve for only five years. At the end of my sixth year I came home one evening and said to Kay, "Brace yourself. I turned in my resignation today."

Kay looked startled and hurt. "What's happened, Ernest? You've never made a decision affecting our lives without talking it over first."

I tried to lie manfully, but after forty-two years of married life, I could not deceive my Kay. As we both knew, Kay's health was the dominant reason. She had a severe medical problem that necessitated several trips to New York and Seattle to consult specialists. Although there was no immediate danger, the prognosis was not good. When I tendered my resignation, I had given the regents a year's notice to allow them ample time to choose a new president. But I had urged them to start the search for my successor imme-

254

diately, since I preferred to leave before the year was out.

During the time left to me at the university, I had hopes of making an old dream of mine come true. I wanted to establish a school of oceanography. The regents already had granted me permission to go ahead with the plan. Alaska has more coastline than the other forty-eight continental states combined. Fishing, its most important industry, is based principally on the production of salmon and halibut. Shrimp were underutilized; the king crab industry was just starting to develop and large stocks of pollack, hake, cod, and other bottom fish were essentially unused by American fishermen.

Fishing fleets from Japan and Russia, equipped with cannery ships and sophisticated gear, were crowding our three-mile limit to take halibut and were making sweeps across the continental shelf of Alaska for crab and bottom fish. Japanese and Russian nationals are not conservation-minded. There were many Alaskans who felt that to conserve the resources, we would have to extend fishing restrictions to the limits of the continental shelf or, failing that, to set twelve-mile limits for other nationals.

Whether this came about or not, to develop and preserve our offshore resources, we needed a better understanding of the ocean. The project would require a research laboratory on the seacoast and an ocean-going research vessel, both too costly to be financed entirely by the state. The plan was submitted to the Office of Naval Research, the National Science Foundation, and private foundations. The response was so encouraging that the state legislature granted us an initial appropriation of $50,000 to get the project off the ground.

With this we were able to employ four scientists to act as consultants. When I sat down at a meeting in Juneau with them and with representatives from the governor's office, the

255

Navy, and the Coast Guard, I was astonished to learn how much needed doing in the area of marine science. Only a small portion of the ocean had been surveyed, I learned. Additional information on bottom topography was needed for precise submarine navigation. For fisheries and other ocean uses, data on such matters as ocean currents, ocean life, climates, water temperatures, acoustics, and mineral resources should be assembled systematically. It was decided to organize an Institute of Marine Sciences that would include both fisheries and oceanography. The academic training would be given at the university, but fundamental research would go on in the ocean itself.

It sounded like a very big order. To begin, modern facilities in the very heart of the fishing industry, in Kodiak, for example, would have been splendid but any such ambitious plans had to wait for future years. The mayor of Douglas, a town just across Gastineau Channel from Juneau, offered us, rent free, an unused school building for office quarters as well as a good dock and an idle cannery that could be converted into a laboratory. When our consultants examined these facilities, they approved them, no doubt with some unspoken reservations, since they were a far cry from the modern laboratories and offices where they were accustomed to work.

The first job was to find an outstanding scientist to serve as director of the institute. We wanted a man of national reputation who would be able to secure foundation grants and who could tempt other scientists to join him in the new venture. He had to be a tough, pioneering, optimistic man. All we had to offer him was a good salary, our moral support, and an ocean brimming with research problems.

I had no idea where to look for such a man so I took the problem to Dr. Roger Revelle, director of Scripps Institute of Oceanography at La Jolla, California. To my surprise he set aside a full day for me. As he explained, "What you're trying to do is much more important than you realize. Your area is a virgin laboratory. The science is so new that only two or three dozen men in the country are qualified to take over the program."

As was to be expected, the men he spoke of were all hip deep in vital research. Finally Dr. K. M. Rae, director of marine laboratories at the Agricultural and Mechanical College of Texas, surfaced and looked at the bait we were offering him. He was cautious but he agreed to come to Alaska and look us over. My last official duty for the university was to persuade him to throw in his lot with us; then my part of the job was done.

In the meantime, after the search of applications and half a dozen interviews, the regents had selected Dr. William R. Wood of the University of Nevada as the next president of the university. I knew that they had made a wise choice.

That year we had the largest graduating class in the history of the university. It was late that night before Kay and I could be alone. I relaxed, reviewed the past seven years, and let myself wallow a little in a sense of accomplishment. We had taken on the job rather reluctantly and from unselfish motives, and yet it had proved to be a wonderfully satisfying period. "We've paid off part of the debt we owe to Alaska," I told Kay. "Our end product has been young people . . ."

I stopped there because Kay was smiling across at me. Perhaps I had begun to sound sentimental, possibly grandiloquent.

"Come on, Ernest," she said, "your Boy Scout deed for the day is finished. It's time to get some sleep."

When the new president arrived, we toured the campus together. The heart of any university is its work on campus, but a state university also becomes involved in a myriad of off-campus activities. Our work already extended to the shores and borders of a big land in the shape of scientific research and extension work.

As I ticked off the various projects to Dr. Wood, the weight of his new responsibilities must have seemed heavy. In his inaugural address, he said, "Where but in Alaska could you find a single university with a fur farm, a musk-ox herd, a square mile of glacier, several tons of bones of prehistoric animals, an ice station on the polar ice cap four hundred miles north of land's end; a world famous scientist with a special alarm system to awaken him when the aurora borealis flashes across our northern skies, two satellite-tracking stations, no fraternities or sororities, and no losing football team for the alumni to use as an excuse for firing the president!"

So the time had come to fold our tents. As we were driving to the airport I stopped at the entrance to the campus and turned for a last look. My thoughts must have showed in my face because beside me, Kay said, "Don't look back, Ernest," and I could hear the compassion in her voice.

As we flew south on the Boeing jet, I felt as if we were flying over bits and pieces of our lives. The flash of blue below us was Harding Lake where we had a summer cabin. The shadow of our plane was flitting over glacier-carved valleys and serrated ridges. I had back-packed across a good many of them.

"This is Captain Joslyn speaking," a voice said over the intercom. "We are now cruising at thirty thousand feet; weather ahead is clear and unlimited; our estimated flight time to Seattle is three hours and five minutes."

I squeezed Kay's hand and smiled. Captain Joslyn indeed. Eons ago I had been his first passenger on a bush flight. We had shared some tight spots in those days. For an instant I was back in that puny little plane, Joslyn fighting

258

the controls to gain altitude after an uphill take-off from a landing strip in the brush. It had been close. The top of a spruce tree had ripped the canvas on the underside of one wing.

We had left Alaska, I saw, and were skirting the town of Whitehorse in Yukon Territory. Not far away was the Watson River country. I once discovered a fox den there when I was back-packing to examine a silver-lead prospect. I wondered if the family of foxes still lived there below us.

In a few more minutes we had crossed the jagged coast range under its white blanket of glaciers and were back over Alaska again. There was Juneau and the picturesque inland passage stretching hundreds of miles southward. Boats were threading their way along the narrow channel. From the air they were toy boats. It had been nearly forty years ago when Kay and I had stood at the rail of the old *Northwestern,* gazing awestruck at the mighty coast range. From thirty thousand feet the coast range was dwarfed and we could see behind it and hundreds of miles into British Columbia.

Right on schedule, Captain Joslyn put the plane down in the Seattle airport. We came eagerly into the terminal and our sons, their wives, and our grandchildren rushed to meet us. I felt as if we had come full circle.

And so the retirement days began. It was a wonderful luxury after breakfast to take an hour to read the morning newspaper. But the greatest dividend was the time Kay and I now had to enjoy a relaxed companionship with no outside pressures forcing us into action. Kay decided to redecorate and refurnish our Seattle home. I damned the interior decorator when he banished all our prized Alaskan paintings from the living room and library and I had to carry them downstairs and rehang them in the recreation room.

The first year was a joyful time, one of the happiest of

our years together. True, there were frequent checkups with the doctors, but Kay did not seem to be losing ground and we refused to notice the puzzled frowns of the doctors as we went our happy ways. We even discussed spending part of the following winter in Honolulu.

In June we motored to California to be present when our youngest son, Dale, received his master's degree at Stanford University. The next day we were in the car, ready to start home, while Dale and his family stood around to bid us goodbye. Suddenly Kay said, "Get started, Ernest."

There was such urgency in her voice that I pulled away and left the family standing bewildered at the curb. I glanced at Kay. She was crying and I knew that she never expected to see them again.

Within a few weeks the doctors decided on additional surgery. She survived this, but eleven days later her brave heart stopped and she went alone over the last summit. I knew that if possible she was looking back over her shoulder.

When I finally left the hospital to drive home, I threaded my way mechanically through the traffic. There were many traffic lights, but I have no memory of them. I only remember the feel of the empty house when I walked in and the abject loneliness. Thank God I had two sons and eight grandchildren who still needed me.

So what now? I felt a pressing need for physical and mental activity. Trimming shrubs and working in flower beds did not fill the bill. Occasionally I was offered consulting work and it was a relief to get into my field clothes, climb around in a mine, and concentrate on the problems involved.

When the University of Alaska invited me to the campus where a new building was to be named after me, it was hard to speak with composure. I, as well as hundreds of our friends in the audience, knew that Kay should share the hour with me. My brother- and sister-in-law had come to Alaska with me. After the ceremony we flew over the North Pole to Scandinavia, spent several weeks in Europe, and then continued on around the world.

One of my many trips back to Alaska was a sort of pilgrimage to look again at a mountain. At the suggestion of some of our thoughtful Alaska friends, the U.S. Board of Geographic Names had designated this mountain to be named in Kay's honor, a 4,305-foot peak, looking down on the headwaters of Coal and Woodchopper Creeks. In the old days, from our mining camps, Kay and I used to gaze up at that peak and watch the sun tint it. Now it is Mount Kathryn, rising in beauty, Alaska's tribute to her fine, dear life.

Chapter XXIII

TODAY AND TOMORROW

EVEN after we had moved to Seattle we never felt separated from Alaska. Every morning we used to check the weather report from Fairbanks, open letters from northern friends, and read avidly any reference to the continued advance of the university, to the building of a pulp mill, to the discovery of an oil well or of a mineral deposit.

I still follow the development of the new state as intently as if my own well-being were involved. Sometimes I remember the men who opposed statehood because Alaska, they felt, did not have a broad enough economic base. There is irony in the thought now. Just two years before statehood, it was discovered that in Alaska, buried thousands of feet beneath the surface, imprisoned in porous beds of marine sediment, were vast reservoirs of petroleum and natural gas.

For years geologists had guessed that it must be there. They had mapped large basins of sedimentary rocks where oil and gas could occur. They guessed and guessed again, but each time their hopes were dashed.

As far back as the 1920s a few shallow wells, drilled near Katalla, adjacent to the Gulf of Alaska, yielded a limited quantity of high-grade oil. A crude refinery was built and

262

154,000 barrels of oil were treated, but when the refinery burned in 1933, it was not considered economically feasible to rebuild it.

In 1923, a deep well was drilled at Cold Bay on the Alaska Peninsula. Although there was a nearby oil seepage, nothing came of it but a dry hole. Several other favorable structures on the Alaska Peninsula were tested. They all resulted, not in oil but disappointment, until July 1957. At that time, the Richfield Oil Company, drilling in the Swanson River district of the Kenai Peninsula fifty miles from the city of Anchorage, brought in a gusher, and Alaska's oil boom was on. Most of the major oil companies began moving into the area, convinced that an important new oil field had been discovered and ready to spend millions of dollars to develop it.

When the oil-bearing structures were traced to the shores of Cook Inlet, the next step was to drill under the waters there. It took courage and keen engineering as well as millions of dollars to build the drilling platforms. Vicious tides, sometimes thirty feet high, bear down Cook Inlet. In winter they carry crushing ice floes. Yet today Cook Inlet is dotted with a dozen drilling platforms, anchored to the bottom by steel legs. Oil and natural gas flow up through the drill casing to pipelines extending from the platforms to refineries and other installations on shore where the oil can be loaded into tankers. This one field pushed Alaska into eighth place among oil-producing states. It has required an investment, since 1959, of $1.2 billion, a husky chunk of bait to cast into Alaska. As it turned out, it was cheap at the price. In 1967, the production from seventy wells in the Kenai area had a value of $88.2 million, with years of future production assured.

Such large reserves of natural gas were tapped that nobody knew what to do with it. A pipeline was laid to

Anchorage but that city could use only a small fraction of the output. Many of the gas wells were capped. Then Collier Carbon & Chemical Company started building a chemical complex near Kenai to use the gas for the production of ammonia and prilled urea, planning to ship much of the output of fertilizer to Japan.

By 1970 a Phillips-Marathon liquefied-gas plant, being built near Kenai at a cost of over $100 million, should go on the line. The gas will be compressed at the unbelievably low temperature of −248 degrees Fahrenheit, transforming it into a liquid state. The liquefied gas will be rushed across the Pacific to Japan in refrigerated tankers. At Tokyo the tanker will be hooked onto storage tanks, temperatures will rise and the natural gas from Alaska will feed into the mains of the world's largest city. Hawaii, too, is interested in this supply of gas.

Yet all this is only the beginning. Other large basins of marine sediment are known in Alaska. It does not require undue optimism to predict that new oil-producing areas will be found.

One of the great basins is north of the Brooks Range on the Arctic slope. This basin, extending from the range to the shores of the Arctic Ocean, was set aside as a Navy Petroleum Reserve in 1923. Between 1945 and 1953, the Navy drilled seventy-five holes to test the area. They discovered the Umiat oil field and Gubic gas field, as well as a small gas field near Point Barrow, but because of the isolated location work was suspended.

In recent years a portion of the vast area was opened to commercial development. There is probably no place on earth where exploration costs are so high. It is a treeless area, swept by winter storms, and in continuous darkness for several months of the year. The land is pitted with hundreds of small lakes and in summer, when the tundra becomes swampy, surface travel is unbelievably difficult. But difficulties do not stop an oil company when the stakes are high. Several of the major companies arrived with geologic field parties. Later, using huge cargo planes, they moved in their drilling equipment.

Once again the gamble paid off. In 1968, Atlantic Richfield Oil Company in a joint venture with Humble Oil & Refining Company brought in a spectacular wildcat well near Prudhoe Bay near the Arctic Coast, just three hundred and seventy-five miles due north of Fairbanks. Later in the same year, they hit the jackpot again with a second well. The two wells, seven miles apart, apparently are on the same structure.

That second well, known as Sag River State No. 1, encountered three hundred feet of oil sand. Perforations in the bottom fifteen feet of sand showed a flow rate of twenty-three hundred barrels of high-gravity oil per day. So the first two wells drilled in that remote area were winners. Those two major oil companies hold a block of leases on ninety thousand acres in the very heart of the field. If the estimates of their consultants are correct and the field does indeed contain five to ten billion barrels of oil, it would rate as one of the largest petroleum accumulations known to the world today. This may prove to be the greatest economic thrust in the history of Alaska.

It will take years of drilling to test the Arctic field. In the meantime, other major companies will turn their attention to favorable areas in different locations, the Bering Sea for example, or the shelf area along the Gulf of Alaska. It could easily happen that Alaska will develop into one of the most important of the oil-producing states. It is expected to be in fifth place by 1970. A new source of fuel discovered within the confines of our own country is naturally a cause for rejoicing. It is also a healthy development for the new state. In 1967 the petroleum payroll in Alaska came to more than $41 million. In the first nine years of statehood, Alaska took in almost $177 million from the industry. By 1968, the state's oil royalties alone amounted to $41,000 a day. As my son Stanton put it, "Alaska's assets are no longer frozen." With all that wealth pouring into the State Treasury, the university is no longer starved for funds. Whenever I return to the campus, I look around me, unbelieving, trying to visualize the lone frame building in its clearing on the hill back in 1922. In the past seven years, the on-campus enrollment has more than doubled. More than four thousand students work part-time for university credits in the community colleges, correspondence courses, and evening classes. The faculty has doubled in the same time, and some beautiful new buildings have been built. For the past ten years, the annual growth rate on campus has averaged twelve percent and the same growth can safely be projected for the future.

While oil-field workers come pushing up North, tourists, too, have been discovering Alaska in increasing numbers. Some of them come by boat, cruising along the great, wild coastline, and some come by jet, just over two hours from Seattle to Anchorage or three hours to Fairbanks, where feeder airlines scatter them out to far-flung spots—Kotzebue, Nome, or Barrow. Others come by car and trailer, driving up the Alaska Highway through British Columbia and Yukon Territory, always astonished to discover when they arrive that all major highways in Alaska are paved.

Since the coast of southeastern Alaska is too rugged for highway construction, the state has established a sort of "marine highway" in the form of four car-ferries with overnight accommodations. People drive aboard at Prince Rupert in British Columbia, cruise up the Alaska coast, and drive off again at Haines or Skagway, then through the

Coast Range to the Alaska Highway. During several months, the ferries run as far south as Seattle. Before long the service from Seattle will be year round.

Last year about 100,000 tourists spent $25 million in Alaska and every year the numbers grow. The primitive wilderness and the great wild mountain ranges speak to the soul of modern man, surfeited with crowds and too-civilized living.

There are areas in Alaska where no man has ever trod. Some of the world's greatest ice fields are up there, mysterious fjords indenting the coastline, broad intermontane valleys, and the bleak tundra of Eskimo land, all too vast, and varied to be changed by the work of man. They will stand in their primitive grandeur a hundred years from now.

So will our forests. The heavy rain forest, stretching for hundreds of miles along the coast of southeastern Alaska, was guarded jealously for years by the U.S. Forest Service which controlled a good part of it. According to the estimates, seventy-four percent of the timber is hemlock, twenty percent Sitka spruce, and six percent red cedar, most of it within three miles of tidewater, making for favorable logging and rafting conditions. Several Alaskans dreamed of building a pulp mill to use the timber and a few traveled East to promote the idea, but without success.

When the late B. Frank Heintzleman was put in charge of the Forest Service's huge timber domain in Alaska, he had different ideas from many public servants. Some of the forests, he saw, already were dying of old age. There should be selective harvesting of the timber crop on a perpetual yield basis, not only for the health of the forest, but to provide a new industry for Alaska. Although he prepared background data to alert the pulp industry, it took years to catch their interest.

Finally, in 1954, the first modern pulp mill was built

267

near Ketchikan. The mill now employs eleven hundred Alaskans and annually processes two million board feet of hemlock and spruce into high-grade dissolving pulp. Carefully planned and engineered logging will perpetuate the timber resource for generations to come.

When, in recognition of his efforts, Heintzleman was appointed territorial governor of Alaska by the Secretary of the Interior, he encouraged a combination of Japanese and American capital to build another pulp mill at Sitka. The product of this mill is exported to Japan. The two pulp mills, and some recently built sawmills, now turn out a product totalling $84 million annually. In 1968, the U.S. Plywood-Champion Paper Company signed a contract for 8.75 billion board feet of timber. They plan to build a pulp mill, probably near Juneau, at an estimated cost of $70 million and will employ 1,250 people in the mill and woods. This third mill will raise the combined value of forest products to well over $100 million a year. Yet there are even greater pulpwood resources in interior Alaska, in its forest of birch and soft woods. Timber will be an important future part of Alaska's economy.

As to minerals, while the petroleum and timber industries boom, gold mining has fallen on sorry days. The rich placer gold camps of interior and western Alaska, once known as "Alaska's Golden Heart," are empty now. Before World War II the annual production of gold from Alaska was about $25 million. Today it has dwindled to less than $1 million annually—not because the gold reserves are all mined out, but because gold mining no longer is profitable.

Shortly after the turn of the century, when the Klondike gold fields became overcrowded, a thousand hardy and experienced miners spread out westward into Alaska, searching for new fields. There are thousands of stream valleys in interior Alaska. In each you can find evidence of the men who have been there, to sink prospect holes and pan the gravels. Most of them failed, and sometimes you stumble on brush-hidden graves. But a few struck it rich and placer camps at Fairbanks, Iditarod, Nome, and in a dozen other locations, yielded millions of dollars in new wealth.

Years after the individual miners had skimmed off the rich cream, mining organizations such as mine brought in dredges, draglines, and other mechanical equipment to mine the lower-grade gravel and to dig again through the old workings of the pioneers. But the government fixed the price of gold at $35 an ounce while production costs soared. One after another the gold mines were forced to shut down.

Yet it is common to refer to Alaska as a great storehouse of untapped mineral wealth. If this is true, as I firmly believe it is, there will be rich and extensive mineral deposits discovered in future years that can be worked at great profit. In Alaska we have hundreds of occurrences of deep-seated intrusive rocks which can give birth to mineral-bearing solutions. We also have host rocks to enclose and localize these minerals. This has been the pattern in famous mining districts scattered over the Western states and western Canada.

Alaska is one of the last areas in the West where it is still possible for a sharp-eyed prospector to find new mineral outcrops simply by walking over the surface. The famous Kennecott Mine in the Copper River country was one of the richest deposits of high-grade copper ores ever discovered. Yet the first prospector to explore this wild country behind the ranges was led to it by the characteristic green stains of copper salts on the limestone cliffs towering above the valley floor.

Two very large, low-grade lode deposits of gold, the Treadwell Mine and the Alaska-Juneau Mine, were worked for years and yielded millions. Both outcrop within a stone's throw of the coastline and were easy to find. There must be others as rich hidden in the back country.

Many areas have not been adequately prospected and some have never felt the crunch of a prospector's boots. The rugged mountain fastnesses are difficult and sometimes dangerous to traverse. Some areas are covered by a rank surface growth that could conceal mineral deposits. It will take sophisticated geochemical and geophysical prospecting to ferret them out.

The men who fanned out all over the interior of Alaska in an early day were placer miners. They gave all their attention to testing stream gravels, and seldom got up on the ridges to prospect for lodes hidden away in the country rock, although the mother lodes, from which the placer gold was eroded, were located there. That is a job for a new generation of men. Some will be prospectors scratching over the surface looking for outcrops, but most will be trained men, using new scientific methods of ore finding, men with test tubes and a kit of chemicals sensitive enough to detect traces of metals, a few parts per million, in the stream sediments or the hillside soils. From these minute indications they will work upstream or up the hillsides, hoping to find "hot" spots that will lead them to new wealth.

Other men will cruise slowly over favorable areas in helicopters equipped with delicate electrical equipment. The anomalies that they detect will be traced with ground traverses.

Each time I fly over Alaska my eyes keep searching the cliffs for bright-colored stains that can indicate mineralization. When I look down at the covered areas, I am haunted by the thought that somewhere below the airplane a rich mineral deposit may be hidden. Someday the signals will be read. A diamond drill will be set up on the hillside and finally the drill will bite into nice, bright ore.

Not long ago I was in Nevada directing a drilling operation to test a large mineral deposit. That afternoon I was surveying in the drill holes, at an elevation of six thousand feet, getting ready to plot them on a map. As I was walking up a hillside, transit over my shoulder, I suddenly remembered that it was my seventieth birthday. My first impulse was to mention it to my companions but I immediately thought better of it. I did not want them warning each other, "We'd better watch out for the 'Old Man.' This altitude might be too much for him."

That evening I walked out from the camp into the desert. The air was clean and crystal clear, and the night full of stars. It seemed only yesterday that Kay and I with our first baby had set out for the North. We had been through some dark valleys, Kay and I, but we had crossed some splendid summits, too. There had always been useful work to do and there had always been some other summit just ahead. I thought of those days and of our family gathered snug against the Arctic night, of friends, adventures, the unusual and stalwart people we had met. Standing there in the Nevada desert, I conjured up Alaska around me again. I stretched the desert mountains thousands of feet higher, capped them with snow and glaciers, and added the muffled roar of a glacier-fed river in a distant valley. In my mind I stood on the shores of a fjord, trimmed near the water's edge by scattered spruce trees. Waves spattered at my feet. The outgoing tide was rafting icebergs calved from the glacier nested at the head of the fjord. Except for the swish of a small waterfall, the mountains were locked in an ancient silence. That land I loved would always be part of me, I knew.

271

Seventy years, I thought. And I remembered an expression I had heard many years ago: "Old age is a bad habit developed by people who have nothing to do." I would like very much to believe it.